# The Azerbaijanis

**Other titles from Bennett & Bloom:**

The Georgians: People, Culture and History *(forthcoming)*
*edited by Nicholas Awde*

The Armenians: People, Culture and History *(forthcoming)*

In the Shadow of Aliyev: Travels in Azerbaijan
*by Jason Thomson*

Tattooed Mountain Women and Spoon Boxes of Daghestan:
Magic Medicine Symbols in Silk, Stone, Wood and Flesh
*by Robert Chenciner, Gabib Ismailov & Magomedkhan Magomedkhanov*

The Tattooing Arts of Tribal Women
*Lars Krutak*

Carved and Coloured Village Art from Tsarist Lands
*by Robert Chenciner & John Cornall*

Georgia: A Short History *(forthcoming)*
*edited by Nicholas Awde*

Historical Atlas of Georgia *(forthcoming)*
*Edited by David Muskhelishvili*

Circassian Culture and Folklore: Hospitality Traditions, Cuisine, Festivals & Music (Kabardian, Cherkess, Adigean, Shapsugh & Diaspora) *(forthcoming)*
*by Amjad Jaimoukha*

Racism in Russia *(forthcoming)*

Women in Islam: An Anthology from the Qur'an and Hadiths
*Translated and edited by Nicholas Awde*

Witness through Troubled Times: A History of the Orthodox Church of Georgia, 1811 to the Present
*edited by Tamara Grdzelidze, Martin George & Lukas Vischer*

Georgian Monks on Mount Athos: Two Eleventh-Century Lives of the Hegoumenoi of Iviron
*translated & edited by Tamara Grdzelidze*

Georgians in the Holy Land *(Iberica Caucasica Volume 2)*
*edited by Tamila Mgaloblishvili*

Maximus the Confessor and Georgia *(Iberica Caucasica Volume 3)*
*edited by Tamila Mgaloblishvili*

The Roses of Jericho: Diary of a Journey through the Holy Land and Syria,
5 July-28 September *(Iberica Caucasica Volume 4)*
*by Grigol Peradze*

The Wellspring of Georgian Historiography:
The Early Medieval Historical Chronicle 'The Conversion of Kartli' and 'The Life of St Nino'
*translated & edited by Constantine B. Lerner*

The Mediterranean Legacy in Early Celtic Christianity: A Journey from Armenia to Ireland
*by Jacob G. Ghazarian*

The History of Bishop Sebeos: Redefining a Seventh-Century Voice from Armenia
*by Gabriel Soultanian*

The Pre-History of the Armenians, Volume 1
*by Gabriel Soultanian*

The Pre-History of the Armenians, Volume 2: The Proto-Armenian Hieroglyphic Inscriptions of Aram
*by Gabriel Soultanian*

The Pre-History of the Armenians, Volume 3: The Anatolian Hieroglyphic Inscriptions of the Proto-Armenians
*by Gabriel Soultanian*

Arabic-English/English-Arabic Dictionary
*by N. Awde & K. Smith*

Afghanistan: The Taliban Years
*S. Iftikhar Murshed*

Arabic Verbs: For Revision and Practice
*by John Mace*

Basic Arabic Workbook: For Revision and Practice
*by John Mace*

Intermediate Arabic Workbook: For Revision and Practice
*John Mace*

# The Azerbaijanis
# Azərbaycanlılar

## People, Culture and History

Edited by
Nicholas Awde &
Fred James Hill

BENNETT & BLOOM

First published
in 2009 by
BENNETT & BLOOM
www.bennettandbloom.com
PO Box 2131
London W1A 5SU
England



Typeset and designed by Desert♥Hearts

Printed and bound by
Marksprint/Zrinski D.D.

*British Library Cataloguing in Publication Data*
A catalogue record for this book is available from the British Library

ISBN 978-1-898948-54-4 (paperback)
ISBN 978-1-898948-34-6 (hardback)

# Contents

## The Azerbaijani alphabet

| Azerbaijani letter | Transcription in this book | Sounds like... |
|---|---|---|
| **A a** | [a] | c***ar*** |
| **B b** | [b] | ***b***ox |
| **C c** | [j] | ***j***et |
| **Ç ç** | [ch] | ***ch***urch |
| **D d** | [d] | ***d***og |
| **E e** | [e] | p***e***t |
| **Ə ə** | [a/e] | ***a***pple |
| **F f** | [f] | ***f***ox |
| **G g** | [g] | Ma***gy***ar |
| **Ğ ğ** | [gh/g] | French: Pa***r***is |
| **H h** | [h] | ***h***at |
| **İ i** | [i] | s***ea***t |
| **I ı** | [i] | h***u***rt |
| **J j** | [zh/j] | lei***s***ure |
| **K k** | [k] | ***k***ite |
| **L l** | [l] | ***l***et |
| **M m** | [m] | ***m***ap |
| **N n** | [n] | ***n***et |
| **O o** | [o] | British: c***o***t |
| **Ö ö** | [ö/o] | French: f***eu*** |
| **P p** | [p] | ***p***et |
| **Q q** | [q/g] | ***g***ot |
| **R r** | [r] | 'rolled' ***r***adio |
| **S s** | [s] | ***s***it |
| **Ş ş** | [sh] | ***sh***ut |
| **T t** | [t] | ***t***en |
| **U u** | [u] | sh***oo***t |
| **Ü ü** | [ü/u] | French: t***u*** |
| **V v** | [v] | ***v***an |
| **X x** | [kh] | Scottish: lo***ch*** |
| **Y y** | [u] | ***y***es |
| **Z z** | [z] | ***z***ebra |

# Preface

THIS HANDBOOK is an introduction to the Azeri, or Azerbaijani, Turks and their culture and history. Today they live principally in the Republic of Azerbaijan and the northwestern provinces of Iran. The chapters of this book are designed to be read not only as a unified work but also as independent parts, and we hope this will prove to be of wider benefit since there is still little comprehensive material in the English language on the Azeris.

In order to make this book as accessible as possible, the transliteration of Azeri names and terms mostly follows a simple easy-to-read system that is approved internationally. The modern Latin Azeri alphabet is also used in a few instances that relate to the Republic of Azerbaijan after 1991. For details of the modern alphabet, see the facing page.

The editors would like to thank Thea Khitarishvili, Tina Joyce, Bernard & Gillian Joyce, Ian M. Carnochan and Stephen Zimmer for their help, as well as Adil Bagirov and Zaur Rzakhanov for their support in the very early stages of compiling this volume.

*Nicholas Awde &*
*Fred James Hill*

AZERBAIJAN
GEORGIA
Zaqatala
Sheki
Qazakh
ARMENIA
Mingechevir
Reservoir
Ganja
Lake
Van
Yerevan
NAGORNO-
KARABAKH
Khankendi
(Stepanakert)
Lachin
TURKEY
NAKHCHIVAN
Nakhchivan
IRAN

## Map of Azerbaijan Today

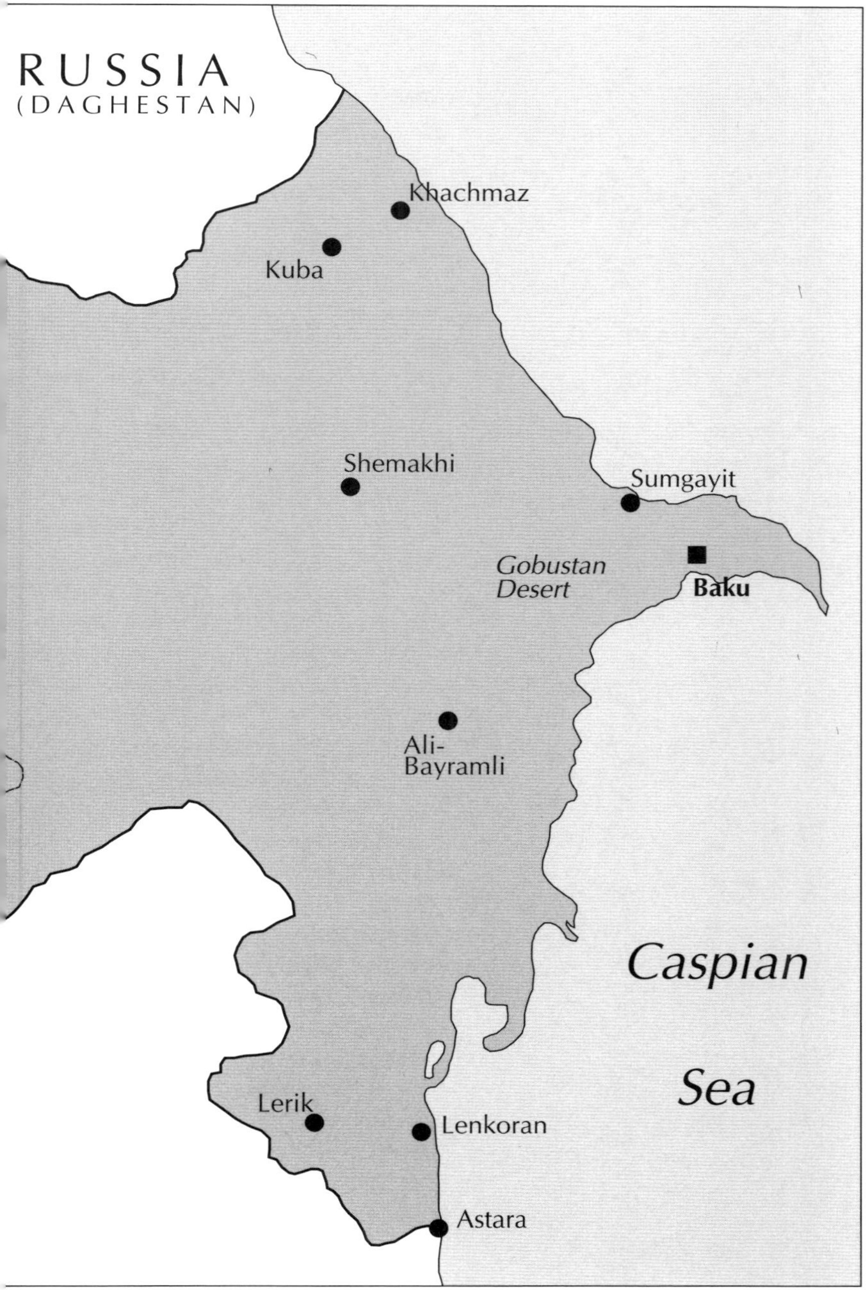

# Khans, Tsars and Commissars: The Making of the Republic of Azerbaijan

Nicholas Awde & Fred James Hill

THE REPUBLIC of Azerbaijan belongs to the immensely complex and historically turbulent region of the Caucasus. It is surrounded by Iran to the south, Turkey, Armenia and Georgia to the west, and Russia to the north. Its eastern flank runs down the coast of the energy-rich Caspian Sea, a huge salt-water lake (the world's largest inland body of water) that lies 28 metres below sea level. The Republic has been historically connected to a larger more loosely defined territory that has long been closely identified with the Azeri (Azerbaijani) people and which covers not only much of the eastern section of the South Caucasus region but also northwestern Iran.

Azerbaijan's history has been woven from a wide network of relationships established over the course of centuries by an array of cultures and changing political allegiances. The many states and kingdoms of varying sizes and power that sprang up locally always depended on their survival by allying themselves to the major empires of the day. As a result of imperial rivalries, the latter often saw to it that the Caucasus region remained an unstable and war-torn buffer zone.

Adding to the dynamism of Azerbaijan's past are the countless nomadic peoples and warlike tribes that took advantage of the busy migratory route from the northern steppes that ran southwards along the western shores of the Caspian down into Iran. Such a past is reflected in the present-day inhabitants of the Republic of Azerbaijan, who are themselves descendants of the various Turkic, Iranian and Caucasian peoples that have inhabited the region.[1]

While the empires of Persia exerted a powerful and sustained influence over the region, the Azeris successfully established their own cultural traditions and in turn made an enormous contribution to the Persian world, producing great leaders, poets, artists and other influential figures.

During the first half of the 19th century an international border was imposed as a result of war between Russia and Persia which led to the eventual creation of two entirely separate Azeri territories—often referred to as Northern and Southern Azerbaijan. The Azeris in the north, who lived in a patchwork of khanates, found themselves incorporated into the Russian Empire and it was their descendants who would eventually carve out for themselves the modern Republic of Azerbaijan. Meanwhile, those in the south were destined to remain within Persia. Southern Azerbaijan is generally considered to consist of the Iranian provinces of Western Azerbaijan (with its capital at Urumia), Eastern Azerbaijan (its capital at Tabriz) and Ardabil (its capital also called Ardabil).

Northern Azerbaijan's first taste as an independent republic came in 1918. It was the first time that the terms 'Azerbaijan' and 'Azerbaijani' were officially used in the sense of describing a unified Azeri territory and its people. Previously, under the tsarist regime, the region lay divided under the imperial provincial system and the Azeris were officially referred to in the official documents and literature of the Russian Empire as 'Caucasian Tatars' (as opposed to the Crimean or Kazan Tatars) or simply 'Turks'. The First Republic proved a short-lived experience, lasting a mere 23 months before being smothered by the new regime of the Soviet Union. It would take decades of languishing under Soviet control before the Azeris were once again able to proclaim a new independent republic, which they did in 1991.

Like the other Caucasian nations, the Republic of Azerbaijan has had to come to terms with the hand it was dealt by Soviet Russia. Not only has it had to reconstruct its economy and reverse the damage wrought by decades of cultural and religious repression, but it has also had to struggle hard to reassert its territorial integrity in the face of rival claims by its neighbour Armenia—an ordeal that has brought war, a refugee crisis and a significant loss of land.

Despite such upheavals, the viability of Azerbaijan as a modern state with a clear sense of national identity is in no doubt. Today the majority, though by no means all, of the Republic's population identify themselves culturally as Muslim Azeris, a key element of which is their language, Azeri (or Azerbaijani). Now the Republic's official language, Azeri is a form of Turkish similar to that spoken in Turkey and is also closely related to languages spoken today in Central Asia from where it originated. Another characteristic of the Azeris is the predominance of the Shi'ite creed of Islam. The Republic of Azerbaijan is one of only a handful of states where Shi'ite Muslims outnumber Sunnis, a feature it shares with Iran, Iraq and Bahrain.

## Imperial rivalry in the Caucasus

A convenient starting point from which to pick up the complex threads that would eventually be woven together to form the modern state of Azerbaijan is the beginning of the 18th century. It was a time that saw the Persian Empire of the Safavid dynasty crumble and imperial Russia's interest in the South Caucasus become more clearly defined. From the time of their first shah, Ismail (*ruled* 1501-1524), the Safavid rulers of Persia had seen the South Caucasus as their own domain, claiming suzerainty over its local rulers. They divided their possessions in the region, which included territory now in modern Azerbaijan, Armenia and northwestern Iran, into numerous provinces and districts run by *beglarbegis*. Persian Georgia (i.e. Kartli and Kakheti) was ruled by its own special hereditary *vali*, or viceroy.

The Safavids themselves were an Azeri-speaking dynasty whose original power base was in Tabriz, in Iranian Azerbaijan, and it was they who were responsible for installing Shi'ite Islam as the official state religion. For two centuries they had waged an exhausting and largely fruitless war against their Sunni archrivals, the Turkish Ottomans, whose own empire to the west was ruled from Istanbul. In the midst of their bitter imperial rivalry, Russia saw a window of opportunity in which to make its move on the South Caucasus.

Having already raised Russia's standing in Europe, Tsar Peter the Great (1672-1725) had further dreams of dragging his backward state onto the world stage as a great power that could rival the European empires. In this, the Caucasus had a considerable amount to offer—not only was the region a bustling production centre of goods such as silk (especially at Shemakha [Shemakhi]), carpets and other fabrics, it was also a vital channel for trade. Dominating the land and Caspian Sea trade routes that connected Russia with the Middle East would enable it to monopolise European-Persian trade—an especially appealing proposition and, given the condition of the ailing Safavid Empire, seemingly a viable one.

The region also had a wider strategic value. The Russians had already secured two major naval routes to the outside world: the Baltic and the Black Sea. But neither was satisfactory since both routes could be easily blocked by a hostile state—the Ottomans in the case of the Black Sea. Getting a foothold in the South Caucasus would strengthen Russia's hand against the Ottomans, enable it to gain influence in Persia, and, so the hope was, to gain a way to the Indian Ocean and create a so-called 'warm-water port'.[2]

Meanwhile, the strategically placed city of Baku, situated along the north-south route with well-established links to inland regions and boasting the finest natural harbour in the Caspian, became of special interest to Russia. Writing at the beginning of the 18th century, Cornelius de Bruyn remarked in his *Travels* that Baku's 'very fine port' had been 'lately fortified by the Persians'. He added that the town 'stands in the western part of Persia, in the country of Shirwan [Shirvan], upon the Caspian Sea, and still preserves its ancient walls'.[3]

In de Bruyn's opinon, such an acquisition would prove 'very commodious' for the tsar since:

> ...it lies contiguous to his [i.e. the tsar] dominions, and is very advantageous to those of his subjects who traffic there for any considerable time. It might likewise be preserved without any difficulty, after it had been conquered, by erecting forts there.[4]

Peter the Great spent the first two decades of the 18th century bolstering Russian trading posts in the Caspian and overseeing the construction of a Caspian trading fleet, based at Kazan on the Volga. He also strengthened Russian-Persian relations. Envoys were sent to Persia, ruled then by Shah Husain (*r.*1694-1722), to discuss trade and military co-operation with Iran and Georgia against the Ottomans, thereby permitting him to establish consulates in the Persian capital Esfahan, as well as in Gilan and Shirvan.[5]

The initial pretext for sending Russian troops into the Caucasus came about in 1721. That year, in reprisal for Iran's anti-Sunni policies, Daghestani mountain tribes, adherents of Sunnism, descended on Shemakha, the provincial capital of Shirvan, killing a number of Russian traders and massacring around four to five thousand Iranian officials and other Shi'ite Muslims.[6]

However, the following year, while Peter made preparations for an assault on the South Caucasus, Persia was thrown into crisis following a major Afghan invasion led by Mahmud of Kandahar. After a lengthy siege of the Persian capital Esfahan, which fell in October that year, Shah Husain was forced to abdicate and recognize Mahmud as the new ruler. The following month, Husain's choice of crown prince proclaimed himself Shah Tahmasp II of Persia and set about challenging the Afghan invaders.

The Russians, now with the pretext of coming to the rescue of the beleaguered Persian throne, began their march down the western Caspian coast and took a number of key cities and towns including Derbend (Derbent), Baku (described by Tsar Peter as 'the key to all our business')[7] and the southern Caspian province of Rasht.

Tsar Peter was well aware of the value of Baku's oil, ordering the general who had seized the city, Mikhail Matyushkin, to send a thousand puds (1 pud = 16.38 kg) of white petroleum or 'as much as possible, and find [there] a refining master'.[8]

According to de Bruyn, the region of Baku produced:

> ...the best oil in the world, both brown and white, the first of which is carried into Gilan, and a hundred leagues beyond in to Persia, and the white they send to all parts. They assured me, that at the distance of two or three leagues from that town, the land burns continually, because of the abundance of saltpeter it is impregnated with. The governors of this province never fail to enrich themselves in a short time.[9]

However the threat of a military confrontation with the Ottomans, who had seized the chance to muscle in on the Caucasus and marched into Georgia in 1723, was becoming an ever more worrying prospect for the tsar. Russian troops were now desperately low on supplies and suffering a staggeringly high loss of life from disease. Ignoring pleas from Tahmasp for recognition, Russia opted to broker a deal with the Ottomans and the two powers signed a treaty in June 1724 providing for the division of western Persia.[10] Under the terms of the agreement, known as the Treaty of Constantinople, the Caspian territory already in Russia's possession would remain so, while Southern Azerbaijan and a good part of the South Caucasus would go to the Ottomans.[11]

Peter's death in January 1725 emboldened the Ottomans to go beyond the limits imposed by the treaty, and, despite protests by Russia, by late summer they had occupied all of Georgia, Armenia and the lion's share of Azerbaijan and Shirvan.[12] That same year, the Safavid dynasty suffered a catastrophic blow. Mahmud unleashed a vicious campaign of violence in Esfahan, massacring most of the Safavid princes, along with countless others who incurred his wrath. The deposed shah, Husain, was beheaded the following year. The Afghans were only finally checked in 1729, when they found their match in Tahmasp Quli Khan, who would soon rule Persia under the name Nadir Shah. A general from the branch of the Afshar (of Oghuz Turkish descent) who has been likened to a 'Persian Napoleon', Nadir Shah's military successes enabled Tahmasp II to return to Esfahan and take the throne, albeit briefly.

Now hoping to undermine Ottoman influence in the Caucasus, Russia signed a peace treaty with Persia in February 1732 agreeing to restore territories south of the Kura river. Derbend and Baku were returned in a separate treaty signed in Ganja in 1735, at a time when

Nadir Shah was making gains against the Ottomans in the South Caucasus. While it marked a temporary end to Russia's political ambitions in the region, there were still economic gains to be had—Russian merchants were able to enjoy good trade terms with Persia, including being exempt from the payment of tariffs.

Once Tahmasp II had served his purpose, Nadir Shah denounced him as a 'drunkard'[13] and deposed him in 1732, choosing briefly to reign through the fallen shah's eight-month-old son, Abbas III. Then, in 1736, he took the throne for himself. In 1740, he had both Tahmasp and Abbas executed. Nadir Shah went on to establish a sizeable empire making gains from Kandahar to Delhi, in northern India. Furthermore, as war resumed with the Ottomans, he notched up another series of victories against his Turkish rivals. A Sunni himself, he also nurtured dreams of imposing Sunnism on the Shi'ite Persian Empire, but to no avail. He was assassinated in 1747.

## Independent khanates during the 18th century

After Nadir Shah's death, the once centralized Safavid Empire disintegrated, descending into anarchy as various contenders fought for the throne. As Persian power weakened throughout the Caucasus, a number of feudal khanates, ruled by an array of Muslim strongmen (including those of Karabakh, Baku, Sheki, Quba, Ganja, Shirvan, Derbend, Erivan [Yerevan] and Nakhchivan), vied with each other to assert their dominance in the politically turbulent region. The population over which such rulers were attempting to impose their authority was not homogeneous, but:

> ...mixed in terms of ethnicity, religion, sect, and nomadism-sedentarianism. The largest component of the population of eastern Caucasia has been called 'Turcoman tribes', some of whom were nomadic, some semi-nomadic, and other settled as farmers or town dwellers. Among the settled were the Javanshirs of Karabakh. Kurds, Lezghi, and Avars were found throughout the region... There were also non-Muslim minority communities of Georgians, Armenians, and Jews in all regions except Talysh near the Caspian coast.[14]

During the latter part of the 18th century, the khanate of Shirvan, which prior to Safavid rule had been a larger and more important regional state, began to enjoy a temporary new-found revival of its fortunes.[15] Meanwhile, Baku, once a part of the Shirvanshah state, had found itself under the rule of the descendants of an Iranian garrison commander who

Khanates of the South Caucasus in the 18th century.

was prominent during the upheavals of the 1720s. Despite its small size, it was able to capitalize on its strategic position.

Nevertheless, the tattered Persian Empire's fortunes began to wax towards the end of the 18th century and its new rulers vigorously re-asserted Safavid claims of suzerainty over the South Caucasus—territory without which no shah could ever consider Persia to be complete. Asserting authority over such a complex and diverse region ultimately 'depended on the ability of a particular Shah to make his will felt, and the determination of the local khans to evade obligations they felt were onerous':[16]

> Naturally, it was those khanates located closest to the province of Azerbaijan which most frequently experienced attempts to re-impose Iranian suzerainty: the khanates of Erivan, Nakhchivan and Qarabagh across the Aras, and the Cis-Aras khanate of Talysh, with its administrative headquarters located at Lankaran and therefore very vulnerable to pressure, either from the direction of Tabriz or Rasht.[17]

Though more difficult to influence, the khans of Ganja, Sheki and Shirvan were considered to be vassals of the Shah, as were those of Baku and Quba, although contact between Persia and these two khanates was effectively limited to 'maritime commercial links with Anzali and Rasht'.[18] Of great concern too was Christian Georgia, also beyond the direct reach of Persia, but which had likewise traditionally come under the Empire's suzerainty. It was here that Persian and Russian interests would clash head on. Georgia, whose survival was continually threatened by its Muslim neighbours, would soon become the conduit through which Russian military power would be re-channelled into the South Caucasus, paving the way for Russia's eventual annexation of the region.

## The Russian conquest of the Caucasus

Like Peter before her, the Russian Empress Catherine II (*r.*1762-1796), had viewed Persia with considerable interest, not least because of its links to India—it had long been held in Europe that 'trade with India could make any nation rich'.[19] Catherine would not shy from exploiting religious tensions to increase her country's influence in the Muslim dominions to the south. She assumed the mantle of protector of Orthodox Christians living under Ottoman rule—the Treaty of Kuçuk Kaynarci, signed in 1774 after the Russian defeat of the Ottomans, would provide the basis for such a claim.

Pond and mosaic façade at the Khan's Palace in the former khanate of Sheki.

Meanwhile Christian Georgia, which had been fighting a war of liberation against both the Persians and the Ottomans, gained a new sense of purpose after its core kingdoms of Kartli and Kakheti were united in 1762 under King Erekle II. The Georgians were now willing to test the sincerity of Russia's avowed goodwill towards Christians in the region.

Accordingly, in 1783, Erekle II optimistically signed the Treaty of Georgievsk, which placed his kingdom under the protection of the

Russians, constituting a formal renouncement of Georgian allegiance to Iran.

A plan for an active Russian presence in the Caucasus was hatched by Catherine's right-hand man, Prince Grigori Potemkin. He envisaged a two-state bulwark against the Ottomans consisting of Georgia, enlarged by the territorial addition of Ganja and other parts of the eastern Caucasus, and a new Armenian state forged from the khanates of Karabakh, Qarajadagh, Erivan, and Nakhchivan. Military intervention was planned for 1784 but was effectively scuppered by the outbreak of war with the Ottomans the previous year.[20]

Meanwhile, in Persia, the bid to drag the territories of the South Caucasus back into the Persian fold was launched by Agha Muhammad Khan, the future Shah of Iran and the man responsible for establishing the lengthy rule of the Turcoman dynasty of the Qajars. Since 1779, Agha Muhammad Khan had been consolidating his hold over Persia, managing in the process to seize central Persia from the ruling dynasty of the Zands, which had come to power in the middle of the century. It was under the Qajars that Tehran became the capital of Iran. Eager to crown his achievements, in spring 1795, Agha Muhammad Khan duly launched a major campaign to rein in the Caucasian territories, with his eye set firmly on the prize of Georgia. A three-pronged attack followed: the left wing marched towards Erivan, the right up along the Caspian shore towards Shirvan and Daghestan, while in the centre, Muhammad Khan himself led a force towards Georgia.[21]

Ibrahim Khan, the ruler of Karabakh, famously attempted to prevent Agha Muhammad Khan's advance through his territory. Nevertheless, despite having planned well for such an eventually, Ibrahim was forced to retreat to his fortress capital of Shusha. Unable to count on the support of Baku and other allies, which had surrendered to the Qajar's terms, Ibrahim was forced to yield. On August 9, 1795, the month-long siege of Shusha came to an end. Although he accepted Qajar suzerainty, agreeing to pay tribute, Ibrahim nevertheless remained defiant and refused to allow his enemy's troops into his capital. Eager to continue with his campaign, Agha Muhammad Khan subsequently seized Ganja, from where he issued an ultimatum to Georgia, insisting it pledge its allegiance or face the consequences.

King Erekle II stood his ground, yet there was little he could do without the aid of Russia, which, overconcerned with its own wars against the Ottomans, was little disposed to fulfil its obligation to its Christian protectorate. In September 1795, Georgia was abandoned to its fate. Tbilisi was subjected to a major onslaught at the hands of Agha

Muhammad Khan's forces—the city was sacked and a massacre of its inhabitants unleashed. Nevertheless, Russia subsequently launched a punitive campaign under Count Valerian Zubov, who set out to 'chastise the Shah' by annexing the Kura-Aras region.[22] Zubov's forces occupied Derbend, Baku and the districts of Salyan and Talysh, followed by Shemakha. Zubov's apparent destination was Tabriz, yet the expedition was promptly recalled following the death of Catherine II in November 1796 and the accession of Tsar Paul I, who disapproved of his mother's policies in the Caucasus.[23]

In a renewed attempt to assert Qajar authority over the Caucasus, Agha Muhammad Khan, now Shah of Persia, opted first to settle the score with Ibrahim of Karabakh, who had by now forged links with the Russians. Ibrahim subsequently fled to Daghestan and, in June 1797, the Shah was finally able to enter Shusha. It proved a fateful move: just days after his arrival the Shah was murdered by his own servants.

Russia's decisive response to the Caucasian question was not long in coming. Rather than fulfil its responsibility to defend Georgia, it embarked on a policy of outright annexation, beginning with Eastern Georgia (Kartli and Kakheti) in 1801. Russia was now in a position to conquer the rest of the South Caucasus, which it would do so with a combination of direct military action and ruthless exploitation of the fractious relations between the Caucasian khanates—co-opting local rulers, creating divisions and further weakening unity in the region.

The man who spearheaded the invasion of the region was Paul Tsitsianov, a Russian of Georgian aristocratic descent who had been handpicked to oversee the annexation of key Georgian territories. Harbouring strong imperialistic sentiments and with deeply ingrained anti-Persian attitudes, Tsitsianov haboured ambitions to go beyond Russia's planned objective to establish a secure frontier with Persia along the Kura and Aras rivers. Opposing 'every attempt at a peaceful settlement of the conflict between his country and Iran',[24] the new viceroy also had his sights set on the northwestern provinces of Khuy, Tabriz, and Gilan.

Tsitsianov was Russia's star in the Caucasus—described by the government as 'our prince', it was said he made music with 'bombshells and bullets' forcing every khan to 'dance to his piping'.[25] Summing up Tsitsianov's short but vigorous career in the South Caucasus, General Potto wrote in the 1890s that:

> In the short time he passed there [in the South Caucasus] he managed to completely alter the map of the country. He found it composed of the

> minutely divided, independent Muhammadan states leaning upon Persia, namely, the khanates of Baku, Shirvan, Shekeen, Karabakh, Ganja and Erivan, to which must be added the territory of the Djaro-Bielokani Lesghians, the pashalik of Akhaltsikh, and the Turkish fortresses situated on the shores of the Black Sea. All these khanates, territories, and fortified places constituted a hostile ring, encircling on three sides the Georgian countries... Three years passed, and Tsitsianov left Transcaucasia in extent almost as it is now [i.e. the 1890s]: peaceful... and submissive from sea to sea.[26]

In fact, the South Caucasus would remain less than 'peaceful' until well after Tsitsianov's death, and yet he unquestionably laid the ground for Russia's ultimate domination of the region. Amidst claims that, from the time of Georgia's 'Golden Age' under Queen Tamara (*r.*1184-1213), Ganja had belonged to Georgia but had been lost owing to the 'weakness of her rulers', Tsitsianov's troops stormed the city in January 1804 after a month's siege. Its ruler Javad Khan was killed and the khanate annexed. In the course of the sacking of the city, between 1,500 to 3,000 people were massacred.[27]

In a report to the tsar, Tsitsianov described a brutal act of revenge that resulted in the slaughter of a large number of inhabitants who had taken refuge in a mosque:

> Five hundred Tatars shut themselves up in a mosque, meaning, perhaps, to surrender, but an Armenian told the soldiers that there were some Daghestanis amongst them, and the name was a death-signal for all, so great is the exasperation of your Majesty's troops against those people for their raids into Georgia and the robber war they carry on.[28]

Tsistianov added that 'all the women in the town were spared—a rare occurrence in Caucasian warfare...'[29] He immediately renamed Ganja 'Elizavetpol', in honour of the Russian Empress and the city's main mosque was converted into a church. In the ensuing chaos, large numbers of the local population fled to the safety of Persian-controlled lands.

Unsurprisingly, the success of the Russian advance in the Caucasus had been viewed with alarm by the both the Persians and Ottomans. Fath Ali Shah, who had become ruler 1797 following Agha Muhammad Khan's death, was no less adamant than his predecessors that the Caucasian khanates were part of Persia. Like his Ottoman rivals, he saw that direct military confrontation with the Russians was inevitable.[30]

Fath Ali Shah resorted to a time-honoured way of bolstering his image as suzerain over the khanates before the outbreak of war with the Russians. Following in the footsteps of Agha Muhammad Khan, he had gold or silver coins minted in Erivan, Ganja and Nukha (the capital of Sheki) to defiantly declare his legal authority there.[31] Such acts had been perfectly natural for both leaders, who, just 'as the Safavids and Nadir Shah had done', regarded the cities as utterly Persian.[32]

War between Russia and Persia inevitably broke out in July 1804 at Erivan, where Tsitsianov had earlier issued an ultimatum to its ruler, Muhammad Khan, to 'recognize the Russian candidate as Catholicos of the Armenian Church at nearby Echmiadzin, to give hostages, to pay 80,000 roubles of tribute annually and surrender all military supplies'.[33] Heading the Persian force was Abbas Mirza, heir to the Persian throne and governor of Azerbaijan. Although Tsitsianov's forces, outnumbered three to one, defeated those of Abbas Mirza, his bid to take the khanate was ultimately unsuccessful. He was forced to retreat northwards to Georgia, leaving Erivan temporarily to the Persians.

Turning to diplomatic means, Tsitsianov subsequently gained the allegiance of the rulers of Karabakh and Sheki. He then fatefully turned his sights on the khanate that held the key to the domination of the Caspian Sea—Baku. On January 30, 1806, after successfully annexing Shirvan, he crossed over into Baku, then ruled by Husain Quli Khan, and demanded its surrender. On February 8, after being hoodwinked into thinking that the city was about to be handed over to him, the Russian commander set off to meet the khan only to be turned on and killed:

> Tsitsianov's head and hands were cut off and sent in triumph back to Teheran; his body was buried under the walls of Baku, to be disinterred later on when that city was finally captured by the Russians under Boulgakoff, and, eventually, in 1811 committed to its last resting-place in the venerable church of the Sion monastery in Tbilisi.[34]

The tsar reacted quickly to the news of the demise of his viceroy and immediately approved a new expedition to rein in Baku. Skilfully exploiting local rivalries, on their march down the Caspian coast the Russians managed to annex Derbend in June 1806. A rebellion had broken out in the city and its unpopular ruler Shaykh Ali was forced to flee, with the result that the city capitulated 'without a shot being fired'.[35] With an emboldened Russian army now poised to march southwards, both Baku and Quba declared they would surrender.

Meanwhile, war in the South Caucasus raged on as Russia found itself fighting on two separate fronts against not only Persia, but also the Ottomans. Nevertheless, Russia's disciplined and well-equipped modern army was destined to have the upper hand. Its two rounds of war against Persia culminated in landmark treaties, each of which helped consolidate its position and confirm it as the dominant power.

Fath Ali Shah.

The first Russo-Persian War ended in the Treaty of Gulistan in October 1813, which established the border between the two powers along the Aras (Arax) River and formalized Russia's dominion over Baku, Karabakh, Ganja, Sheki, Shirvan, Derbend and Quba, together with part of Talysh and the fortress of Lenkoran. Persia also gave up its claims to Georgia, and Daghestan. It also confirmed Russia's domination of the 'Persian' or Caspian Sea.[36]

Despite subsequent diplomatic attempts by Persia to regain its lost territories, Russia was resolute that it would not give up any of the land now in its possession. A telling insight into the Russian mind-set regarding the khanates and their inhabitants is given by the following advice from a Russian commander in 1816:

> Upon arriving in the Caucasus, be sure to follow these guidelines in dealing with the natives:
> —Refrain from anything that could weaken their perception of our power, the principal source of our strength in these regions.
> —Establish commercial relations so as to generate among them needs that they still do not feel.
> —Maintain a continuous state of dissent among their diverse nations and never forget that their unity could be fatal for us.
> —Introduce among them the light of Christianity.
> —Absolutely prevent them from the possibility of links with Turkey and Persia.[37]

In the midst of these hardening attitudes and a new provocative move by Russian troops into territories still held by Persia, including part of the Khanate of Erivan, it was inevitable that war would once more break out—which it did in July 1826. A Persian offensive on Karabakh and Georgia ended in a Russian victory and another redrawing of the map with the Treaty of Turkmanchai on February 22, 1828. In addition to a host of punitive measures inflicted on Persia, the treaty allowed for the Russian annexation of the Khanates of Erivan and Nakhchivan, which had until then been held by Persia in accordance with the terms of the Treaty of Gulistan. This finally brought down the curtain on Persia's centuries-old domination of the Caucasus. Crucially for the future of the region, Russia had firmly in its possession the territories that would eventually become the modern republics of Azerbaijan, Georgia and Armenia.

The Azeri people now found themselves permanently separated by an international boundary. Azeris to the north now lived in territory dominated by the Russian Empire (from which the modern Republic of Azerbaijan would emerge), while those to the south remained under Persian rule. Nevertheless, relative freedom of movement across the borders continued, although merchants on both sides were subject to various taxes.

At first, the Russians opted for indirect rule over their new territorial acquisitions—allowing the local khans loyal to the tsar to maintain order. Yet this gradually changed as the Russian government changed its policy and opted for tighter administrative control over the region. Inevitably, a concerted effort was made to incorporate the khanates into the imperial political and economic system. As part of the drive, the Russian rouble was introduced (thereby doing away with punitive internal tariffs) and weights and measurements were standardised. In December 1867, the South Caucasus was divided into five provinces: Kutayis (Kutaisi), Tiflis (Tbilisi), Erivan (Yerevan), Elizavetpol (Ganja) and Baku—the last two provinces closely corresponded to the present-day Republic of Azerbaijan.

With the notable exception of oil-rich Baku and the Apsheron Peninsula, Azerbaijan experienced little in the way of cultural or beneficial economic change under the tsarist regime. Remaining a predominantly peasant land, the overwhelming majority of the Azerbaijani population languished in poverty in the countryside. While Alexander II had officially abolished the ingrained rural slavery of Russian serfdom with the Emancipation Act of 1861, 'the peasants of Transcaucasia received only partial freedom, being placed in the category of "half-serfs". Their obligations were not well-defined and proved the source of continuous quarrels and riots.'[38]

The Russians were well aware of the gravitational pull of much of the South Caucasus towards the wider Islamic world. With its overwhelmingly Muslim population, heavily influenced by mullahs educated in Ottoman Turkey or Iran, ultimately only a heavy-handed approach backed squarely by military muscle would prevent the Caucasus from slipping away from the clutches of the tsar.

It was the Russia's readiness to exploit Muslim tensions that had the unintentional effect of finishing off the work begun by Shah Ismail in the 16th century—that of making Shi'ite Muslims the majority in Northern Azerbaijan. At war with the Sunni Ottomans, the Russians looked more favourably on Shi'ites, while imposing a host of discriminatory measures on the Sunnis. The result was that Sunni numbers declined significantly as huge numbers made their way to Ottoman territory. Meanwhile, Shi'ite numbers were bolstered by the large influx of labourers from Shi'ite Iran.

Important ethnographic change also took place amidst Russia's strong desire to develop its agriculture and industry and so compete with the more advanced countries of Europe. Settlers, many of whom were from Christian communities such as the Russians, Ukrainians and Armenians, were encouraged to move to the region.

Armenians, who already had an ancient and important presence in the Caucasus and who had been key allies to Russia, were especially encouraged to settle in the former Yerevan and Karabakh khanates.[39] By the middle of the century their numbers had reached into the hundreds of thousands. The region of Karabakh would go on to be the scene of major warfare between Azerbaijan and Armenia in the 1990s.

Meanwhile, attempts to settle Russians in Azeri territory were not a great success. Russian settlers were given a decidedly frosty, if not outright menacing, reception by the local population. Often harassed and hounded, many left out of fear for their safety. A new drive to settle Russians in the early 1900s also failed to bring the desired results and again many simply threw in the towel and left for home.

## Baku and the oil industry

In the last two decades of the 19th century, Baku followed an astonishing trajectory that was altogether quite different to the rest of Azerbaijan. It saw itself dramatically transformed into a major state-of-the art oil-producing centre where, against the backdrop of derricks, slicks and smoke, Azeris and large numbers of immigrants (particularly Russians, Armenians and Iranians) came together to create a highly charged cosmopolitan cocktail.

Baku and the Apsheron Peninsula, the famed 'Land of Fire' with its natural oil seepages and flames that burned from the ground, had enjoyed a long history in the trade of oil. Across the centuries, local rulers had taken a keen interest in the commodity, while Arab historians had been reporting on oil production and extraction techniques in the region since the ninth century. The area was also a prime source of oil obtained from seals hunted in the Caspian waters. The skins of the seals were used as containers in which to transport both types of oil.

Although he never actually visited the region, the 13th-century Venetian merchant Marco Polo reported that Baku 'lamp oil' (the primary use for the product) was hauled off in bags by camels where it found its way as far as Baghdad. Up until the 19th century, oil was still being transported by ox and cart.

In the 1700s, the khans were reported to have been making a tidy sum from oil wells, which they leased to independent contractors. Production was estimated at a total of around 1,500 to 3,500 tons a year.[40] A visitor to Baku in 1735, the same year the khanate was restored to Persia, wrote:

> At Balakhani there were 52 oil wells, which were a great source of wealth. The oil from wells is collected in large and deep stone-made ponds and carted to Baku in large leather bags. The oil is used in all houses as a fuel (all houses are blackened by the dense smoke) and as a remedy for rheumatics and skin diseases, while, used internally, it cured gravel [kidney stones]. It is quite likely that the fact that the Black Death did not touch Baku was due to the presence of petroleum.[41]

Other uses for the oil included lubricating the axles of heavy carts, waterproofing flat-roofed buildings and even encouraging silk worms to produce cocoons. (In Azerbaijan today, oil is still used for medicinal purposes, especially 'naftalan', a rare form from the Azeri town of the same name, which is prescribed as a serious remedy for variety of skin, joint and bone diseases.)

By the end of the 19th century, Baku had changed beyond recognition. Thanks to the injection of huge amounts of foreign investment, it was now by far and away the greatest oil producer in the world. In keeping with its status as the first true oil-boom centre, it boasted all the trappings of a modern European city, complete with luxury hotels, casinos, public transport (in the form of a horse-driven tramway) and telephones.

Ludvig Nobel, the Swedish 'King of Oil' and pioneer of the Baku oil industry, credited with creating the Russian oil industry. With his brother Robert, he operated their Baku oil company Branobel, which at one point produced 50% of the world's oil.

The turning point had come in 1873, with new regulations that allowed free competition in oil-producing regions. Baku soon began to boast illustrious names such as the Nobel brothers, Rothschilds, Rockefellers, Shell, and Royal Dutch. Writing from first-hand experience in 1905, J. D. Henry felt compelled to echo what was by now only too apparent. 'Baku,' he declared, 'is greater than any other oil city in the world. If oil is king, Baku is its throne.'[42]

Not only did Baku lead the world in terms of the volume of production—by 1900 it was extracting 11.5 million tons a year, compared to 9.1 million in the United Sates—it was a trailblazer in production techniques too, pioneering methods of extraction (including steam drilling), refinery, storage, and transportation. Credited with laying the foundations of the modern oil industry in Baku were the energetic and ever inventive Swedish Nobel brothers Robert and Ludvig (their illustrious brother Alfred was the inventor of dynamite who left his fortune to fund the famed Nobel Prizes). It was they who pioneered deep drilling, laid the region's first pipeline, and, in 1877, gave the world its first oil tanker—a Swedish-built steel steamship that sailed on the Caspian, which they fittingly named the 'Zoroaster' after the founder of Zoroastrianism, the ancient fire-venerating religion that once thrived in Azerbaijan.[43] The Nobels also had an image of the famous Surakhani fire temple (near Baku), complete with burning flames, as a logo for their company.

Nobel fire temple logo.

Not to be outdone by such competition, by 1883 the Rothschilds had a fully operational railway line transporting oil from Baku to Batumi on the Georgian Black Sea coast. Travelling on the same line en route to Iran in the 1890s, the British military attaché

Late 19th-century scene of Batumi, the Georgian Black Sea terminal for Azerbaijan's oil. First proposed in 1878, onstruction on the Baku-Batumi pipeline began in 1896 and on completion in 1906, it was the world's longest.

and oriental secretary General Sir T. E. Gordon observed the changes in Baku and was clearly impressed by what he saw:

> Baku has immensely improved in every way of late, and now has good streets, hotels, and shops. The rise in the value of house property and building sites within the last ten years has been enormous. The town is growing in size, and new buildings are rising, which give it an appearance of prosperity and increasing trade. The harbour is crowded with steamers and sailing vessels, and the wharves present a pretty sight. The loading and unloading is quickly done by steam-cranes and powerful porters who come in numbers from the districts of Khalkhal and Ardabil.[44]

Offshore, on the waters of the Caspian, things were bustling too, with the likes of Swedes and Finns crewing some of the best steamships in the world. A major company in the region was the Volga Steam Navigation, founded by a Scotsman named Anderson. One branch of the company operated vessels on the River Volga, the other the Caspian. The latter ran six large steamers—captained by Russians and with German officers from the German colonies that had settled along the Volga—which were each capable of transporting 60,000 to 80,000 puds of oil (900-1,200 tons).[45]

While Baku played host to ever-increasing numbers of self-made oil

Oil tankers crowding the Caspian Sea at the turn of the 20th century. Ludvig Nobel had built the world's first successful oil tanker, the *Zoroaster*, which made its maiden voyage in 1878 from Baku to Astrakhan. The venture was so successful that Nobel ordered two more tankers that year of the same design: the *Buddha* and the *Nordenskjöld*.

millionaires and international tycoons, the overwhelming majority of the city's native Azeri population, now a minority, faced the daily struggle to make ends meet. The oil boom had brought them nothing, least of all jobs. Skilled posts were mostly taken up by Russians, Armenians and other foreign Europeans, while a flood of imported labour, especially from Iranian Azerbaijan, squeezed them out of unskilled work.[46] The influx of Iranian workers was noted by General Gordon, who wrote: 'Baku swarms with Persians, resident and migratory. They are seen everywhere—as shopkeepers, mechanics, masons, carpenters, coachmen, carters and labourers.'[47]

Nevertheless, the industrial boom in Baku did have the effect of creating a small yet well-educated native middle class. A few Azeris also joined the ranks of the wealthy Western oil magnates and some were conscientious enough to plough a part of their oil earnings back into Azerbaijani society. One of the best-known Azeri philanthropists was Haji Zeinal Abidin Taghiyev, who escaped a poverty-stricken upbringing to become one of the richest oil barons in Baku after establishing his own oil company in 1872. Taghiyev's money supported a

## Baku in the oil boom years

The huge influx of oil money during the late 19th century created a construction boom of impressive mansions and public buildings in Baku. Designed by top architects from Europe and America, many have survived to give the city a unique character. *This page (clockwise from top right):* City Hall; an ornate seafront block contrasts with the ancient simplicity of the Maiden's Tower; the Philharmonia. *Opposite:* the Seadat mansion.

Devastated wasteland of the Apsheron oil fields at the turn of the 20th century.

huge range of charitable projects, especially those relating to education, and he can be given credit for establishing the world's first Muslim boarding school for girls in 1901.

It was Azeris such as Taghiyev who also created the funds that enabled students to study abroad in Russia and Europe, thereby helping to nurture a new intellectual elite that would shape the burgeoning Azeri political life of the early 20th century and the eventual creation of the First Republic. Taghiyev was also responsible for the construction of the first western-styled drama theatre in Baku, built in the 1880s.

## The road to independence

From the arrival of the Russians to the close of the 19th century, there was little in the way of locally organized political activity in Azerbaijan, yet the situation was set to change dramatically. In 1905, Russia was rocked by a revolution instigated by opponents of the tsar who aimed to replace his autocratic rule with a democratic constitution. As elsewhere in the Empire, the First Russian Revolution sparked major political developments in Azerbaijan. Throughout the Caucasus there were outbreaks of civil disorder as peasants took advantage of the crisis to rise up against their landlords. Baku itself was rocked by outbreaks of violence, some of which spilled over into bloody ethnic confrontation and massacres.

In an attempt to defuse the empire-wide crisis, the tsar was forced to make concessions and allowed the creation of an elected parliament, known as the Duma. Despite being highly restrictive in terms of democracy, the Duma helped to fuel political activity across the empire —and no less so than in Azerbaijan, where the political and social upheavals had helped focus nationalist sentiments that had been quietly growing over the previous few years. Themes such as Muslim unity, independence and the region's Turkic heritage struck a resonant chord in the Azeri people. Tensions and competition between Azeris and Armenians (the Russians fatally manipulated the situation by favouring the latter) added a further dimension to this new sense of Azeri nationalism.

Relaxation of tsarist censorship laws in the aftermath of 1905 paved the way for an explosion of the Azeri-language press. Although the first Azeri newspaper, *Ekinchi* (*The Sower* or *The Ploughman*), was published in Baku as early as 1875, it had been shut down by the authorities only two years later. Other journals followed but Azeri-language publications were banned in the early 1890s. Now, in the new climate, Baku became the leading centre of

The aftermath of street violence in Baku—the man nearest the telegraph carries a revolver while a dead body lies in the street.

Greek-Russian style church at Balakhani—at the start of ethnic massacres in September 1905, its bell was said to have mysteriously tolled on its own.

Muslim journalism throughout the Russian Empire and a huge variety of Azeri newspapers, books and magazines flew off the city's thriving press.

Baku, a city that was aloof from European Russia and which had a raw and rapidly expanding oil industry and a hitherto unorganized workforce, was also becoming a natural and irresistible haven for Socialist activists escaping the long arm of the imperial Russian authorities. Amongst these was Leonid Krasin, a key player in the creation of the Bolshevik movement, who arrived in 1900.[48] The city was also the schooling ground of another Socialist agitator, a Georgian by the name of Ioseb Jughashvili, better known to the English-speaking world as Joseph Stalin.

Stalin first arrived in the city in 1904 in order to set up a new Bolshevik committee after the powerful Russian Social-Democratic Worker's Party had split into two factions, represented by the Bolsheviks and the more moderate Mensheviks. (In fact, Stalin's first article as an activist had already been published in Baku in 1901, in the first edition of the Georgian-language newspaper *Brdzola* ['Struggle'], the underground publication of the revolutionary wing of the Georgian Marxists.) At the time in Baku, a vanguard organization led by the charismatic agitator Ilya Shendrikov was busy organizing a general strike to secure workers a package of benefits including pay rises, sick pay and better working conditions.[49] Shendrikov's movement was severely criticized by the squabbling Bolsheviks and Mensheviks on account of its preoccupation with the immediate needs of the workers rather than 'higher' political Marxist Socialist objectives:

> The demagogue Ilya was never tired at mass meetings of discussing minor questions like the provision of aprons, etc, by the employers, without touching upon the real significance of the strike. As a result, the more backward workers left these mass meetings without being enlightened as to the true nature of the struggle and went away determined to fight only for mitts and aprons. They would leave the meeting with a hatred towards the Bolsheviks, for whom mitts and aprons were a minor problem and not the vital question.[50]

In fact, the Shendrikov strike succeeded in winning its demands. Ending on December 13, 1904, it proved to be the 'first collective agreement between workers and employers in the history of the Russian Empire'.[51]

By 1907, the Bolsheviks, dominated by the likes of Stalin (whose *nom de guerre* had changed from 'Koba' to 'Gaioz Nisharadze') and an Armenian by the name of Stepan Shaumian, had made Baku their base in the Caucasus. In the seclusion of the working class Muslim Azeri district they set up their secret printing press.[52] Recalling those days, Stalin was later to write:

> Two years of revolutionary work among the oil workers of Baku hardened me as one of the practical leaders. In contact with the advanced workers of Baku, in the storm of the deepest conflicts between workers and oil industrialists, I first learned what it meant to lead the workers' masses. There in Baku, I thus received my second revolutionary baptism in combat.[53]

Azeri Marxists had reservations about being subsumed by the Social Democratic Party, on account of its close identification with the Russians and Armenians. Accordingly, in Baku in 1904, a party known as the Muslim Socialist Democratic Party emerged, founded amongst others by the writer and future leader of Soviet Azerbaijan, Nariman Narimanov. Popularly known as Hummet (or Hemmat, 'Endeavour'), the party added Turkic nationalist elements to Socialist ideas, using the Azeri language to get its message across. The party was careful, however, to keep close ties with the Bolsheviks, and, despite the zealous ring to its name, it was in no way preoccupied with the religious aspects of Islam. The party expanded rapidly, but a sweeping political crackdown in 1907 by the Viceroy of Transcaucasia, Count Vorontsov-Dashkov, and the fact that its political ideology was ultimately of limited appeal to Azeris, resulted in a loss of influence in Azeri politics—for the time being at least.

Another important party emerged in Baku around 1911 with the secret foundation the Muslim Democratic Party, known as Musavat ('Equality'), by a group of intellectuals that included breakaways from Hummet. Less revolutionary in tone, the party based its core values on a more conventional interpretation of democracy. While it saw itself as a political vehicle for the growing sense of Azeri nationalism, Musavat was sensitive to the realities of the complex cosmopolitan climate of the city and remained cautious in its demands, pushing for secular nationalism and autonomy rather than fully-fledged independence. Despite an uneventful first few years, its leader, the journalist Mammad Amin Rasulzade (1884-1955), ensured that the party would later go on to achieve great popularity.

Nationalist political activity was not merely restricted to Baku. To the west, Ganja had also seen an increase in political activity driven by an open sense of Azeri-Turkish nationalism. There a secret militant organization known as Difai, which emerged in 1905 amid bloody Azeri-Armenian ethnic strife that had engulfed the region, had been carrying out armed attacks against the Russian authorities. In fact, it would be Ganja, not Baku, that would become the first capital of the Republic of Azerbaijan.

The turning point came in 1917, when Russia was once again rocked by revolution, this time with a vengeance. In March of that year, in the midst of an ever-worsening economic crisis and popular resentment over Russia's participation in World War I—a conflict that had brought unimaginable suffering and loss—Tsar Nicholas II was forced to abdicate. The tsar's fall brought an end to 300 years of rule by the Romanov dynasty and the Russian Empire slid uncontrollably into anarchy and chaos. A landmark event was the October Revolution, which saw the Bolsheviks seize power in St Petersburg. As the revolt spread, Azerbaijan found itself split into two opposing power centres: Baku and Ganja.

Baku simmered as Azeris, Russians and Armenians vied through a kaleidoscope of parties to take over the city amidst the gaping power vacuum. With a lack of external support, it was clear that the losers would be the Azeris. The main force in the crumbling Russian Empire was now the Bolsheviks, under the leadership of Vladimir Lenin. In Baku, the Bolsheviks were predominately Russians and Armenians and they wasted no time in using underhanded tactics to prevent the Musavat Party, despite its attempts at conciliation, from gaining fair representation on the city's ruling revolutionary council, or soviet.[54]

The governing of Baku therefore quickly passed into the hands of an entirely Bolshevik 'Council of Commissars', headed by Stepan Shaumian. Lenin, desperate to keep Russian control over Baku's oil, ordered the Armenian Shaumian to vigorously oppose any moves towards independence in Azerbaijan or, indeed, the rest of the Caucasus. By March 1918, with the Bolsheviks pulling no punches to control the entire city, relations between the various Baku factions had degenerated into bloody conflict. Russian troops, acting on behalf of the Baku soviet, and armed Dashnaks (Armenian revolutionary nationalists) attacked the city's Muslim (i.e. Azeri) areas, quashing resistance and forcing the community to recognize the authority of the Bolshevik soviet. After the surrender, the Dashnaks then embarked on a three-day rampage, slaughtering large numbers of ethnic Azeris and sparking off an exodus as thousands fled the city in fear of their lives. The notorious event, dubbed the 'March Days', would go down in the annals of Azeri history as a chilling act of Armenian aggression towards themselves, and it still stirs passions in the context of the present-day Azeri-Armenian conflict over Nagorno-Karabakh.

## Mammet Amin Rasulzade

One of the fathers of the modern Azeri nation, Mammet (or Mammad) Amin Rasulzade was born on January 31, 1884, in Novkhana, not far from Baku. As a journalist and activist in Baku in the early 1900s, he became involved in the Hummet party and the social democratic movement, which called for the national autonomy of Azerbaijan and naturally aligned him with the future communists. During this period, he also completed his first dramatic work, entitled *The Light in the Darkness* and which was staged in Baku in 1908.

He moved to Iran in 1909 to participate in the Iranian Constitutional Revolution (1906-1911), a period that saw the rise of nationalist and social democratic movements in Iran and the adoption of a constitutional monarchy.

Iranian Azerbaijan played an immensely important role in the rebellion. Sattar Khan, the leader, of the Tabriz anjuman, or council, led a historic uprising in the city that spread throughout the country and ultimately led to the downfall of the despotic shah, Muhammad Ali, and the restoration of the constituion.

While in Iran, Rasulzadeh founded the country's key social democratic newspaper *Iran-e No* (*New Iran*), which paved the way for modern European-style journalism in Iran. After he was forced to leave in 1911, he spent a period of time in Turkey before returning to Baku in 1913, where he became a major figure in the newly created Musavat Party, eventually becoming its chairman in 1917.

As an influential editor and contributor of the the Azeri journal, *Açiq Söz*, Rasulzade referred to Azeris as 'Turks' which led to the choice of 'Azerbaijani Turk' as a nationalist term for the people of his country (under the Russians they had simply been called 'Tatars' or 'Muslims'). After the dissolution of the Transcaucasian Federation, he was unanimously elected as chairman of the Azerbaijani National Council government in 1918.

Rasulzade is popularly held to have saved the young revolutionary Stalin from the clutches of the police in Baku in 1905 – a fact that is said to have helped him survive the excesses of the Bolsheviks after his arrest following the fall of the Azerbaijani Republic in 1920. He was subsequently taken to Moscow where he worked for two years as a press representative for the Commission on Nations. In 1922, he was seconded to Finland and would never return to his native Azerbaijan. He lived in exile for the rest of his life, first in Poland and Romania and eventually in Turkey after World War II.

Up until his death, Rasulzade led the Azeri opposition movement to Soviet rule and continued to write vigorously in support of the nation he helped to create. He died on March 6, 1955, and was buried in Ankara.

It was natural that Ganja should now be the centre for the Azeri nationalists. Unlike Baku, with its large Russian and Armenian population, in Ganja the majority of Azeris had been settling their differences under the united banner of their by now well-defined nationalist cause. While coming to terms with the city's highly influential Armenian minority and conceding them entitlement to representation in Ganja's government, the Azeris began to sever imperial ties, excluding Russian settlers from their plans and ordering all Russian troops to leave the territory.[55]

Meanwhile, there had been hopes that unity might be fostered across the South Caucasus and that a common approach to dealing with the chaos in Russia might be found, yet such expectations looked increasingly over-optimistic. Relations between the main Caucasian nationalist groupings—the Azeris, Armenians and Georgians—had been deteriorating. With little harmony evident between the groups, the atmosphere became increasingly militant. Nevertheless, a final push for unity somehow brought about the creation of an independent Transcaucasian Federation, created on April 22, 1918. The move brought instant condemnation from the Baku soviet, which declared itself utterly opposed to any decision to break away from 'Mother Russia'.

Perhaps inevitably, the new patchwork nation was doomed to failure from the outset. The following month, on May 26, the Georgians pulled out of the Federation and within the next two days both the Azeris and the Armenians had followed suit. On May 28, the authorities in Ganja declared the creation of the independent Azerbaijan Democratic Republic. This marked the first time that Azerbaijan was concretely and officially adopted as a political name for the territory and the term Azerbaijani used for its citizens.

The Musavats set up a provisional government in Ganja, headed by Fath Ali Khan Khoiski. A Sheki-born lawyer and judge who had graduated from Moscow University, Khoiski had been elected to the Second Russian Duma in February 1907 as a representative of the Muslim section. However, after the tsar decreed the Duma's dissolution in June the same year, Khoiski remained aloof from politics. Nevertheless, after the Russian Revolution of 1917, he was elected to the Transcaucasian Seim, or parliament, and served as minister for justice in the government of the Transcaucasian Federation.

The Ganja government immediately set about establishing political ties with their Muslim cousins in the Ottoman Empire and appealed to them for help in wresting Baku from the Bolsheviks. The Ottomans, still embroiled in World War I and allied to Germany, jumped at the offer.

Apart from Baku's oil, the invitation offered the Ottomans the irresistible opportunity of regaining some of their former glory by toppling the final bastion of Russian power in the Caucasus. The idea of helping the Azeris also fuelled romantic dreams of Turanism, or Pan-Turkism: uniting the various Turkic peoples who occupied lands stretching from the Balkans all the way to China.

Fath Ali Khan Khoiski (1876-1920): prime minister of the Azerbaijan Democratic Republic from May 1918 to April 1919.

From an Azeri point of view, such a partnership was not entirely comfortable—the Ottomans had so far not formally recognized the independence of Azerbaijan and few Azeris relished the prospect of absorption into the Ottoman Empire.[56] Nevertheless, in June 1918, a 7,000-strong Ottoman force, led by the Turkish commander Nuri Pasha, entered Ganja where it joined forces with thousands of Azeri and other volunteers who were dubbed the 'Army of Islam'.

Meanwhile in Baku, still reeling from the recent bloody inter-ethnic fighting, Shaumian and his Commissars repeated their opposition to any separation of Azerbaijan from revolutionary Russia and vowed to crush the national government in Ganja as well as its allies. In the meantime, the Baku soviet continued to ensure a ready supply of its oil to Russia.

Russia pulled out of World War I on March 3, 1918, after signing the Brest-Litovsk Treaty with Germany. A deal between the two powers was soon on the table whereby fuel-hungry Germany, still at war with the Allies, was to secure supplies of Baku's oil for itself, to be transported via Russia. Had Germany managed to persuade its Ottoman allies to call off its attack on Baku (a condition laid down by Russia), the city may well have ended up oiling the German war machine. As it happened, however, the Ottomans were clearly following their own agenda and the agreement fell through.

With Baku on the brink of collapse, surrounded and with no military or material support forthcoming from Soviet Russia, the possibility of

Scene depicting the shooting of the 26 Commissars, Shaumian is pictured top.
Note the Azeri-language caption, written in Perso-Arabic script.

inviting a British force in to help protect the city was now fiercely debated. The force in question, commanded by General Lionel Dunsterville, had been waiting in the wings in Iran, armed with authorization from the British government to enter the Caucasus on a reconnaissance mission.

Following the direct orders of Lenin and Stalin, the Bolshevik Commissars did all they could to persuade the Baku soviet not to allow the British in. Their efforts failed and instead the soviet turned on the Commissars. They were forced to relinquish power on June 31 and a new government, the so-called Centro-Caspian Dictatorship (made up mainly of Russians backed by Armenians and dominated by the more moderate Mensheviks), took over. While reaffirming its support for unity with Russia, the lacklustre government branded the twenty-six Commissars as traitors and blamed them for the recent disasters in the city. (Shaumian and his cronies were later arrested, deported to Turkmenistan and, in a somewhat murky sequence of events, shot and their bodies dumped in the Turkmen Desert.)

The new Baku government then called on the help of what they believed was a sizeable and willing British force that would help them withstand the onslaught of the Turkish attack. Their optimism was misplaced. General Dunsterville, leading a force of some 2,000 men, arrived by ship in August. Finding the city in upheaval and the task of defending it an overly risky proposition, he promptly ordered his troops to abandon it and, sailing back into the Caspian horizon, left Baku to its fate.

Inevitably, on September 15, Baku fell to the Ottoman-Azeri force. Three days later, the government of Azerbaijan arrived from Ganja and Baku was declared the capital of the Azerbaijan Democratic Republic. Parliamentary elections were held in November of the same year, bringing in a Musavat majority. It was a landmark event—the Republic could now lay claim to being the first modern Muslim democratic parliamentary state in history and one that also saw Muslim women able to vote for the first time, a rare phenomenon in any country, Muslim or otherwise, at this early stage in the 20th century (women in the USA and Great Britain would have to wait until 1920 and 1928 respectively to gain their full voting rights).

The newly-created Azeri Parliament reflected not only the various political parties of the different provinces but also represented the dominant ethnic groupings. Out of a total of 120 deputies to the Baku parliament, Azeris numbered 85, Armenians 21, Russians 10, the rest being Polish and Jewish. Fath Ali Khan Khoiski remained prime

Detail of official map issued by the Azerbaijan Democratic Republic in 1919.

minister until April 1919, after which time the post went to Nasib Yusuffbayli.

Meanwhile, the Ottomans were forced to withdraw from Baku. As their forces marched out, an Allied occupation force marched in, led by Major General W. H. Thompson on November 17, 1918. (The Ottoman Empire's role in World War I had ended a little earlier on October 30 with the signing of an armistice with the victorious Allies.) Charged with keeping a watchful eye over Azerbaijan, the force remained until the summer of the following year.

As the post-World War peace process got underway at Versailles, the Azeris spent many anxious months wondering how sympathetic the British and its Allies would be to their cause. Having sided with the Ottomans, the general feeling amongst the Azeris was that their independence would be ignored and their country simply be treated as a part of Russia. In the event, the Allied Command accepted the legitimacy of the government of Azerbaijan and in January 1920, amidst great relief, it recognized the Republic's independence, along with the other South Caucasian Republics of Armenia and Georgia.

## The early Soviet years

The First Republic of Azerbaijan was destined to be short-lived. With the British now gone, Azerbaijan was once again headed towards political disintegration, fatally undermined by Bolshevik agitation. The Russian government had no intention of simply sitting back and letting the fledgling Caucasian states enjoy their newfound independence.

Desperate and controversial attempts by Azeri politicians to win official recognition of their nation by Russia, which included offering a generous oil deal, led absolutely nowhere. Choosing its moment, the Russian government ordered the invasion of Azerbaijan, and in April 1920 its troops marched into Baku. A Soviet government was immediately established under Nariman Narimanov. Members of the national government were rounded up, arrested and prominent leaders executed. Rasulzade, Musavat's leading light, was himself arrested and, after a period of exile in Moscow, fled to the West, living in Germany, Poland and Rumania, before finally arriving in Turkey where he died in 1955. Both Georgia and Armenia suffered a similar fate to Azerbaijan and were brought under Soviet control in this same period.

A failed yet spirited campaign of resistance throughout Azerbaijan, especially in Ganja, led to serious conflict and heavy loss of Azeri life. Members of the Hummet Party were absorbed into the Russian Communist Party and, though they played key roles in the new Azeri government as well as the Communist Party, they were never fully trusted by the central government in Moscow. Many of them were later handed down death penalties in Stalin's Great Purge from 1936 to 1938.

The upheavals had left Azerbaijan in a desperate social and economic state. In the countryside poverty and neglect had led to the near total destruction of crops and infrastructure.[57] Villages were deserted as ragged peasants flooded in and out of cities in a desperate search for food and work. Yet the cities proved of little comfort: in post-war Baku, oil production had seriously declined, the oil barons had fled, and workers attempted the near impossible task of keeping up with a hugely inflated cost of living.

Meanwhile, the Soviet authorities set about the territorial, political, and economic restructuring of the troublesome Caucasus, binding Azerbaijan, Armenia and Georgia in half-communal, half-tailor-made institutional straitjackets, the straps of which were collectively tied up in Moscow. Azerbaijan now joined its neighbours as a member of the Transcaucasian Soviet Federated Socialist Republic (TSFSR), created in December 1922.

Crucial in Moscow's eyes because of its oil, Azerbaijan was given little say in the functioning of the TSFSR and few Azeris actually held posts in its governing bodies. Within Azerbaijan itself, the pervasive influence of the Azerbaijan Communist Party ensured that the Azeri government operated strictly within the bounds of Soviet acceptability—less than half of its members were Azeris, the rest being Russians along with a good number of Armenians. The Transcaucasian Federation was eventually dismantled in 1936 and Azerbaijan became a union republic, or soviet socialist republic, in its own right.

Azerbaijan had had a far from tranquil history yet there was little to prepare it for the sustained and intense trauma of Communist rule. In 1929, the Communist Party set into motion a campaign to enforce the collectivisation of agriculture. Lands were confiscated and peasants forced en masse into collectivized farms, bringing about widespread discontent in the countryside and regular uprisings that were brutally suppressed by the Soviet Red Army.

Added to this was the suffering caused by a prolonged campaign of purges against dissenters. Well before Stalin's notorious and much publicised trials during the 'Great Purge', which peaked between 1936 and 1938, the Azeris had already been subjected to oppression and fear—as was the situation in every other corner of the Soviet Union. In the early years of Soviet rule, anyone considered an opponent of the regime, especially the Musavats and others who had played a prominent part in Azeri nationalism, were under the constant threat of arrest and execution. The regime's ideological attack on religion, which gathered momentum towards the end of the 1920s, also brought Muslim leaders into the official line of fire.

Stalin had taken over the leadership of the Soviet Union after Lenin's death in 1924, and Narimanov clashed with the leader's close associate Sergo Orjonikidze (a Georgian like Stalin), who led the Communist Party in Transcaucasia. To remove him from the Caucasus, Orjonikidze had Narimanov transferred to Moscow where he died in 1925 under suspicious circumstances. The man who now stepped forward to eagerly do the new leader's bidding in Azerbaijan was an ethnic Azeri by the name of Mir Jafar Bagirov (Baghirov), Commissar of Internal Affairs, and, from 1933, First Secretary of the Azerbaijan Communist Party.

Bagirov emulated his master's ruthlessness and during the 'Terror' years he presided over a climate of fear in which anyone in Azeri society could suddenly find himself branded an enemy of the state. Politicians, writers, artists and poets in their droves were executed or exiled to Siberia and probable death. Loyalty provided little immunity from the witch-hunt. At the height of the Terror, even high-ranking officials of the

Nariman Narimanov (1870-1925, centre in white suit), leader of Soviet Azerbaijan.

Communist Party of Azerbaijan were dragged before courts to answer trumped-up charges and promptly shot. The total number of victims of the purges in Azerbaijan will never be known, but in the late 1930s alone the figure may well have exceeded 100,000.[58] (Bagirov himself would eventually fall from grace, accused of treason after Stalin's death.)

## The Great Patriotic War

Though Azeri life may have been of little value to Stalin, Azerbaijan's oil was not. On the eve of World War II—or the Great Patriotic War as it became known in the Soviet Union—Baku was responsible for the bulk of Soviet oil production. Furthermore, its prodigious output was not overlooked by the other global powers. When international conflict erupted, concerns that Azerbaijan's oil supply might fall into German hands had been sufficiently worrying to the British and French that they had even discussed contingency plans to pre-emptively destroy Baku's production facilities.

As the war progressed, Hitler did in fact become convinced of the vital need to acquire Azeri oil and accordingly drew up plans to march across the Caucasus to seize Baku—code-named 'Operation Blue'—and setting the attack date for September 1942. Anticipating success, Hitler's generals presented him with a 'Victory Cake' in the shape of the region, an event that was even filmed for posterity. As his entourage tucked into pieces of the Caspian Sea, the choice slice was saved for Hitler: Baku.

In the summer of 1942, bracing itself for an imminent attack, the Soviet government took drastic pre-emptive action. It ordered the wells in Baku to be sealed and began to transfer personnel, machinery and equipment—lock, stock and barrel—out of the region where it could be deployed to increase production in other parts of the Soviet Union more distant from the war front.

As in World War I, the Germans in fact never reached Baku and its oil. Yet this is not to say that Azerbaijan escaped lightly in the war. The deliberate scuttling of its oilfields had left its industry in ruins and although oil production was eventually resumed in 1943, it was a blow from which Baku would never recover fully. Furthermore, although fighting never came to Azeri territory, it had contributed as many as half a million men to the war effort elsewhere, suffering an appalling loss of life in the process.

Meanwhile, an event at the end of World War II unexpectedly brought Iranian Azerbaijan into the international limelight—one that proved to be one of the earliest incidents in the oncoming Cold War and which prompted Churchill to make his famous 'Iron Curtain Speech' of 1946. Early on in the war, Iran had been occupied by Soviet and British troops, becoming a key supply route between the Soviet Union and the Allies. The arrangement was intended to be strictly temporary, with agreements on both sides to evacuate the country within six months of the end of the war.

However, by 1945 the Russians had clearly made themselves at home, having decided to remain and support two nationalist movements in northwestern Iran: the People's Republic of Azerbaijan governed from Tabriz and the Kurdish Republic of Mahabad. After the Soviets ignored the withdrawal deadline of March 1946, the alarm was raised. There was little doubt that the Soviet Union was muscling in on the oil-rich Middle East and aiming for the same 'warm-water ports' that had eluded the tsars in previous times, and the West had no intention of standing idly by. A combination of heavy diplomatic pressure and appeals by Iran to the newly established United Nations, backed by menacing threats from the United States to expel Soviet troops by force from the region, finally persuaded the Red Army to withdraw in May. By the end of the year the Iranian separatist movement had crumbled, along with Soviet plans for the region. The event is considered one of the first episodes in the Cold War.

## Collectivisation and the economy

The collective farms or *kolkhozs* imposed by the Soviet authorities in the 1930s replaced privately owned or rented individuals farms in Azerbaijan. Although landless or very poor villagers applauded collectivisation, independent farmers and landlords, particularly in the richer mountain areas, put up fierce and sometimes bloody resistance.

Eventually it was the Soviet introduction of modern farming machinery, with its obvious advantage over traditional methods, that won most of the populace over to the new collective system. (The new machinery was so impressive that, for a brief period in the 1930s there was a fashion among the farmers of giving children names such as 'Tractor' and 'Cultivator'.)

Azerbaijan continued to grow all the grain it needed until Soviet agricultural planning in the 1950s forced each republic to specialize and cultivate a limited range of crops, a measure designed to make the satellite republics more dependent on both each other as well as the central government. With sufficient grain supplies coming from Kazakhstan and the Ukraine, Azerbaijan's duty was to supply cotton, grapes and, for the most part, vegetables—the latter explains its label as the 'USSR's pumpkin field'. Such changes made Azerbaijan into a grain importer for the first time in its history.

'Gathering Hay', 1966, by artist Alakbar Rezaguliyev (1903-1974).

In the 1960s, the collective farms, which were (in theory at least) owned by the farmers and run by locally elected directors, gave way to the new Soviet system of *sovkhoz* (from the Russian *Sovetskoye khozyaystvo* or 'Soviet venture'), in which farms were now openly state-owned and operated. These larger, more mechanised farms were devoted to cotton or viticulture, while more traditional small-scale activities such as beekeeping, tobacco growing, silkworm breeding and forest farming began to die out.

The change was actually welcomed by many, since *kolkhoz* members were paid a share of the collective farm's earnings each year, often in produce rather than money, which inevitably varied with the success of the harvest. *Sovkhoz* employees, on the other hand, had constant salaries paid in cash, along with paid leave and holidays.

Mikhail Gorbachev's *perestroika* during the 1980s with its promise of a return to private land ownership and independent farming, was at first met with great enthusiasm in Azerbaijan, but the corruption that was endemic in the Soviet system proved intractable. The need to bribe so many people, both in and out of government, in order to get land and ensure a trouble-free existence meant that many newly independent farms soon went bankrupt or were simply abandoned.

## The post-war years

After Stalin's death in 1953, his successor Nikita Khrushchev lost no time in ordering the Soviet Union's past to be officially reviewed. Khrushchev, head of the Communist Party from 1953 and premier of the Soviet Union from 1958 to 1964, denounced Stalin for mass murder and crimes against the Soviet People, thereby beginning a process of 'de-stalinisation'. With the tables of Soviet justice turned, Azerbaijan's villain Bagirov was able to experience first-hand the kind of courtroom ritual that had chillingly sent so many of his own victims to their fate. Arrested and tried on charges of engaging in anti-Soviet activities, he was denounced as traitor and shot in 1956. Somewhat belatedly, his victims were publicly absolved of any wrongdoing.

In the new climate, there was a substantial relaxation of control over the media, education and literature. This was not extended to religion, however. Since the late 1920s, religion had become the focus of a sustained campaign that saw the closure of mosques and the persecution of the Muslim clergy. A new ideological atheist attack was now pursued with vigour, and Islam was driven underground although it was far from eradicated.

Economically, Azerbaijan was destined to languish in the doldrums. Apart from the construction of the offshore oilfield Neft Dashlari, or 'Oil Rocks', which started production in the 1950s, the Azeri oil industry found itself in a pitiful state—production was woefully under-exploited and investment from Moscow negligible. In the post-war years, the Volga-Ural region and then Siberia replaced the Caspian as the centre of the Soviet Union's oil production (by the end of the Soviet era Baku oil production accounted for a mere three per cent of this, generating an income that was 'not sufficient even for the maintenance of existing oil installations').[59] Meanwhile, little was done to promote alternative industries. Although products such as Azeri carpets and caviar were important 'Soviet' exports, the rewards failed to reach Azerbaijan itself.

It was under Heydar Aliyev, First Secretary of the Azerbaijan Communist Party from 1969 onwards, that there was a significant shift in economic policy. A native of Nakhichevan from humble origins, Aliyev had worked his way up the Kremlin ladder, becoming the first Azeri to reach the rank of major-general in the KGB. As a result of Aliyev's careful guidance, by the late 1970s Azerbaijan had managed to record the highest industrial growth rate in the Soviet Union. Wheat and cotton production rose dramatically, and the republic became the Soviet Union's main grape producer.[60]

Aliyev was made a member of the Communist Party's ruling

Politburo in Moscow in 1982—no other Azeri had reached such political heights in the history of the Soviet Union. However, he fell from grace in 1987, after failing to fit in with the spirit of USSR leader Mikhail Gorbachev's new campaigns of *perestroika* ('restructuring') and *glasnost* ('openness') and he found himself abruptly 'retired' on health grounds. Returning to his birthplace of Nakhichevan, he spent the next few years campaigning against Gorbachev and was destined to return to the political centrestage as president of a once-more independent Azerbaijan.

In the meantime, however, the Soviet Union was staggering towards its demise by the end of the 1980s. As it began to falter, tensions in the Caucasus, which for so long had been suppressed, inevitably began to resurface and the republics of Azerbaijan and Armenia soon found themselves locked in a bitter conflict with each other.

## Nagorno-Karabakh

The eye of the storm was the hotly contested region of Nagorno-Karabakh ('Mountainous Karabakh'), which covers an area of approximately 5,000 square kilometres (roughly the size of Luxembourg) and lies in western Azerbaijan in the mountainous region of the Lesser Caucasus, close to the border of Armenia. Azeris and Armenians both lay claim to the region, based on their own conflicting interpretations of history, ancient and modern.

A major theme in the unfolding controversy was the Russian policy of inviting Armenians from the Ottoman and Persian Empires to resettle in the Caucasus following the Persian and Ottoman wars of the 19th century. The Azerbaijani argument is that such a policy altered the ethnic balance of lands traditionally associated with historical Azerbaijan and that present Armenian claims to such territory are unjustified.

The early 20th century saw serious clashes between Azeris and Armenians, particularly in Baku. The chaos that followed the failed revolution in Russia of 1905 unleashed a round of ethnic bloodletting in Azerbaijan, resulting in serious loss of life and major disruption and damage; and then, in the aftermath of the 1917 revolution and the collapse of tsarist Russia, ethnic tensions exploded once more. A particularly bitter event in the collective Azeri memory is the 'March Days' of 1918, when Armenian Dashnak troops, supposedly enforcing the Baku soviet's authority, went on the rampage and slaughtered large numbers of Azeris in Baku.

Nationalist passions also came to the fore during the brief period of independence (1918-1920) in the Caucasus as the newly established Azeri

## Azeris Worldwide

Determining the precise number of Azeris outside of Azerbaijan is a somewhat daunting task owing to the varying criteria used to define ethnic groups in the many countries where they live. Varying data, or the simple lack of it, add to the problem, meaning that present estimates of the total population of ethnic Azeris worldwide reach anywhere up to 46 million. The overwhelming majority live in Iran (est. 23-30 million)—where Azeris constitute a little under a third of the population—followed by the Republic of Azerbaijan with around 7.5 million. Three other countries with significant Azeri populations are neighbouring Turkey (c. 800,000), Russia (c. 650,000) and Georgia (c. 285,000). Armenia's significant Azeri population prior to the break-up of the Soviet Union is now minimal after Azeris fled or were expelled between 1988 and 1991. Figures from the United Nations High Commissioner for Refugees from 2003 put the number of exiles at 200,000. Azeris have also moved further afield in growing numbers, creating a diaspora of between 250,000 to 1 million, spread across countries such as Kazakhstan, Germany, Ukraine, Netherlands, Canada and the United States. Official census figures, where available, will inevitably be far smaller than the real total. Conversely, the data of international 'ethno-linguistic' projects tend to overestimate numbers, often as a result of incorrect classification of related Turkic peoples such as the Iraqi Turkmens as well as the use of unverified sources. Thanks to the creation of the Republic in 1991, combined with increased migration and a comparative easing of restrictions on ethnic groups in Turkey and Iran along with the international proliferation of Azeri press, radio and TV channels, there has been rapid growth in a sense of common identity amongst Azeris worldwide.

### Azeris in Iran

The Azeri (or *Âzari* آذری) population of Iran live mainly in the northwest provinces of the country—East Azarbaijan (= Azerbaijan), West Azarbaijan, Ardabil and Zanjan—forming an ethnic and geographical continuum with the Azeris of the Republic of Azerbaijan. Significant numbers also live in and around the capital Tehran as well as Kurdistan, Hamadan and Markazi. Iranian Azeris are Shia Muslims and have formed an integral part of the multi-ethnic Iranian state since the 11th century. It is a status quo however that has not been without its problems since the Azeri homeland lies on such an politically sensitive faultline. The traditional territory of Azerbaijan was divided definitively as a result of the struggle between the Russian and Iranian empires, and, later, Soviet support for nationalist movements in Iran continued for much of the first half of the 20th century. The increasing autocracy of the Pahlavi regime over the whole country included repressive policies towards groups such as the Azeris, Kurds and Balochis (the latter two peoples being Sunni Muslims who are similarly divided by sensitive international borders) but the 1979 Iranian Revolution, although just as repressive, did bring a degree of respite—notably some restoration of Azeri language publication, broadcasting and education rights. (Note that Iran is a country where more than 60 languages are spoken.) Concern in Iran has grown in recent years over the rise of calls for union between the two Azerbaijans, while the Republic of Azerbaijan has become increasingly concerned by what it sees as the threat of religious fundamentalism imported from Iran. Despite such pressures, Azeris have always been a stable part of Iran, evidenced by a historically continuous presence in the political and military leadership: modern top Iranian Azeris include Supreme Leader Ali Khamenei, fifth President Mohammad Khatami and Mir-Hossein Mousavi.

### Azeris in the Republic of Azerbaijan

In the Republic of Azerbaijan, Azeri Turks constitute approximately nine-tenths of the population. The remainder includes distinct groups of Daghestani peoples such as

Avars, Udins and Lezghins, as well as Russians, Armenians, Mountain Jews and Tats, Talyshs, Kurds, Turks, Georgians, Ukrainians, Germans and Iranians. The principal language is Azeri, although Russian is widely spoken and used in education, particularly in Baku. There continues to be a large number of displaced Azeris from Nagorno-Karabakh and its surrounding areas as well as Armenia.

### Azeris in Turkey

Since ethnicity is a fluid and sometimes controversial concept in Turkey, it is impossible to determine how many ethnic Azeris currently live there. Accepted guesstimates suggest a minimum of 800,000 Azeris, and reports indicate that as many as 300,000 of this number hold Republic of Azerbaijan nationality. Their presence is due to a long, complex history of settlement and migration that continues to the present day, aided by geographical proximity and closely related languages. What sets many of Azeri origin apart is the fact that they are Shia Muslims (Turkey is a Sunni country).

### Azeris in Georgia, Russia and the Former Soviet Union

The Azeri communities in Georgia total almost half a million and are concentrated in the capital Tbilisi and the three provinces bordering the Republic of Azerbaijan: Dmanisi, Bolnisi and Marneuli (just under 285,000 according to the 2002 national census). They comprise one of the two largest ethnic minorities, the other being the Armenians. In the Russian Federation estimates put the number of Azeris living at more than two million with the majority centred in and around Moscow (the official 2002 census figures of c. 129,000 may be up to four times more when assimilated and non-legal residents are taken into account) and St Petersburg (officially 17,000 in 2002 but unofficially estimated far higher). Another million live in the other countries of the former Soviet Union (excluding Georgia and Azerbaijan), particularly Ukraine, where economic migration is a growing phenomenon (46,000). Significant numbers of Azeris also live in Central Asia, especially in Kazakhstan, mostly as a result of the sustained campaigns involving purges and deportations of opponents of the Soviet regime from the 1930s. The majority of the first exiles were the wealthier farmers ('kulaks'), who resisted, or were perceived to resist, Soviet collectivisation of their land. Later, most of the exiles were intellectuals who had fallen victim to Stalin's Years of Terror during the 1930s and '40s. However, since many were regrouped in a limited number of places, they were able to retain their sense of community and therefore their identity. Even after the central government's decision in 1957 to allow deported ethnic groups such as the Chechens to return home, substantial numbers of Azeris opted to stay in their adopted land.

### Azeris in the West

The European population of Azeris may be as high as one million or more. The largest community is in Germany, with groups of varying sizes in every other country in the European Union, notably Netherlands, France, Sweden, Norway, Denmark and Greece. From 1920 onwards, after the Soviet take-over in the First Republic of Azerbaijan, political motives were the main reason for leaving the country. Shortly after the Second World War, Azeris from Iran also began arriving in the West, fearing reprisals after the collapse of their short-lived Soviet republic. A later influx of Azeris to Europe—mainly to Germany, Belgium and the Netherlands— began in the 1960s. Most of these were part of the Azeri community in Turkey who came along with the so-called Turkish 'guest-workers', who were employed in industry and public services as a cheap labour force. From 1991 to the present, there have been new movements of migration from the Republic of Azerbaijan to Europe. Initially, they tended to be to other former socialist countries such as Poland, Bulgaria and Hungary, where there were ample trade opportunities. Soon, however, this expanded to include Belgium, Germany and Scandinavia, where living standards are higher. Meanwhile, in the USA, the most significant concentrations of Azeris are to be found in California, New Jersey, New York, Michigan and Pennsylvania.

Anti-USSR independence slogans daubed on a Baku wall, 1990.

and Armenian republics mixed diplomacy with military threats to enforce their historical claims over territories with mixed ethnic populations. Not only did this include Nagorno-Karabakh, but also the region of Nakhchivan—now part of Azerbaijan but separated by Armenian territory—and Zangezur—a strip of land that connected Azerbaijan and Nakhchivan but which became part of Armenia. These lands, once part of the patchwork of South Caucasian khanates that were absorbed into the unsatisfactory tsarist system of provinces, failed to fit neatly into the equally problematic borders of the newly created republics.

Amid much wrangling and frequent violent confrontation, Armenia had little choice but to accept the decision made at the Paris Peace Conference in 1919-20 (involving diplomats from more than 30 countries, this was an attempt to form a lasting peace after World War I by resolving territorial disputes), which officially recognized Azerbaijan's claim to Nagorno-Karabakh. However, the Soviet invasion of the same year left a new question mark hanging over the fate of the region.

The Soviet government soon began carving up the Caucasus to its own satisfaction. Nagorno-Karabakh, with its large Armenian population, was on the point of being handed by the Bureau for Caucasian Affairs to Armenia but Stalin reversed the decision, using his first-hand experience in the Caucasus to guide his personal policy of 'divide-and-rule'. And so, in 1924, Nagorno-Karabakh instead was officially designated an autonomous region of the Azerbaijan Soviet Socialist Republic (SSR). Meanwhile, although the Armenian SSR received Zangezur, its claims on Nakhchivan were rejected. Instead Nakhchivan was granted the status of an autonomous republic within the Azerbaijan SSR, despite being geographically separated. That done, the Soviet authorities deemed the matter closed.

Azeri-Armenian ethnic tensions remained dormant, though by no means forgotten, under the oppressive Soviet regime. While there were rumblings of discontent during the 1960s, the new dialogue created by Gorbachev's *perestroika* and *glasnost* in the 1980s—a time when most of the Soviet republics seriously began to contemplate the possibility of a future outside the clearly decaying Soviet Union—intensified nationalist fervour and saw the issue resurface with a new urgency.

Matters came to a head on February 20, 1988, when a vote was passed in the Nagorno-Karabakh soviet to transfer the territory from Azerbaijan to Armenia. In response to the swift rejection by the Azeri and Soviet authorities, huge pro-Armenian demonstrations were staged in Armenia and Nagorno-Karabakh. Amidst general uncertainty and increasing rumours of ethnically motivated attacks, Azeri and Armenian passions began to flare once more. On February 27, in Sumgait, an ethnically mixed town in Azerbaijan where large numbers of Azeri refugees had been arriving, gangs of young Azeris went on the rampage. When the situation was finally brought under control two days later, the official death toll stood at 32 dead—twenty-six Armenians and six Azeris—although many believed this to be far higher.[61] The subsequent arrest and sentencing to death in a Moscow court of a young Azeri for his role in the killings intensified the highly charged atmosphere and led to further incidents and protest.

Increasingly incensed over the unfolding events in Nagorno-Karabakh, Azeris soon turned on Moscow and the puppet regime in Azerbaijan. Their anger finally found expression in a huge demonstration that took place in Baku during November. In January 1989, amidst the heightened tension and ever-growing numbers of refugees, the Soviet authorities sent in the Red Army and suspended the Nagorno-Karabakh parliament. A special committee under the direct control of Moscow was set up to help resolve the situation. But matters only worsened, and in May 1989, the Armenians in Nagorno-Karabakh began a four-month strike. Azerbaijan countered by imposing an economic blockade. Then, in December 1989, both the Armenian and

Nagorno-Karabakh parliaments adopted a resolution to make Nagorno-Karabakh part of Armenia, setting the scene for open conflict.

## Independence and war

One of the effects of the crisis in Nagorno-Karabakh was to galvanize political activity in Azerbaijan. Of the new parties created in 1989, the Azerbaijan Popular Front (APF) proved especially influential. Created by Azeri intellectuals, the APF had a broad popular appeal. Its elected chairman was Abulfaz Elchibey, a firm supporter of pan-Turkism who called for closer ties with Turkey. Like Heydar Aliyev, he was a native of Nakhchiven and also shared the same surname (he only took the name Elchibey, meaning 'envoy of the people', in the late 1980s). Firmly behind reasserting Azeri control over Nagorno-Karabakh, the APF's agenda was a bold one that pointed to a new future for Azerbaijan. It demanded a secular democratic constitution for Azerbaijan and, though it stopped short of insisting on full independence from the Soviet Union, it nevertheless called for a high degree of political and economic freedom.

The APF tapped into the popular disenchantment and bitterness over the republic's management by the ruling elite, which had left the country amongst the poorest in the Soviet Union—a state of affairs that was scandalously at odds with the favourable trade performance it enjoyed with its fellow republics. The APF accordingly promised major reforms and vowed particularly to undo the damage caused by Soviet agricultural policies, epitomized by collectivisation.

In the late summer of 1989, the APF was behind a series of major strikes and demonstrations aimed at getting its demands heard and in October, it managed to gain official recognition as a party—by no means an easy feat.

In 1990, a bleak period in Azeri history known as 'Black January' took place. After ethnic clashes had left a number of Armenians and Azeris dead, Moscow announced its intention to send troops into Azerbaijan and Armenia. Curfews were imposed in the major Azeri cities including Baku and a state of emergency was declared in Nagorno-Karabakh. Soviet troops and tanks rolled into Baku on January 20 and a bloodbath ensued. Scores of civilians were killed and many more wounded. Gorbachev justified the use of troops as a necessary measure to counter extremists in Azerbaijan—by which he meant APF leaders, many of whom had been arrested in the operation. The event left Azerbaijan profoundly traumatised. Indeed, even the Azeri authorities saw fit to condemn what they termed an illegal act of aggression. Across the board, relations with Moscow had now reached an all-time low.

In August 1991, the Soviet Union was rocked by an attempt to depose

Gorbachev. While the bid failed, it nevertheless dealt the regime a mortal blow and shattered the illusion of a Supreme Soviet authority over the USSR once and for all. Soon there was a stampede of Soviet republics rushing to leave the Union, led by Georgia and the Baltic states. In Azerbaijan too, events moved swiftly. On August 30, the Azerbaijan Supreme Soviet voted to restore independence to Azerbaijan—a decision that was formalized on October 18. The Communist Party of Azerbaijan (CPA) immediately dissolved itself.

It may have seemed that Azerbaijan had shrugged off the Soviet regime almost overnight, but the tentacles of Moscow were still long and active and the Communist legacy was not about to vanish as rapidly. The Azeri ruling elite in particular was not prepared to relinquish the reins of power and let in new blood. The following month, Ayaz Mutalibov, the Moscow-backed Communist leader, was elected president of independent Azerbaijan. As the only runner in the elections, his investiture was greeted with mass demonstrations.

Abulfaz Elchibey (1938-2000), the Republic's first elected president.

Meanwhile, the situation in Nagorno-Karabakh was on a knife-edge. Negotiations to resolve the situation foundered and Armenia (which had also gained independence in 1991) began to pour troops into the region. In January 1992, Armenians in Nagorno-Karabakh declared the territory the Republic of Mountainous Karabakh and began to consolidate their hold over the region.

Mutalibov was forced to resign in March 1992 over his bungled handling of the crisis. Nevertheless, two months later he was reinstated—an act that was greeted again by huge protests, led by the APF, which culminated in the occupation of the Majlis (National Assembly) and presidential palace by demonstrators. Having clearly outstayed his welcome, Mutalibov duly packed his bags for Russia.

Elections were held in June 1992 and, with a majority of more than 60 per cent, Abulfaz Elchibey stepped into the presidency. Pledging to end the war in Nagorno-Karabakh, the new Azeri leader also declared his ambition to steer Azerbaijan away from its ex-Soviet partners and to reject membership of the Commonwealth of Independent States (CIS), created by Russia to maintain control over the ex-Soviet republics. Instead, he believed, Azerbaijan should forge ever closer links with Turkey.

Under Elchibey, an intensive military campaign in Nagorno-Karabakh was launched, but, despite making initial gains, the Azeris were unable to withstand the huge counter-offensive. The cost to Azerbaijan was immense. Armenia managed to seize of most of Nagorno-Karabakh along with areas of its surrounding territory.

Meanwhile, the country's sharp descent towards economic ruin was matched only by Elchibey's plummeting popularity. By June 1993, the Azeri campaign had all but collapsed and a colonel by the name of Surat Husseinov promptly staged a military rebellion. As he marched towards the capital, the beleaguered president fled to his native Nakhchivan. In the meantime the old political stalwart Heydar Aliyev chose his moment to emerge from his own Nakhchivan exile and occupy the political centrestage once more.

Called on by Elchibey for his support, Aliyev confidently assumed the powers of presidency in his absence. This did not prevent the march of Husseinov's army into Baku, although this was carried out without any shedding of blood. In the frantic negotiations that ensued, Aliyev duly appointed the colonel prime minister and handed him responsibility for the military. (Husseinov was subsequently dismissed and later imprisoned for allegedly taking part in an attempted coup.)

Elchibey watched on horrified and, refusing simply to disappear, he demanded to be handed back his right to take up the the presidency. A referendum was held in August to settle the matter. He fared disastrously: the Azeri people almost unanimously turned in a vote of no-confidence and he was officially dismissed. In the elections that followed on October 3, Aliyev, at the head of his party, Yeni Azerbaycan (YAP—New Azerbaijan Party), won the presidency in a landslide victory.

After further failed attempts to win back Nagorno-Karabakh over the following months, a Russian-brokered cease-fire was declared in May 1994. The conflict had cost more than 30,000 lives to that date alone and the accompanying social, economical and territorial cost of the war to Azerbaijan was immense. When the dust settled Azerbaijan had lost control of between 15 to 20 per cent of its territory, while nearly a million of its people were displaced, a situation that continued to place an enormous burden on the country as it entered the 21st century.

The Baku metro system, although built in Soviet times, continues to contribute to the capital's international standing as a symbol of efficiency and public service.

## The new Republic

Regardless of these internal disclocations, in November 1995 Azerbaijan adopted a new secular constitution backed by popular referendum. Aliyev continued to hold onto power for the duration of the 1990s, during which time Azeri political life remained decidedly stormy. There were several attempted coups linked to Husseinov and Elchibey while former president Mutalibov was also accused of planning to overthrow Aliyev's leadership in September-October 2001, backed by a group of opposition parties and other groups.

Aliyev's response to the challenges was to tighten his control over the government and military, removing many of his opponents from power and ensuring a central rule for his ruling Yeni Azerbaycan party, with its key positions as often as not reserved for his close relatives. Aliyev's critics condemned him for suppressing political freedoms, rigging elections and turning a blind eye to rampant corruption among his cronies, yet he was undeniably regarded with affection by many Azeris who knew him by the nickname 'Baba', or 'Grandfather'.

Economically Azerbaijan continued to face great hardship. Apart from endemic corruption, the war with Armenia had left it with the huge burden of supporting hundreds of thousand of displaced Azeris. The impasse in the Nagorno-Karabakh dispute, described as a 'frozen conflict', was enough to keep even the boldest of foreign investors at arm's length.

Nevertheless, there was ground for some optimism. In September 1994, Aliyev brokered what was described as the the 'Deal of the Century' between the State Oil Company of the Azerbaijan Republic (SOCAR) and major Western oil companies, which led to the injection of massive foreign investment into Azerbaijan's energy sector and to the republic's return, in 1997, to the world oil markets. Meanwhile, another boost was the discovery in 2000 of significant gas reserves in the Shah-Deniz offshore field, which promised to make Azerbaijan a major future gas exporter

With the Soviet era behind it, Azerbaijan began to re-evaluate its relationship with the wider world. Russia was viewed with suspicion and accordingly there was a general desire amongst Azeris to place as much distance as possible between themselves and their former Communist rulers. Azerbaijan's joining of the newly created Commonwealth of Independent States (the economic union originally comprising 12 of the 15 former Soviet republics) had only been made possible after President Mutalibov had overriden the National Assembly's unanimous vote not to do so—a decision that helped contribute to his downfall.[62] After Azeri membership was finally ratified in 1993, Aliyev was still careful to pursue a policy of independence regarding military matters, distancing his country from any CIS common defence agreements.

After independence, Azerbaijan was free to explore its relations with its once hugely influential neighbouring Islamic states, Iran and Turkey. Relations with the latter were especially productive. With its related language and heritage and a distinctly secularist outlook, Turkey was a state with which the Azeris could confidently establish political, economic and cultural ties.

Iran, however, presented a number of problems. Despite many important agreements struck with Teheran relating to judicial and

Generations of oil derricks are a constant reminder of Azerbaijan's natural wealth.

legal matters and economic co-operation, the relationship between the two states nevertheless remained uneasy. Given the secularist culture that had developed in Northern Azerbaijan since the 19th century, as well as a tendency towards Western culture and ideals, the Islamic revolutionary ideals prevalent in Iran held no attraction. Rather, uncertain of Iranian ambitions in the region and deeply

Presidents Ilham and Heydar Aliyev with the capital's panorama behind them.

concerned about Iran's potential to export Islamic fundamentalism, Azeris continued to view their neighbour with a degree of suspicion. Iran, for its part, held back from stirring up politico-religious agitation in Azerbaijan owing to its desire not to antagonize Russia. Relations between Azerbaijan and Iran were not helped by the latter's siding with the Armenians on the Nagorno-Karabakh issue as well as key differences over the legal status of the energy-rich Caspian Sea and conflicting national oil and gas policies (in fact, Aliyev was branded a 'tool of the Great Satan' by the Iranians on account of his oil deals with the US).

The relationship was further complicated by differing views of history of the Azeri people. It is a commonly held belief in Iran that Azeris inhabiting Iranian Azerbaijan are in fact Iranians who, by an accident of history, happened to have adopted a Turkic language—accordingly, their rightful place is with the Iranian nation. The argument can then be extended to justify calling the Azeris of the Republic of Azerbaijan 'Iranians', who were separated from Persia as a result of 19th-century Russian imperial expansionism.

In Azerbaijan, on the other hand, Azeris living in Iran are considered to be ethnic Turks who share a common history in a land that has, over the centuries, been forcefully occupied by foreign powers. Taken to its own logical conclusion, for some this would mean that Iranian

View of the old city walls of the ancient and symbolically important city of Shusha.

Azerbaijan should be reunited with the Republic of Azerbaijan. Elchibey, who died in 2000, was one of those who argued such a case before finding it necessary to moderate his tone in the interests of political correctness.[63] Such views kept Iran vigilant and mindful that overly friendly relations between the two groups of Azeris could bring with it certain long-term dangers.

On December 12, 2003, Aliyev died at the age of 80, but not without having laid plans to ensure a smooth transition of power to his son Ilham Aliyev, who had already become president in October 2003. Born in 1961, Aliyev junior was a graduate from the prestigious Moscow State Institute of International Affairs. He later worked as a vice president of Azerbaijan's state oil company and became co-chairman of his father's ruling party, YAP. Despite being portrayed as a reformed playboy and gambler, many (including oil-rich Western companies) saw in him a way in which to fill a looming power vacuum quickly and peacefully, and thus to maintain the status quo—or perhaps even to undertake genuine reforms.

The future of the Azeri economy rests on its ability to extract and export oil and gas. In 2003 the energy sector accounted for 90 per cent of exports. Azerbaijan now figures amongst the twenty top oil-rich countries in the world. Maximizing its potential depends on foreign investment and expertise as well as regional stability and the ability to export its energy—to which end the success of the Baku-Tbilisi-Ceyhan pipeline, which began transiting oil to the Mediterranean via Georgia and Turkey in 2006, is especially important.

Meanwhile, finding a solution to the conflict with Armenia is of vital concern for Azerbaijan. Several internationally sponsored initiatives to find a settlement have failed—ranging from granting substantial autonomy for Nagorno-Karabakh within Azerbaijan, to Azerbaijan giving up claims to Nagorno-Karabakh in exchange for other territory (such as the Zangezur region in Armenia, which would create a corridor connecting the Azeri heartland with Nakhchivan).

During inconclusive talks between the Azeri and Armenian governments held in 2001, the region of Shusha, of great symbolic importance to Azeris, became pivotal in any resolution of the crisis. The city of Shusha's historical role as the capital of the Karabakh khanate still symbolizes the Azeri spirit of independence and resistance to foreign occupation, as epitomized by Ibrahim Khan's stand against Agha Muhammad Khan in 1795. The city, including a number of surrounding villages, was lost to regular Armenian forces in May 1992, resulting in the exodus of the entire Azeri population. (According to a 1989 official Soviet census, the total population of the Shusha region had been 23,156 of which around 92 per cent were Azeris and 7 per cent Armenians.)[64]

The strength of popular feeling over Shusha was summed up by Azeri foreign ministry official Elchin Amirbayov, who declared that the nation felt that:

> No settlement is possible without restoration of Azerbaijani sovereignty over the Shusha region. In addition, they [the Azeri people] believe that the Azerbaijani people evicted from Nagorno-Karabakh, including the people from the Shusha region, should be given the right of return and provided with the same security guarantees that will be provided for the Armenian population of Nagorno-Karabakh.[65]

The loss of territory aside, even if international attention lessens over the Nagorno-Karabakh stalemate, its displaced population will continue to be a harrowing reminder for the Azeri people.

*

# History Mirrored in Words: Language Policy in Azerbaijan[1]

Çiğdem Balım-Harding

*Along came the tongues of the Quran,*
*The voices of the Prophet, the language of law.*
*They put you behind the door.*
*You asked for justice, they robbed you.*
*But you were not destroyed, my mother, my dear language,*
*You made armies tremble, my hero Tongue!*
—Sabir Rustemkhanli (from *Sağol, ana dilim*)[2]

AZERI, OR AZERBAIJANI Turkish (*Azərbaycan dili*), is the national language of Azerbaijan.[3] It is also spoken by the Azeris in northwestern Iran, Afghanistan, Iraq, Syria, Turkey, and by the Azeri communities in other parts of the world. Linguistically classified among the Southern (or Oghuz) branch of the Turkic languages along with Turkish (Osmanli), Turkmen and Gagauz (Balkan Turkish), Azeri has been written in the Latin alphabet (Roman script) since December 25, 1991.[4] The adoption of a new alphabet to replace the Soviet Cyrillic was one of the first decisions of the Parliament of the new Republic of Azerbaijan.

Changing alphabets is a form of language planning which would be an almost unthinkable decision for many nations. However, alphabet reforms have been an inseparable part of Azerbaijan's social and political history since the 19th century. Baku itself was the centre of debates over language reforms and alphabet changes among the Turkic-speaking peoples in the early 20th century. As the first republic to change its alphabet from Cyrillic to Latin, Azerbaijan led the more recent round of alphabet reforms among the Turkic-speaking peoples of the former Soviet Union. Such changes illustrate the fact that languages are conceived by their speakers not only as instruments of communication but also as symbols of group or national identity and social and political change.

The Azeri language has a well-established literary tradition dating from the 14th century. Azeri, along with Chagatai and Ottoman Turkish was one of three literary forms of the Turkic languages. As a written language it was widely used by the peoples of the North Caucasus and Transcaucasia and, like the languages of other Muslim peoples of the time, it was written in the Perso-Arabic script.

The Treaty of Turkmanchai in 1828 marked the final division of the Azerbaijani population between Iran and Russia, giving rise to the birth of Southern and Northern dialects of the language. During the 19th and early 20th centuries, in Russian-controlled Azerbaijan there was a period of rediscovery of Azeri history, literature and identity. Azeri intellectuals, many of whom were educated in Russia, Istanbul and Paris, contributed to movements of reformation and cultural renaissance in the Turkic world. Amid fierce debates about religion and morality and the role of education for modernization, the use of the Arabic alphabet was a key issue. It was recognized that the Arabic script was cumbersome for representing the vowel sounds of Turkic languages and therefore of Azeri. Accordingly, it came to be seen as a major hindrance to mass literacy in society. As Azeri became the medium of education, the reform of the Arabic alphabet gathered momentum.

The adoption of an alphabet based on Latin was a daring and radical proposition. Arabic was not simply the established medium of writing for the Turkic languages. It was a unifying force throughout the Islamic world. Being the medium of the sacred Quran and the lingua franca of the ethnically and linguistically diverse Muslim peoples, the Arabic language and script enjoyed a status that was second to none.

A key player in the language reform movement in Azerbaijan, which was intimately linked with similar movements among the other Turkic-speaking peoples of Russia and the Ottoman Empire, was the dramatist Mirza Fatali Akhundov (1812-78). Akhundov represented the modernist Azeri intellectual who associated language use with social reform and development. He favoured a literary language that was closer to the colloquial form and which could be used by all levels of society. His plays, which were satires of traditional religious morals written in colloquial language, made a significant contribution to the modification of the literary language. Like his colleagues, Akhundov aimed to modernize and westernize society and believed mass literacy was achievable only by means of a struggle to free all the non-Arab Muslim peoples of the 'Orient' from the Arabic alphabet. He was especially keen for Iran and the Ottoman Empire to join the cause.

Akhundov prepared a reformed Arabic alphabet where each sound could be represented by a letter that would enable people to write as they speak. During the same period, intellectuals of the reformist Tanzimat movement in the Ottoman Empire were also discussing the possibility of an alphabet reform. Writers such as Namik Kemal were against a total change but backed the reformation of the existing Arabic alphabet. Ali Suavi, an Ottoman publisher, was already using a reformed version of the Arabic alphabet in works published in Ottoman Turkish.

Akhundov came to Istanbul in 1863 from Tbilisi and submitted his proposal, 'The Reform of the Alphabets of Islam', to the Ottoman Scientific Society, supported by its head Mehmed Munif Efendi. While the society agreed that the Arabic script was indeed unsuitable for writing and reading Turkish, it was unable to approve Akhundov's proposal on the grounds that a new alphabet would alienate the people from their heritage and render it impossible for younger generations to read the literary works of the past. Akhundov was nevertheless awarded a medal and the promise that his works would be published in Ottoman Turkish.

During his stay in Istanbul, Akhundov met the Iranian Ambassador Mirza Husain, with whom he had been corresponding since 1857. Through him, Akhundov got to know the Iranian journalist Mirza Malkum Khan, who was also a strong proponent of alphabet reform. Between 1868-78, Akhundov worked with Malkum Khan on a Latin-based alphabet. In 1873, through the Ottoman newspaper *Hakayik*, he presented the Ottomans with another alphabet based on a combination of Cyrillic and Latin. Again the response was not positive.

Meanwhile, the press in Azerbaijan was becoming an important vehicle for the spread of spoken Azeri as a written language. The first Azerbaijani newspaper was *Ekinchi* (*The Sower* or *The Ploughman*). Published between 1875 and 1877, it was edited by Hasan Bey Malikov Zardabi (1837-1907) who was a naturalist and an educator. *Ekinchi* was closed in 1877 for alleged pro-Ottoman sentiments during the Russo-Ottoman War of 1877-1878. While three periodicals subsequently appeared, in the uncertain period leading up to the First Russian Revolution of 1905, Russia enforced a ban in 1904 on all periodicals published in Azeri.

The crackdown meant that the Azeri publishing centres shifted to Iran and Tbilisi, the latter being second principal media centre after Baku. Nevertheless, after 1904, there was a sudden proliferation of newspapers using Azeri or a modified form of Ottoman, which were edited by westernized reformist intellectuals with secularist and anti-colonialist sympathies. Prominent among them were Jalil M. Mammadghuluzade, editor of the popular satirical magazine *Molla Nasraddin*, and Ali Bey Huseynzade, editor of *Fuyuzat* (*Bliss*), a literary periodical. Since Azeri intellectuals were not only thinking of an alphabet reform for Azerbaijan but of one that would encompass the Muslim world, they had hopes of organizing a conference among the Muslims of the Orient to reform their alphabets.

Similar movements had started among the Tatars, inspired by 19th-century Russian nationalism. Tatar intellectuals in Kazan, Ufa and Orenburg joined forces with Ismail Bey Gasprinsky, a Crimean Tatar intellectual, to establish a common literary language for all Turkic peoples. They envisaged that this should be a modified form of the Kazan dialect. However, the Tatar scholars did not support any moves to replace the Arabic alphabet. They believed that each religion had an alphabet as its symbol and therefore any change would have a significant impact on religious and cultural traditions—in this case, those of Islam.

In 1883, Ismail Bey, now editor of the newspaper *Terjuman* (*The Translator*) in the Crimean city of Bakhchisaray, argued along the same lines as his Azeri contemporaries that traditional Islamic society was ready for reform. However, while the secularist Azeri intellectuals saw reform of the alphabet as a means to achieving modernization and social change, Gasprinsky wanted to reform Islamic society using the religion of Islam itself, and he was not convinced that an alphabet reform was necessary. He formulated a 'new method' (*usuli-jedid*) which aimed at reforming the traditional *mektebs* ('maktabas' or Quranic schools) with the introduction of secular subjects and a phonetic method which made literacy in the Arabic alphabet easier to achieve.

Gasprinsky's ideas found resonance in Azerbaijan. At the beginning of the 20th century, a time when literacy was no more than ten percent, the language of education was a constant bone of contention. In secondary schools a few courses might be in Azeri but the rest were in Russian. Meanwhile, higher education was entirely in Russian. Native language instruction was offered only in religious schools, leaving students unqualified for higher education or jobs. Parents wanted to keep their Azeri traditions and language, but if their children were to succeed in life and have better jobs they had to be educated in Russian.

Discontent among Azeri teachers grew. They complained of the Russification of their language and poor preparation of students for work in their own language. Therefore, they called for the use of Azeri (or 'Tatar' as the Russians called it) as the language of instruction in the schools, demanding textbooks in Azeri and the introduction of the new system of *jedid* schools for teaching reading.

In 1906/7, a Baku-based committee comprising respected members of the community and chaired by the nationalist Nariman Narimanov attempted to address these concerns. It recommended a programme of study that would be conducted in Azeri, including language, literature, religious studies and a variety of secular subjects. Russian would also be taught and used as the language for certain courses such as accounting. A comprehensive plan for the nationalization of education was also produced by the committee, a large proportion of whose members belonged to the Russian Social Democratic Workers' Party (the forerunner of the Communist Party) or were affiliated to the Socialist movement.

During the short-lived 1918-20 Azerbaijan Democratic Republic there was renewed interest in the study of national history, literature and culture along with a new-found pride in the Azeri language and a keen desire to promote its use (for example, it became the language of instruction at Baku University in 1918). As discussions of alphabet reform gained new impetus, the adoption of a Latin-based alphabet was seriously considered. Under the Musavat government, Latin alphabet projects were prepared by Mahammadagha Shakhtakhtinski, Tagizade and Sajidov, and another by Abdullah Bey Afandizade Azagbeyli in 1919. In 1920, Afandizade's project was submitted to the new republic's parliament and discussions started on whether to reform the Arabic alphabet or to change to a Latin-based one.

After the Russian seizure of power in April 1920, the new Bolshevik government was overwhelmingly in favour of the Latin alphabet, yet the Azeri elite remained divided on the issue. Supporters of alphabet change claimed that a Latin-based alphabet would make education and communications easier and therefore lead to a better rate of literacy and social development. It was argued that, unlike the Arabic script, the Latin script was international in character and easier to write and print. However, opponents interpreted this enthusiasm for change as a desire on the part of the Communists to alienate Azerbaijan from other Turkic-speaking peoples and the wider world of Islam. They insisted that changing alphabets would cut future generations off from their past and prevent them from accessing their literary heritage. Furthermore, with the adoption of a Latin alphabet, religious leaders and other literate people would be made illiterate overnight and be alienated from the Tatars in the rest of the Soviet Union and the Turks in Ottoman Turkey.

| *Letter* | *Value (IPA)* | *Letter* | *Value (IPA)* |
|---|---|---|---|
| A a | [a] | Ŋ ŋ | [ŋ] |
| B b | [b] | O o | [o] |
| C c | [dʒ] | F f | [ö] |
| Ç ç | [tʃ] | P p | [p] |
| D d | [d] | Q q | [k] |
| E e | [e] | Ƣ ƣ | [ɣ] |
| Ə ə | [æ] | R r | [r] |
| F f | [f] | S s | [s] |
| G g | [g] | T t | [t] |
| H h | [h] | U u | [ü] |
| İ i | [i] | V v | [v] |
| I ı | [ɯ] | X x | [x] |
| J j | [j] | Y y | [u] |
| K k | [q] | Z z | [z] |
| L l | [l] | Ƶ ƶ | [ʒ] |
| M m | [m] | З з | [ʃ] |
| N n | [n] | ' | [ʔ] |

Table 1: Azerbaijan's first Latin alphabet, 1922

In fact, throughout the Soviet Union many Tatar intellectuals blankly refused to accept arguments for the superiority and ease of the Latin alphabet, nor did they believe it was the key to promoting mass education. For them, there was no reason why Arabic could not be made to represent the vowel sounds of Turkic languages. Similar sentiments were echoed by nationalist Ottoman intellectuals. They were all worried that if one Turkic group began to use the Latin alphabet, they would be cut off from the rest of the Turkic world, with serious ramifications for the future of their commonly-held written script.

It is alleged that a meeting held in the autumn of 1920 between Lenin and leading Azeri politician Samad Aghamalioghlu (1837-1930) changed the course of events in favour of the Latin alphabet. When asked by Lenin as to how the Azeris felt about the Latin alphabet, Aghamalioghlu replied that the Azeri people were only too willing to embrace it, upon which Lenin exclaimed: "Latinization? This is revolution in the East!"

During a teachers' conference in October 1920 in Baku, the alphabet issue was reopened. Azeri intellectuals divided into two main groups: Reformists (*Islahatchilar*) and Pro-Latinists (*Latinchilar*). The chairman of the Azerbaijan Central Executive Committee (TsIK), Nariman Narimanov, set up a committee composed of both opponents and proponents of the Latin alphabet. They worked on the principal of creating an alphabet that would be as phonetic as possible and where each phoneme would be represented by a letter. Thus the first official Azeri Latin Alphabet with 33 letters and an apostrophe came into being in 1922 (see Table 1).[5]

## Turks unite

The new alphabet carried the traces of former projects by different linguists and was influenced by different Latin alphabets. For example, under the influence of French, the letter 'q' was used for the sound 'k' and the letter 'u' for 'ü'. From the Russian alphabet, the letter 'y' was borrowed to stand for 'u'.

Through their weekly journal *Yeni Yol* (*New Way*), the committee announced rules for reading and writing Azeri in the new alphabet as well as a programme for adult education courses. Books were earmarked for publication in the new alphabet. The committee also proceeded to purify the language by Turkifying its lexicon and syntax, removing much of the centuries-old Persian and Arabic influence.

Schools were expected to start using the new alphabet in 1923. However there was a shortage of books and the training of teachers was not yet completed. Furthermore, schoolbooks printed in the Latin alphabet were filled with typographic errors. As a result, education continued to be in the Arabic alphabet, with the Latin alphabet taught alongside it. By 1925, 25,000 people had learned the new alphabet in adult education courses; by 1926, this number had risen to 60,000.

While Azeri intellectuals played an active and central role in alphabet change, the central Soviet authorities also took a great interest in the subject. In 1922, an all-Union commission on Latinization was organized in Moscow. The statute that set up the commission declared that Latinization was a worthy goal, one that was justified on the grounds that Arabic was a religious import and not native to the Turkic-speaking peoples.

In 1926, a newly formed Turkological Congress met for the first time, consisting of 131 delegates, including thirty-two Azeris, nineteen Tatars, seventeen Russians, nine Bashkirs, and eight Uzbeks, as well as representatives from across the Turkic-speaking communities. The agenda of the congress included topics such as the classification, orthography and teaching of Turkic languages and dialects and, most importantly, the proposal to adopt a Latin-based alphabet. The congress passed a resolution to adopt a Latin-based alphabet with 101 in favour, seven against and nine abstaining. The resolution also urged the Turkic peoples to study the experiences of Azerbaijan in implementing a Latin alphabet.

Many of the representatives at the congress had in mind the adoption of a common alphabet for all the Turkic languages and dialects and even the possibility of creating a single literary language. However, there was distinct lack of support from Turkic-speaking communities for a Latin alphabet, let alone for a common literary language. Furthermore, persuading Azerbaijan to alter its own Latin alphabet to fit in with the rest seemed a distinctly tall order.

In May 1927, an All-Union Central Committee for the New Turkic Alphabet (VTsKNTA: *Vsesoyuznuyi Tsentralnyi Komitet Novogo Tiurkskogo Alfavita*) was formed, following a proposal by Samad Aghamalioghlu to the Central Executive Committee of the SSR, of which he became president. The main task in front of the committee was to prepare a common Turkic alphabet. During the first plenum of the VTsKNTA, Aghamalioghlu made it clear that Azerbaijan was reluctant to alter its alphabet. He suggested that first the other republics should learn how to write as they spoke and then the task of unifying the alphabets could be addressed. Meanwhile, the Scientific Council was set up, which was initially based in Moscow but later moved to Baku (like the VTsKNTA itself). During the first meeting of the Scientific Council a unified letter catalogue for Turkic languages was accepted (see Table 2).

## The need to conform

The unified Latin alphabet for Turkic languages was not the same as that used in Azerbaijan and accordingly the republic was asked to change the letters that did not conform. For example, the unified alphabet used 'c' for Azeri 'ç' ('ch'); 'ç' for 'c' ('j'); 'u' for 'y' ('u'); 'ş' for 'з' ('sh'); 'k' for the sound which Azeri previously wrote with 'q' ('k'); and so on.

Azerbaijan was granted the concession to apply these changes step by step since its Latin alphabet was already in use. But a major source of contention among the members of the council centred on the capitalization of letters. Some members claimed that using capital letters would render the new Latinized alphabet as impractical as the Arabic alphabet and merely complicate matters. Nevertheless, Azerbaijan used capitals and would not be swayed by such arguments.

As the argument continued into the second plenum in January 1928, Azerbaijan was already printing schoolbooks in its own alphabet for other states, including the Turkmen republic. The reality was that

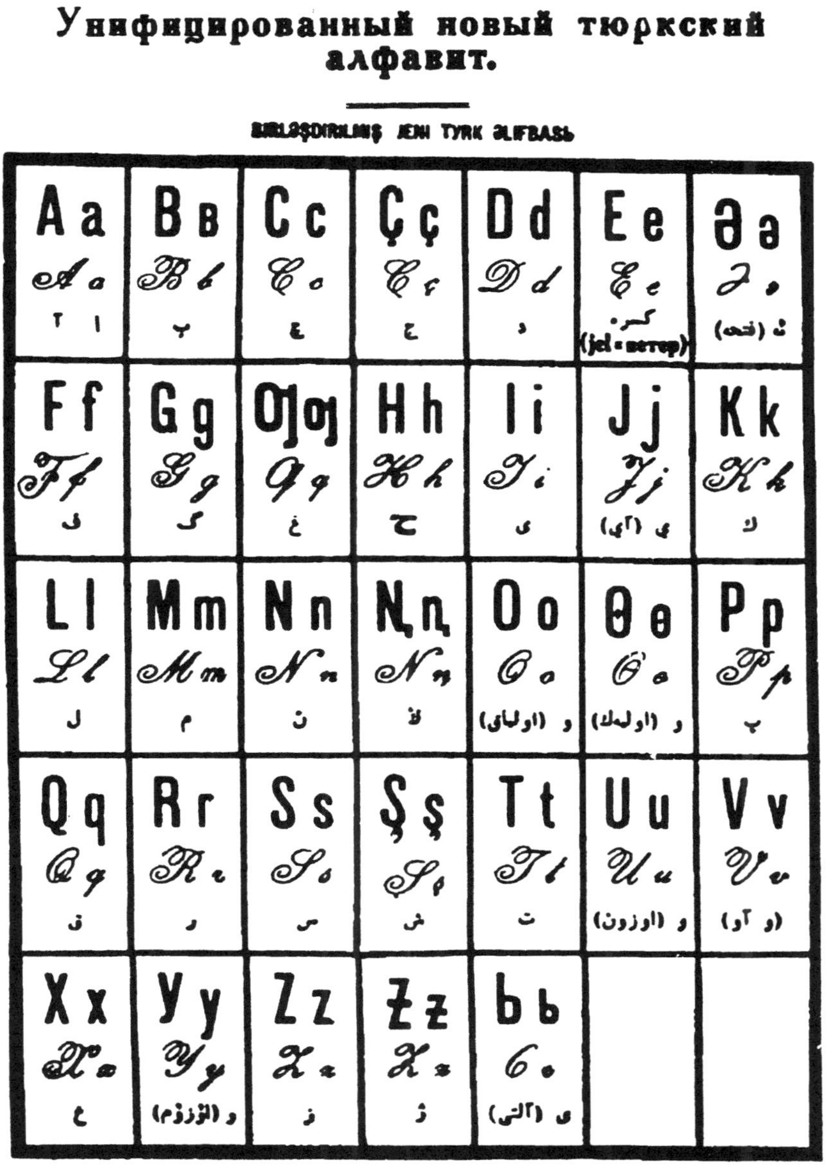


Table 2: the new unified Turkic alphabet, 1927.

| *Letter* | *Value (IPA)* | *Letter* | *Value (IPA)* |
|---|---|---|---|
| A a | [a] | O o | [o] |
| B b | [b] | P p | [p] |
| C c | [dʒ] | Q q | [k] |
| Ç ç | [tʃ] | Ƣ ƣ | [ɣ] |
| D d | [d] | R r | [r] |
| E e | [e] | S s | [s] |
| Ə ə | [æ] | Ş ş | [ʃ] |
| F f | [f] | T t | [t] |
| G g | [g] | U u | [u] |
| H h | [h] | V v | [v] |
| I i | [i] | X x | [x] |
| J j | [j] | Y y | [ü] |
| K k | [k] | Z z | [z] |
| L l | [l] | Ƶ ƶ | [ʒ] |
| M m | [m] | Ь ь | [ɯ] |
| N n | [n] | Ɵ ɵ | [ö] |
| Ŋ ŋ | [ŋ] | ’ | [ʔ] |

Table 3: Latin alphabet, 1929.

printing presses lacked the proper letters and each state had to use whatever it could lay its hands on. Since Azerbaijan was clearly better equipped for the job, it came under increasing pressure to use the letters of the unified alphabet in printing. Agreement to do so was reached during the third plenum and took effect from January 1, 1929 (see Table 3).

## Language and Stalinism

There were minor changes to the 1929 alphabet in later years. In a reversal of the earlier practice, after 1934, the letter ‘c’ now represented ‘ç’ (‘ch’), and ‘ç’ represented ‘c’ (‘j’). The order of the alphabet was changed in 1939 with ‘ƣ’ (‘gh’) following ‘g’; ‘ь’ after ‘i’; ‘ɵ’ after ‘o’; and ‘y’ after ‘u’. Also the letter ‘ŋ’ was dropped from the alphabet.

In 1930, a new phase started in language planning in Azerbaijan. The Latin alphabet was now viewed as an international alphabet, a force which would unite all the ‘Oriental peoples’ of the Soviet Union, including the Buryat-Mongol and Iranian linguistic groups. However, during the years which followed the move of the Scientific Council from

Moscow to Baku, there were constant complaints from the members that the Baku linguists were treating the council as their own exclusive domain—a situation that was resented by Russian academics as well as Tatars, who sought autonomy over their own process of Latinization.

As Baku increased its standing, seeking to establish common training courses for language teachers and a central letter foundry for the printing presses, linguists from Moscow complained that their advice was not sought by the council and that Baku was too far to travel for meetings. Eventually the VTsKNTA and its Scientific Council were moved back to Moscow. The name of the All-Union Central Committee for the New Turkic Alphabet was changed to the All-Union Central Committee for the New Alphabet (VTsKNA: *Vsesoyuznuyi Tsentralnyi Komitet Novogo Alfavita*).

The new Committee was placed under the jurisdiction of the Presidium of the Council of Nationalities of the SSR. Following Aghamalioghlu's death at about the same time (1930), the new presidium of the VTs no longer included members from Baku, marking the end of an era. Such a state of affairs was not merely the result of the power struggle between linguists in Moscow and Baku, it was also a time when Moscow was beginning to tighten its control over language planning across the republics.

During the late 1920s and '30s, language policy and planning in the USSR was dominated by the theories of Nikoloz Marr, a Georgian linguist (his father was Scottish). Marr rejected the idea of 'language families' and that languages belonged to ancestral groups that evolved according to Marxist theories of class struggle. According to his 'Japhetic theory', all the world's languages derived from four elements—*sol*, *ber*, *yan*, *rosh*—and all were destined to eventually merge into a single world language. This idea was in harmony with Stalin's theory of one common socialist culture. Nevertheless, like many of their colleagues from other states, many Baku linguists refused to accept Marr's theories, despite his powerful position as 'official' state linguist.

By moving the VTsKNA to Moscow, the Soviet authorities were able to prevent the Turkic linguists from having a say in the Latinization of their alphabets and in the planning and control of their languages. At first, until he proposed his own universal alphabet, Marr was in favour of Latinization and it was on his advice that speakers of non-Turkic languages were also encouraged to adopt it. During the following years, the committee began to include in its ranks more and more dedicated Communist Party members and Marrists who were not necessarily noted for their academic skills as linguists.

In February 1933, the new Scientific Council of the VTsKNA was addressed by Marr. He talked about his 'analytical alphabet' of 69 letters which could be used for writing any language and condemned the Latin alphabet as the 'tool of European imperialism'. After 1934, the Scientific Council neither published nor achieved much and language planning was done more and more by non-linguists. By then, many of the linguists in Baku already had been denounced as pan-Turkists or were disgraced for not being Marrists. In 1935 a Central Institute of Language and Writing replaced the Scientific Committee of the VTsKNA. Finally in 1937, after an increasing number of republics began to abandon the New Alphabet (i.e. Latin), the VTsKNA came to an end.

The 1930s also mark the time of the great purges in Azerbaijan and other parts of the USSR. In fact, the purges had already started in the 1920s when opponents of Sovietization including religious leaders and rebellious peasants were eliminated. By the early 1930s, former political leaders and early Communist activists, especially Musavat Party members, were rounded up and killed. Later, Azerbaijan's old Bolsheviks, along with pre-revolutionary writers and artists, were liquidated. Sources give the number of victims in Azerbaijan between 1937-8 as being 120,000 (in 1926, the population of the country was 2.6 million).

The purges eliminated most of the nationalist language planners. With local nationalism now branded 'dangerous', articles began to appear in the Soviet press praising the Russian alphabet (Cyrillic), dubbed the 'Alphabet of the Great October (Revolution)'. Russia and Russians were becoming increasingly more important in the Soviet Union. In the new climate, the Latin alphabet was no longer regarded as being 'international'. The focus was now on the Russian language and its study became obligatory in schools. It was held that in order to maintain the unity and brotherhood of the Soviet peoples it was necessary for the Russian alphabet to be adopted by all states. The use of different alphabets constituted an obstacle that prevented the Soviet peoples accessing the treasure trove of Soviet literature. Little surprise therefore that in 1937 the Latin alphabet was denounced.

In January 1940, as in other republics, Azerbaijan was required to replace its Latin alphabet with Cyrillic. All spoken and written forms of Turkish became 'official languages' and were assigned Cyrillic alphabets. There is a general lack of literature about this change, which happened swiftly and without resistance. Although the Soviet rulers in Moscow claimed that the Soviet peoples were keen to embrace Cyrillic, the lack of public discussion suggests that this was not a grassroots operation.

| *Letter* | *Value (IPA)* | *Letter* | *Value (IPA)* |
|---|---|---|---|
| А а | [a] | Өө | [ö] |
| Бб | [b] | Пп | [p] |
| В д | [v] | Рр | [r] |
| Г д | [g] | Сс | [s] |
| Ғ ғ | [ɣ] | Тт | [t] |
| Де | [d] | Уу | [u] |
| Ее | [e] | Үү | [ü] |
| Ә ә | [æ] | Фф | [f] |
| Жж | [ʒ] | Хх | [x] |
| Зз | [z] | Һh | [h] |
| Ии | [i] | Цц | [ts] |
| Йй | [j] | Чч | [tʃ] |
| Кк | [k], [k$^y$] | Ҹҹ | [dʒ] |
| Ҝҝ | [g$^y$] | Шш | [ʃ] |
| Лл | [l] | Ыы | [ɯ] |
| Мм | [m] | Ээ | [je] |
| Нн | [n] | Юю | [ju] |
| Оо | [o] | Яя | [ja] |

Table 4: Cyrillic alphabet, 1940.

The debates within the Latinization movement, the disagreement about letters and united orthography, the lack of typewriters and printing presses capable of producing textbooks in the Latin script, can all be regarded as problems which might have acted as ammunition for Moscow to justify the installation of the Cyrillic script.

Yet, if the aim of Moscow was unification and accessibility of Soviet literature across language boundaries, this aim was not apparent in its application. There was no unity in the new alphabets—the same sounds were represented by different letters thereby impeding communication by speakers of similar dialects or languages. The real reasons for the change to Cyrillic had more to do with the Soviet central language planners and with the intended political, social and cultural changes that they desired to bring about through the alphabet.

Accompanying the alphabet change was a new official vocabulary, which more often than not meant Russian words replacing Turkic, Arabic or Persian words—for example *partiya* '(political) party' replaced *firgə*, and *respublika* 'republic' replaced *jumhuriyet*. Words of Russian origin were to be spelled as in their Russian originals and accordingly the new alphabet had to have enough letters to facilitate this (see Table 4).

## A change in direction

After World War II and the Stalinist era, there was a change in the direction of language planning in the Soviet Union. Before 1953, when the object of language planning was non-Russian languages and their Russification, all languages remained equal in importance and education in one's mother tongue was guaranteed in the constitution.

After Stalin's death in 1953, his successor Nikita Khrushchev criticized the Stalinist regime for ignoring the Russian language, which he called the 'second native language' of the Soviet peoples. Russian was needed for communication, science and technology and was the key to Russian culture. Therefore the provision that children should be taught in their mother tongue was replaced and parents were given the choice to decide on the medium of instruction for their children. In reality, the right to choose applied only to non-Russian parents who had to decide whether they wanted their children to learn their native language or study in Russian and thereby find better jobs.

By 1958 there were increasing complaints from Azeri writers and teachers who claimed that maintaining the original spelling of borrowed words was nonsense and that some of the letters in the Cyrillic alphabet rendered the teaching of Azeri difficult. Hence, the Russian Cyrillic letters denoting double sounds, such as ю and я, were dropped and й was replaced by j ('y'). An alphabet composed of 32 letters and an apostrophe was created and stayed in use until 1991 (see Table 5).

## Russification intensifies

During the 1960s and 70s, under the leadership of Leonid Brezhnev, Russian came to be regarded throughout the Soviet Union not only as the bearer of the message of Communism and Sovietization but as the message itself. The press carried new praise of the great Russian people and their language, along with the news that all nationalities had come to fully appreciate and understand such magnificence. The bilingualism of non-Russian nationalities was interpreted as one of choice rather than necessity. Now, armed with the new audio-visual devices of the 1970s, the Russian language was taught with renewed zeal.

However, the increasing pressure to learn Russian gave rise to a new era of nationalism and an urge to preserve national languages and cultures. In the census of 1970, 16.6 per cent of Azeris claimed fluency in Russian. By 1979 this had increased to 29.5 per cent—and yet at the same

| *Letter* | *Value (IPA)* | *Letter* | *Value (IPA)* |
|---|---|---|---|
| А а | [a] | Мм | [m] |
| Бб | [b] | Нн | [n] |
| В д | [v] | Оо | [o] |
| Г г | [g] | Өө | [ö] |
| Ғ ғ | [ɣ] | Пп | [p] |
| Де | [d] | Рр | [r] |
| Ее | [e] | Сс | [s] |
| Ә ә | [æ] | Тт | [t] |
| Жж | [ʒ] | Уу | [u] |
| Зз | [z] | Үү | [ü] |
| Ии | [i] | Фф | [f] |
| Ыы | [ɯ] | Хх | [x] |
| J j | [j] | һh | [h] |
| Кк | [k], [kʸ] | Чч | [tʃ] |
| Ҝк | [gʸ] | Ҹҹ | [dʒ] |
| Лл | [l] | Шш | [ʃ] |
| | | ’ | [ʔ] |

Table 5: Cyrillic alphabet, after 1958.

time, according to the 1979 census, more than 90 per cent gave Azeri as their first language while 80 per cent of parents preferred schools in which Azeri, not Russian, was the main language of instruction. Additionally, although children started out learning Russian in Azeri schools, once they reached secondary school the number of hours of Russian instruction dropped considerably.

Around this time there was a resurgence of national literature and journals in Azeri. After 1979, *Azerbaijan*, the monthly journal of the Azerbaijan Writers' Union, published many articles that referred, using indirect but clear language, to Russia's negative influence on Azeri language and culture. Every writer stressed the importance of their national language, regarding it as a key feature of their identity and equating it with the concept of 'motherland'.

Meanwhile, the Soviet authorities continued to promote Russian. The school reform of 1984, which required children as young as six to study Russian, was designed to ensure that secondary school leavers achieved full mastery of Russian. Nevertheless, the policies of *glasnost* that followed shortly afterwards meant that national language movements

| *Letter* | *Value (IPA)* | *Letter* | *Value (IPA)* |
|---|---|---|---|
| A a | [a] | M m | [m] |
| B b | [b] | N n | [n] |
| C c | [dʒ] | O o | [o] |
| Ç ç | [tʃ] | Ö ö | [ö] |
| D d | [d] | P p | [p] |
| E e | [e] | Q q | [q] |
| Ə ə | [æ] | R r | [r] |
| F f | [f] | S s | [s] |
| G g | [g] | Ş ş | [ʃ] |
| Ğ ğ | [ɣ] | T t | [t] |
| H h | [h] | U u | [u] |
| İ i | [i] | Ü ü | [ü] |
| I ı | [ɯ] | V v | [v] |
| J j | [j] | X x | [x] |
| K k | [k] | Y y | [u] |
| L l | [l] | Z z | [z] |
| | | ’ | [ʔ] |

Table 6: the Azerbaijani alphabet, 1991.

began to gain impetus and the literary scene in Azerbaijan flourished once again. Azeris were determined to openly celebrate their own history, literature and fine arts and writers publicly aired their criticism of the dominance of Russian in Azerbaijan.

By the 1990s, academics and writers were now beginning to play an active role in Azeri political life. During the Third Conference of the Azerbaijan Popular Front, for example, the poet Sabir Rustamkhanli and historian Etibar Mamedov, amongst others, were elected to the party's council. Following the events of 'Black January' in 1990, the occupation of Baku by Soviet troops infuriated Azeris, intensifying their desire to reassert their national identity. Academics and authors began to discuss the possibility of a return to the Latin script. The Democratic Bloc (created by the opposition to the Azerbaijan Communist Party) promised an alphabet reform in its programme, yet elections in May 1990 were won by the Communist Party and it was the latter that duly set up a commission to work on the Latinization of the Azeri alphabet.

Opposition came from those who feared that the adoption of the

Latin alphabet would mean a symbolic dependence on Turkey, ultimately paving the way to Turkish domination, and also from religious leaders who advocated a return to the Arabic alphabet. The latter even started teaching the Arabic script with the help of neighbouring Islamic countries. However, prominent figures such as T. Hajiyev, F. Jalilov, K.V. Narimanoglu, S. Aliyarli, S. Rustamkhanli and others wrote many articles supporting Latin, and presented a series of persuasive linguistic arguments in its favour.

Meanwhile, following the break-up of the Soviet Union, several conferences were organized in Turkey order to encourage the adoption of a common Latin alphabet for all Turkic-speaking peoples. The International Symposium on Modern Turkish Alphabets, held at Marmara University, Istanbul, in November 1991, was attended by delegates from all Turkic-speaking communities and a unified 34-letter alphabet was recommended.

## Adoption of the Latin alphabet

On 25 December 1991, the National Council of the Republic of Azerbaijan officially replaced the Cyrillic alphabet with Latin. The law required the necessary preparations for the transition to be completed by 1993. The actual alphabet accepted by the Azeri Parliament (see Table 6) was not the common alphabet proposed by the Symposium in Istanbul, although it was similar.

In 1992, the letter 'ä' ([æ] in the IPA chart) was replaced by the letter 'ə' as used in the previous alphabets, on the grounds that the dots on the 'ä' were cumbersome to write and created problems in printing.

The transition from Cyrillic to Latin proved a slow process in Azerbaijan, a country where literacy levels in Cyrillic were high. The task of printing volumes of new and old books as well as training teachers was a time-consuming and costly enterprise. In 1992/93, Y. Kərimov's *Alifba* (*Alphabet*), a reader for the first year of elementary schools, came out. However, although all newly printed text books were in the Latin alphabet, old Cyrillic textbooks continued to be used for upper grades. Keen to accelerate the implementation of the new alphabet, the government adopted the Latin alphabet in official documents.

National television also began using the Latin alphabet in written texts from 1992 onwards and leading newspapers followed suit. Furthermore, leading newspapers were required to print presidential decrees and parliamentary news in the new script. Books soon followed: the first publications included a two-volume edition of Fizuli's poetry, a folklore anthology, some novels and various scientific books. The successful move to the Latin alphabet has been sealed by computers and the internet, the growing use of English as a foreign language, as well as a national desire to integrate into the global community. Whatever the cost may have been, the new alphabet is most certainly here to stay.

*

# The Birth of the Independent Azeri Media

Famil Ismailov

ON 22 JULY 1875, against the background of the oil fever that fuelled an unprecedented economic boom in Baku, the very first journal published in the Azeri language, *Ekinchi* (*The Sower* or *The Ploughman*), was launched. The event heralded no less than the birth of Azeri journalism. Founded, edited and published by Hasan Zardabi, *Ekinchi* came out fortnightly and was structured like any regular newspaper. Its various departments covered such things as domestic and international issues, financial and scientific news, current affairs, breaking news and letters.

*Ekinchi*, which used an Arabic-based alphabet, was also the first secular national newspaper to appear in the Eastern Islamic world. In Azerbaijan it functioned as a brand-new forum for non-religious, pro-democratic ideas, publishing stories and opinions which helped to forge a new awareness. Unlike the Muslim mullahs of the time, instead of preaching and patronising its readers, it educated, informed and entertained in language that was simple and direct. It broke down the traditional barriers that had existed between the intelligentsia and the rest of the nation. Classic Azeri literature was generally written in Persian, had very complicated metaphorical images and had to be translated and adapted for a wider, less educated audience. Looking back now to the 1870s, it is clear that Zardabi, who was a teacher by training, was simply following common sense and cornering a niche in the media market of that time.

*Ekinchi* tackled a wide range of issues ranging from criticism of feudal relations and religious control over peoples' lives to the emancipation of women and education for the poor. These were serious issues for Azerbaijan—it was the first time that Azeri readers, the inhabitants of an Islamic province of the Russian Empire, were able to read about such controversial matters. *Ekinchi* also published articles that introduced Azeri farmers to the world of Western agricultural technology, giving them small tips at first and then handing out more substantial advice such as how to make field labour easier. The newspaper's appeal extended beyond Azerbaijan's borders into other regions of the Empire with Muslim populations, including Georgia, Armenia, Daghestan and Uzbekistan.

Without doubt, *Ekinchi* had the best educated and the best known authors. Amongst them were Mirza Fatali Khan Akhundov, a prominent thinker, and Seyyid Azim Shirvani, a writer of the utmost brilliance. Educated in Russia and France, these great minds and eloquent speakers represented a small minority of Azeri society which was prepared to break Islamic taboos, ask questions and look for answers—together they laid the foundation not only for Azeri journalism, but for the Azeri intelligentsia for years to come.

Unsurprisingly *Ekinchi* soon became the subject for the close attention of the tsar's censors. On many occasions the paper had to withdraw stories and delay printing. Finally, in September 1877, on the orders of the censorship department, the publication was closed down. Despite the fact that it had only been in circulation for little more than two years and only published 56 editions, *Ekinchi* had deservedly reserved its place in Azeri history.

Thirty years later saw another cornerstone in the early history of Azeri media: the satirical magazine *Molla Nasraddin*. Founded in 1906 by the prominent writer and intellectual Mirza Jalil Mammadguluzade, it was published in Tbilisi, Tabriz and then Baku. Mammadguluzade had secured the funds to start the publication from his wife Hamida, who came from a wealthy family and owned cotton plantations in Karabakh.

The magazine proved immensely popular, especially for its pamphlets and cartoons, and holds the distinction of being the first satirical magazine in the Muslim East. It outlived tsarist censorship but was closed in 1925 by the Bolshevik authorities and re-issued under a different title. At the time of his death in Baku in 1925, Mammadguluzade had fallen on such hard times that he been forced to burn his writings to keep warm during the freezing Baku winters.

## Soviet style with a national flavour

The drive for independence in the national provinces of the former Tsarist Empire was effectively destroyed by the Bolsheviks, with the aid of military hardware and the machinations of Communist movements within the nations themselves. There was an attempt to eradicate virtually everything that might remind people of the past. Denationalisation of the country meant that media outlets were subject

Founded in 1906, the satirical magazine *Molla Nasraddin* survived censorship by the tsarist and Soviet authorities until 1925.

to collective ownership. Not surprisingly, most Azeri newspapers were closed immediately or simply vanished.

The new Bolshevik-controlled media took over. There was an inevitable development from small, badly written newsletters to imitations of the so-called Russian-language 'central newspapers' printed in Moscow, such as *Izvestiya* (*News*), *Pravda* (*Truth*) and *Trud* (*Labour*). In the course of this development the Azeri alphabet saw two radical changes—the first was from Arabic to Latin, and the second a few years later was from Latin to Cyrillic. Latin was considered to be too close to the emerging young Turkish Republic close by on the USSR's southwestern border, whereas Cyrillic was seen as a demonstration of unity between Azerbaijan and Russia.

In the new scheme of things the media was regarded by the Bolsheviks as an important way of bringing in new recruits 'to fight for a bright future, to fight for Communism'. Lenin described the media as 'the cog and wheel of the great [Communist] party machine' and the newspaper as 'a collective propagandist, collective agitator and collective manager of people'. Every student of journalism at Soviet universities knew these quotes by heart.

However, journalists found ingenious ways of getting around the ideological straitjacket. One such way was to dress the message in metaphor and leave it to the Azeri readers to uncover the intended meaning. Nevertheless many writers still ended up in the NKVD secret service (later KGB) prisons and were executed as 'enemies of the state'. Even an incorrect spelling or phonetic mistake, particularly in major speeches, could cost a newspaper editor his life. In one case the entire editorial staff of a publication was carted off to the labour camps on account of a single, tiny typographical error—the verdict had been 'treason and conspiracy' against the regime and its leaders.

The decision-making and executive process of the media was simple: Stalin decreed in Moscow while Mir Jafar Bagirov, First Secretary of the Azerbaijani Communist Party (ACP), carried out his orders in Baku. Every form of media was an extension of a state structure. For example, the sole news agency Azerinform was merely a division of TASS, the central Soviet news agency. Meanwhile, television and radio operated as a single state-run company. The major newspapers were the ACP-directed *Kommunist* (*The Communist*, in Azeri), the Russian-language *Bakinskiy Rabochiy* (*The Baku Worker*) and *Vyshka* (*The Derrick*), as well as *Molodezh Azerbaijana* and the Azeri-language *Azerbaijan Genjleri* (both translate as *Azerbaijan Youth*) which were organs of the Azeri Komsomol (the youth wing of the Communist Party) and published in both languages.

The 1950s brought official damnation of Stalin's 'personality cult' and the arrest and execution of Bagirov, who was branded 'Azerbaijan's Stalin'. The political atmosphere relaxed significantly but it brought no change in the media industry, which remained under the close scrutiny and tough control of the state. Since newspapers, television and radio were the vital parts of the huge propaganda machine run by the Communist Party leadership, people simply had no choice and therefore no alternative source of information. Very few were able to buy a short-wave band radio receiver and to listen, if jamming permitted, to the 'voices' from abroad such as the BBC World Service, Voice of America and Radio Liberty.

## Outwitting the censors

In Azerbaijan, as well as everywhere else in the Soviet Union, the Russian language was dominant. It was not called the 'state language', but it was compulsory. Whether this was good or bad for national identity is a moot point, but Russian certainly played (and still does so) an important role as a tool for inter-ethnic and in some cases international communication.

The lack of alternative sources and the strict control of information had a quite remarkable and unique impact on the development of Azeri journalism. Whereas journalists in many other parts of the Soviet Union tried to imitate their Russian colleagues, Azeri authors deliberately drew upon their own classic tradition of poetry, which is far better developed in Azerbaijan than prosaic traditions. The censors could not bring themselves to challenge lines penned by famous figures that were lifted and then carefully woven into articles. Azeri tradition demands absolute respect to one's elders (called *aghsaggal* or 'white-beards'). As a result, constant references to Classical Azeri or even international writers worked particularly well. This also proved to be true in my own Soviet-era experience. I was once asked to change the wording of the title of an article which came from a quote by Mark Twain and which was judged to have a double meaning. My response was to argue that it was impossible to change a single word in a classic of world literature since to do so could lead to the corruption of other classics, Marxism for example. The quote remained unchanged.

Working in the Russian-language press brought far more advantages than its Azeri counterpart, providing journalists with better training and career opportunities. Dozens of journalists from Azerbaijan became prominent figures in the Moscow-based national newspapers. Meanwhile, young journalists writing in Azeri had few opportunities to develop: the majority of senior editors usually held their position for decades, right up to retirement age.

Senior posts in the media were decided by the Central Committee of the ACP. Furthermore, they were subject to the strict rules of the Party's totalitarian management: you had to be a member of the Communist Party, to be of certain age and nationality (the latter was intended to maintain a balance in promoting different ethnic groups) and preferably not a divorcee. You also had to have nothing compromising in your 'KGB file', for example no unauthorised contacts with foreigners, especially journalists—those from 'non-Socialist' countries were deemed absolutely off-limits. Even in the late 1980s, it was hinted that my having had foreign 'capitalist' friends while studying journalism in Moscow could have a negative impact on my career.

A plethora of other reasons existed that might prevent a journalist from joining a paper. While attempting to get into the central Soviet media, for example, I was refused a place on one of the major Soviet youth newspapers in Moscow on the grounds that I was too young, not a member of Communist Party, not married and, to cap it all, an Azeri (there were 'too many non-Russians on the newspaper').

In the Soviet system, everyone was supposed to be equal and no one out of the ordinary or outstanding—unless this supported the image of the successful development of socialism. Whatever was introduced in the Moscow media was immediately copied by local outlets. All holiday celebrations, for example, were followed by a late evening programme on television—*Goluboy Ogonyok* (*Blue Light*, *Mavi Ishiq* in Azeri)—which consisted mostly of interviews with leading farmers, scientists and artists, mixed with popular music performances. Azeri Television (as well other broadcasters) produced exactly the same kind of programme without even changing the title, and so *Goluboy Ogonyok* became a veritable TV symbol of its day.

In the late 1970s and early 1980s, when the Soviet system started losing its grip, it was the field of journalism that provided the first tangible signs of a fundamental shift in society. Azeri Television introduced programmes that included videos of popular international pop and rock music stars (*Daha Bir Gorush*, 'One More Encounter') and movies by famous international directors. Another very popular programme was the Sunday entertainment programme *Seher Gorushleri* (*Morning Encounters*) with clips of contemporary satirical sketches that were incisively critical of the Soviet system and which, understandably, proved immensely popular with viewers.

Newspapers started printing long articles on issues related to national history, national identity and culture—a far cry from the usual fare of speeches by Communist leaders. The most used genres were the essay and the travelogue. The majority of newspapers came in A3 format and had only four pages, one of which would typically be filled up by a single huge article, usually without any illustrations. Had this happened in a Western newspaper, the reader might have surmised that the editor was deranged. Not so in Azerbaijan. Such a practice was perfectly acceptable in Azeri journalism since it tapped directly into age-old tradition in which national folk singers (*ashugs*, 'folk singers' or 'troubadours') performed long and highly descriptive stories. Having been suppressed by the regime, Azeri journalists used the same style when discussing a particular issue, hiding their ideas in a creative sea of words.

In 1988, I was in a group of Azeri journalists accredited to a Congress of the Communist Party of the USSR. My reports from this major political forum, as well as those sent by my colleagues from other Russian-language newspapers to Baku, were four to five pages—rather short by the standards of the time. However, my other colleague from the Azeri-language press was working hard, writing reports of ten to fifteen pages. We were consumed by curiosity. What on earth could a talented reporter be doing writing over a dozen pages on such a mundane event? A couple of days later, we managed to get newspapers from Baku and looked through his report. He started with a detailed description of everything around him on his walk to the Kremlin Palace: Muscovites doing their usual shopping, the guards at Lenin's Mausoleum, security people checking his bag and recorder and the Azeri delegation discussing various matters and so on. It was unmistakably written in a travelogue style that would be absolutely unacceptable for a foreign reporter for this type of story. However, Azeri readers could immediately relate to the storytellingstyle of the *ashugs* and would happily read on to uncover the underlying political analysis.

## Nagorno-Karabakh and nationalism

With the arrival of *perestroika* everything in the republic began to change with an awesome speed. There was a fashionable saying in the Soviet media in those days: "*Perestroika* is the fresh wind of change!" The conflict between Azerbaijan and Armenia over Nagorno-Karabakh gave the changes an even stronger impetus.

The present conflict started in 1988 and with it a brand-new generation of young, dynamic, talented and politically rebellious individuals appeared on the media scene. They began raising issues which until then had been taboo, such as political opinions, national identity and cultural heritage. They bravely risked their lives covering events on the front line of the Armenian-Azerbaijani conflict. Among those who lost their lives there were Salatin Askerova, a young reporter from the Komsomol youth newspaper *Molodezh Azerbaijana* who was killed by Armenian guerrillas in 1991 and Chingiz Mustafayev, a well-known cameraman and stringer for international news agencies, who died the following year from wounds inflicted by a mortar while filming in a combat zone.

By the late 1980s, the Azeri authorities were forced to recognise the existence of an independent media. Many of these young people joined forces working for *Molodezh Azerbaijana*, which was led by the prominent journalist Najaf Najafov. Most of these were later involved in the group that created the ideological basis for the national democratic movement led by the Popular Front of Azerbaijan. In 1989 they established the Popular Front newspaper *Azadlig* (*Freedom*) and the news agency Turan. Another group belonging to this new generation, but which did not pursue a political agenda, founded an independent Azeri commercial media organization. It published a weekly newspaper titled *Ayna-Zerkalo* (*The Mirror*), which was launched in 1990 and published in both Azeri and Russian in order to cover a larger readership.

Ironically, however, it was the Communist Party's own *Kommunist* (*The Communist*) that gave birth to Azerbaijan's first purely oppositional newspaper. In 1989 a group of young journalists working on the paper persuaded the editorial management to start publication of a weekend supplement entitled *Seher* (*Morning*). Officially it was meant to be devoted to analysis of the social, cultural and economic problems of the day, but the readers of the very first issue immediately understood that this eight-pager was set to play a significant political role in the life of the country.

The article in the first issue published classified statistics that showed Azerbaijan to be a Soviet republic that owed nothing economically to Russia, while later issues ran articles promoting ideas of independence in virtually everything. For example in a piece devoted to the USSR's football premier league, the idea was put forward for Azerbaijan to have its own national team for world championships as well as for Azeri soccer clubs to play in their own right in the UEFA World Cup. The national anthem, flag and emblem of the first Azeri republic (1918-1920) were restored thanks to the influence of similar-minded articles in *Seher*.

However, the Communist governments in both Moscow and Baku soon had enough and in December 1989 the supplement was banned after it published reports about an incident on the Soviet-Iran border when group of Azeri activists dismantled border fences as a symbolic reunion of the two Azerbaijans. Yet the ban was only in place for a month before the events of 'Bloody January' (when Soviet troops took control of Baku on January 20, 1990, killing many civilians) took place. In the ensuing situation when all the newspapers of Azerbaijan went on strike, *Seher* decided to resume activities without seeking official permission.

The first attempt, however, to hold an editorial meeting on January 21, 1990 in the State Publishing House resulted in the arrest of a *Seher* journalist by the Soviet occupying forces. Later that day, the Soviet commander in Baku demanded that his commands and decrees should be published in the newspaper. And so a bargain was struck: the *Seher* management agreed to publish military statements in return for reporting the events of January 20. The resulting edition ran to 12 pages with a print-run of two million and, most significantly, page-sized images of the Baku bloodbath. Although *Seher* became an independent publication in the years of independence that followed, it printed its last edition in 1996.

Although Azerbaijan had boasted only one true daily newspaper in the early 1990s—the state-owned organ of the National Parliament, entitled simply *Azerbaijan*—the number of dailies has subsequently grown, as have magazines and other journals, with the majority being distributed in Baku as opposed to the rest of the country.

## Broadcast media

Towards the end of the 1990s, broadcast mass media in Azerbaijan was less developed than print media as a result of strong state control and a lack of adequate technology. Forty-seven television and radio companies were registered, yet the number of those actually broadcasting was much less. There were only six local TV-radio stations in operation, with staff of up to ten people and airtime from one to three hours per day. Their transmitters were old and low-powered and electricity supply was erratic.

In the capital, Baku, besides AzTV, the state TV-radio organisation, there were two pioneering independent broadcasters operating: Azerbaijan News Service (ANS) and Sara. Both companies had their own television and FM radio stations but their television and radio programmes could be received only in and around Baku. The state broadcasting company had two television and two radio channels that covered the whole territory of Azerbaijan. There was also a state-owned TV and radio station in Nakhchivan broadcasting two to three hours a day.

Sara-TV and Radio Sara were purely entertainment stations with a Turkish cultural orientation. They did not run news and current affairs programmes, a fact that highlighted the kind of political environment in which broadcast journalists had to work. Although ANS did run news and current affairs programmes, its journalists had to be extremely cautious. It was established by a group of successful stringers working for international news agencies during the political turmoil in Azerbaijan. They started by renting airtime from the state television and later managed to purchase and upgrade their own transmitters.

As in the other republics of the Former Soviet Union, the first decades have seen a rapid expansion of new broadcasting opportunities over cable, satellite and internet not only by local broadcasters but also by external organisations such as the BBC World Service.

## Advertising and censorship

Due to a new flourishing advertising market, the reader, listener and viewer took on a new role, that of consumer. By the late 1990s, up to $8 million was spent annually in Azerbaijan for advertising purposes, and this figure has steadily grown. Most of this money went into print media. Revenue from advertising not only helped journalists weather hard times, but also gave them the chance to develop and grow.

Baku's re-emergence as an oil boom centre—with its growing industrial, commercial and social infrastructure and intensification of business activity—demanded more information exchange. The media market quickly responded to this need. *Ayna-Zerkalo* began to carry an average of twelve to fifteen pages of advertisements out of a total of forty-eight. The FM radio station ANS-ÇM began to run advertisement slots every 15-20 minutes. In the midst of such a rapidly expanding market the Azeri media industry saw improvements. TV and radio companies, for example, were able to begin purchasing upgraded Western-made state-of-the-art transmitters.

However, the internal problems of the republic have had repercussions for the media. For example, following a presidentially decreed state of emergency, which lasted from March 1993 to September 1996, the Azerbaijani media was controlled by military censorship. After President Heydar Aliyev came to power in July 1993, the State Committee for Preserving State Secrets in the Media (known from Soviet times as Glavlit) became a major censorship body. While Azeri legislature actually prohibits censorship, special amendments to the law were passed through the National Parliament (*Milli Mejlis*) making it possible. As a result, in Azerbaijan no newspaper could be printed in the state-owned publishing house—which monopolised all printing at the time—unless it had a censor's confirmation stamp. Very often newspapers were left with blank spaces on their pages where an article had to be taken off at the last moment. Many newspapers kept cartoons at hand in order to replace the stories rejected by the censors, although some papers deliberately left the page blank to make a point.

State television was also closed for representatives of the opposition, while opposition newspapers could be shut down at any time. In March 1995, four journalists who ran a satirical newspaper were kept in custody without trial for six months after it published anecdotes about members of the government including Aliyev. Eventually charged with insulting the image of the president and sentenced to various terms of imprisonment, they were subsequently pardoned by Aliyev himself. Censorship was officially abolished in 1996.

Nevertheless censorship was not absolute. International broadcasters such as the BBC World Service, Voice of America and Radio Liberty, whose programmes were re-broadcast via local independent and government networks, were not interrupted. Furthermore, numerous magazines began to be printed abroad, in Turkey or the United Emirates for example, where the quality of printing was better and the meddling hand of the censor was absent. Private TV and radio stations were also able to operate relatively freely, a fact that many journalists put down to the inherent difficulties involved in interfering with live broadcasts of news and current affairs programmes. The subsequent growth in the economy and increased access to the internet has mostly had the effect of amplifying rather than diminishing this tug-of-war between the state and independent sectors, thus reflecting the contradictory reality of Azeri politics and society.

*

# Heritage of the Epics: A Brief Overview of Literature

Çiğdem Balım-Harding

LITERARY TRADITION in the Azeri language can be traced back to works composed in what can best be described as the Azeri dialect of Oghuz Turkish, such as the *dastan* ('epic') of *Dada Gorgud* (or *Dede Korkut*). Although the first written version of the epic dates from around the 10th and 11th centuries, the stories in it contain elements from pre-Islamic times that date back to at least the sixth and seventh centuries. The epic tells of the trials and tribulations faced by Oghuz tribes and Turkic heroes as told by the sage Gorgud (or Korkut). By the beginning of the 16th century, it had taken on the written form of a prologue and twelve stories—today we have two existing copies of the manuscript, one in the Royal Library of Dresden and the other in the Vatican Library.

However, it was the 12th-century poet Nizami Ganjavi (1141-1209) who gave Azerbaijan its first great literary giant. Writing in Persian, as was the custom of the times, Nizami became especially famous among the Turkic-speaking peoples, from Anatolia to Central Asia, for his *Khamsa* (a collection of five long poems of around 30,000 couplets) and other works including *Leyli and Majnun*, *Khosrow and Shirin*, *Iskandar-Nameh*, *Tohfatul Iraqein* (*Gifts from Iraq*), and *Khabsije* (*Book of the Slave*). The tragic romance of the archetypal lover Majnun and his beloved Layla (or Leyli) of the Banu Amir tribe became especially popular—Majnun is driven mad after Layla's father forbids him from marrying her. The epic love story was retold over and over again across the Islamic world and provided the inspiration for some of the world's greatest works of miniature art.

Another major figure in Azeri literature is the 14th-century Sufi mystic Imadeddin Nasimi (or Nesimi; 1369-1417). Born in Shamaka, Nasimi was an outstanding Sufi thinker and poet who wrote in Azeri,

Persian and Arabic. Critical of the censorship and religious bigotry of the times day, he devoted his life to freedom of expression through his poetry. He belonged to the Hurufi movement, which held that the individual and God are fundamentally One. He was comfortable with various styles of verse, subtly proposing his own beliefs while criticising society, but he particularly excelled in the philosophical *ghazal* (sonnet-like lyrical, erotic or mystical poems usually in the form of five or seven couplets). Actively preaching in the region of the Middle East, Nasimi's mystical beliefs eventually landed him in trouble in Aleppo, Syria, where his poetry was branded blasphemous by the religious establishment. On the orders of the town's ruler he was skinned alive.

Another great master of *ghazals* was the poet Mohammad Fizuli (or Fuzuli; 1492-1556). Born in Karbala (in present-day Iraq), Fizuli wrote in Arabic, Persian and Azeri, masterfully building upon the legacy of his predecessors and producing his own philosophical and lyrical *ghazals*. His major works in Azeri include his *Divan* (or *Collection*) *of Ghazals*, the *Qasidas* (a *qasida* is a lengthy form of ode) and a rewriting of *Leyli and Majnun*. His poetry reflected both personal and popular discontent with the heavy-handed political system, feudal lords and religious establishment.

Shah Ismail, the founder of the Safavid dynasty (1501-1736) in Iran, was a great lover of poetry. Ismail and his successors used their native Azeri as the court language rather than Farsi. Under the pen name of 'Khatayi', Ismail produced his famous *Divan of Khatayi*. During the Soviet times Ismail was even celebrated as the 'poet king' and made the subject of many plays. Ismail and his descendant, Shah Tahmasp, used and developed the literary style known *qoshma*, a form of poetry that fits the structure of Turkic languages perfectly. Composed of three to five groups of four lines and in syllabic metre, a *qoshma* might be about nature, beauty, love, bravery, or even social events:

*Men pirimi hak bilirem,*
*Yoluna gurban oluram,*
*Dün doğdum bugün ölürem,*
*Ölen gelsin işte meydan.*

I regard my pir ['saint'] as the essence,
I'll sacrifice myself in his way,
I was born yesterday, I will die today,
Come, if you're willing to die, this is the arena.

Statues of the great poets line the columns of Baku's Nizami Literature Museum.

## European influence in the 19th century

Two Russo-Persian wars and their resulting treaties, Gulistan (1813) and Turkmanchai (1828), saw the region of Azerbaijan divided between Russia and Persia—the former took possession of Northern Azerbaijan, along with most of the South Caucasus, while the latter retained control of Southern Azerbaijan. As the Russian invasion and colonisation of the South Caucasus got under way, it was Tbilisi that became the centre of Azeri literature. The Georgian city became a centre for free thinking and liberal movements and acted as a conduit through which Azeris were able to come into contact with Enlightenment ideas and Russian romantic literature.

Exposed to the influence of the West through the works of Russian intellectuals, Azeri writers, previously dedicated to mystical and romantic poetry, began to turn to non-native genres such as fiction, drama and short stories. Amongst these new Azeri writers, the highly influential Mirza Fatali Akhundov (Akhundzade) (1812-78)[2] deserves special mention. He was from Iranian (Southern) Azerbaijan and worked as a translator in the office of the Viceroy of the Caucasus in Tbilisi. A well-known language reformer who campaigned for a Latin-based alphabet for Persian and Azeri, Akhundov wrote in both languages and created the first, albeit short, novel in Azeri—*Aldanmysh Kevakib* (*Deceived Stars*, 1857), which was set during the reign of the Safavid shah

Abbas I (1571-1629). Under the influence of Moliere, Shakespeare and Gogol, he also wrote the first European-style plays in Azeri (1850-55). Inspired by Modernist ideas, he satirized the social ills of contemporary society, which for him were rooted in ignorance and superstition and underpinned by the clergy and corrupt governments. Advocating the separation of the state and religion, he believed that the only salvation for society was the guiding light of science and rationality. Akhundov's influence on subsequent generations of Azeri writers and dramatists was profound.

The period also saw the creation of the first Azeri press, a landmark event that did much to help spread the language. *Ekinchi*, launched as a thrice-weekly serial in 1875 under the editorship of Hasan Melikov-Zarbadi (1837-1907), was the first Azeri publication of its kind to be approved by the tsarist government. However, it was closed in 1877 for alleged pro-Ottoman sentiments during the Russo-Ottoman War of 1877-78. Between 1877 and 1903 there were only a handful of periodicals featuring Azeri, including the monthly journals *Ziya* (*Light*), *Ziya-i Kafkasya* (*Light of the Caucasus*) and *Keshkul* (*The Beggar's Bowl*). The journals focused on literary and religious topics, yet their circulation was low.

Also of interest was *Kaspii* (*Caspian*) based in Baku, which was bought by the Azeri oil millionaire Zeinal Abidin Taghiyev. Following the death of its Russian editor, *Kaspii* was edited by the Azeri Ali Mardan Bey Topchubashi (1862-1934),[3] a law graduate from the University of St Petersburg who went on to become the First Republic of Azerbaijan's minister for foreign affairs and speaker of parliament. The paper, which in its heyday enjoyed a circulation of around 100,000, took on a Modernist tone and featured articles by many Azeri intellectuals.

## *Molla Nasraddin* and nationalism

During the first decade of the 20th century there was a proliferation of newspapers either in Azeri, such as *Hayat* (*Life*), or in modified Turkish. The use of Azeri vernacular as the language of literary communication became inextricably linked with a blossoming of nationalist sentiment. In general, the press represented a reformist, Westernized intellectual elite with socialist leanings. Newspapers threw themselves behind the growing secularist and anti-colonialist mood which called for constitutional, social and religious reform.[4]

*Molla Nasraddin* was a satirical journal written in Azeri and launched in 1906, inspired by the 13th-century popular character from folklore who invariably has a humorous answer to explain everything. The publication became the mouthpiece of the secularist nationalists under its editor Jalil Mamadguluzade (1866-1932). Published in Tbilisi and Baku, it enjoyed a circulation well beyond Azerbaijan into Central Asia and Anatolia. Following the introduction of the short story in Azeri literature by Abdulrahim Hagverdiev (1870-1933), Mamadguluzade developed the genre further in *Molla Nasraddin* where his humorous and satirical stories and essays, along with the satirical poems of Tahirzade Sabir, the cartoons of Azim Azimzade and those of the Germans Roemer and Schelling, earned the journal a reputation that has never been surpassed.

Writers, journalists and poets emphasized the importance of education and science as well as raising awareness of the moral dilemmas surrounding human suffering, especially in the wake of the oil boom in Baku, which had led to thoroughly miserable conditions for the working class. The journal also touched upon the debate of the roles of women in traditional and western society—the veil itself came to be portrayed as a symbol of male dominance and control over women. *Molla Nasraddin* ultimately proved to be a crucial forum for those thinkers who eventually helped to shape the First Republic of Azerbaijan.

## The Soviet era

During the early years of the Soviet regime, Azeri literature reflected the imperative to elevate the Soviet citizen and State. After the demise of the First Republic of Azerbaijan and its forcible incorporation into the Soviet Union, the Bolsheviks established their own pseudo-intelligentsia designed to serve socialist realism, the three principles of which were of paramount importance in determining the content of a literary work. A poem or a novel had, first of all, to reflect *khelgilik* (in Russian, *naradost*), or closeness to the life of the working masses, and also *ideyalilig* (Russian, *ideinost*), the correct interpretation of party policies. But by far the most important ideological and aesthetic principle (they were never separate) that socialist realism imposed upon the writer was *partiyalilig* (Russian, *partiinost*), which may be translated as 'spirit of the Party'.[5]

The work of the playwright Jafar Jabbarli (1899-1934), as exemplified by plays such as the comedy *Almas* (1928) and drama *Sevil* (1929), reflects the spirit of the time. Both plays became standard reading material for school children who were now to be educated according to the principals of the Soviet ideal. The liberation and creation of a new and bold breed of Soviet Azeri woman was a key concern of the works. The protagonist of *Almas*, for example, is a young female teacher who returns to her home village to teach at a new school. The combination of drama and folk humour rendered in everyday language made the play popular entertainment. Meanwhile, *Sevil*, the story of a young woman of the same name who manages to gain control over the destiny of her life, was written to persuade Muslim women to abandon wearing the veil. So compelling is the drama that it purportedly inspired many women to part company with their veils as they left the theatre. *Sevil* was filmed and shown all over the Soviet East and was also turned into an opera by Fikrat Amirov (1922-1984), who was awarded the title of 'People's Artist of the USSR'.

The Great Purge between 1937-39, unleashed by Stalin throughout the Soviet Union, saw between four and five and a half million people arrested, of whom nearly a million were sentenced to death. Most of the others were incarcerated in prisons or labor camps from which very few ever returned. Intellectuals, even those who supported the regime, were targets of the purges. In Azerbaijan the overall number of those eliminated in the 1930s has been put as high as 120,000—a staggering loss for a population that in 1926 numbered a mere 2.6 million.

Among the victims was Ahmad Javad (1892-1937), whose poems praised the independence of Azerbaijan and who will always be especially remembered for writing the words to Azerbaijan's first national anthem, with music by the composer Uzeyir Hajibeyov. It has been re-adopted as the national anthem of today's modern republic:

*Azərbaycan, Azərbaycan,*
*Ey qəhrəman övladın şanlı vətəni!*
*Səndən ötrü can verməyə cümlə hazırız.*
*Səndən ötrü qan tökməyə cümlə qadiriz.*
*Üçrəngli bayrağınla mə'sud yaşa!*
*Üçrəngli bayrağınla mə'sud yaşa!*

*Minlərlə can qurban oldu,*
*Sinən hərbə meydan oldu.*
*Hüququndan keçən əsgər*
*Hərə bir qəhrəman oldu.*
*Sən olasan gülüstan,*
*Sənə hər an can qurban.*
*Sənə bir çox məhəbbət*
*Sinəmdə tutmuş məkan.*
*Namusunu hifx etməyə,*
*Bayrağını yüksəltməyə*
*Cümlə gənclər müştaqdır.*
*Şanlı vətən, şanlı vətən,*

*Azərbaycan, Azərbaycan!*
*Azərbaycan, Azərbaycan!*

Azerbaijan, Azerbaijan,
Cherished land of valiant sons!
We are ready to give our heart and life for you.
All of us can give our blood for you.
Live happily with your three-coloured banner!
Live happily with your three-coloured banner!

Thousands of souls were sacrificed for you.
Your chest became a battlefield.
Soldiers who deprived themselves of their lives,
Each of them became a hero.
May you become a flourishing garden.
We are ready to give our heart and soul for you.
A thousand and one endearments are in my heart.
And uphold your honour.
To raise your banner
And uphold your honour,
All the youth are eager.
Cherished land, cherished land.
Azerbaijan, Azerbaijan!
Azerbaijan, Azerbaijan!

Declared a nationalist and pan-Turkist, Javad was subsequently shot. Another victim was the poet Salman Mumtaz, also branded a pan-Turkist for daring to suggest that Azeri literature was indisputably a part of Turkic literature. He met his fate at the hands of the NKVD secret service while in prison in 1938. His collection of rare ancient manuscripts, gathered from all over Azerbaijan, was confiscated by the Soviet authorities but today is archived at the Institute of Manuscripts in Baku. The playwright Husein Javid (1882–1944), who wrote historical dramas, was also accused of being a pan-Turkist, was arrested in 1937 and sent off to a Siberian labour camp where he died. During the *perestroika* period of the mid-1980s his remains were brought back to Azerbaijan. Today, there is a large monument in his honour in Nakhchivan, while in Baku a central avenue is named after him.

Two key figures who helped to shape Azeri literature in the 1930s were the poet Rasul Rza (1910-81) and the poet and dramatist Samad Vurgun (1906-56). Although their works were sometimes questioned by the authorities and periodically taken out of circulation',[6] they became celebrities among Russian intellectuals and officials alike and managed to escape punishment.

Mir Jalal Alioghlu Pashayev (1908-78) also deserves special mention here. Mir Jalal wrote more than a dozen novels and nearly a thousand short stories, covering a wide variety of subjects and characters. While the plots are fairly simple there is wealth of characters, a feature that is typical of the writing of the time. Mir Jalal's much translated first novel, *Bir Ganjin Manifesti* (*Manifesto of a Young Man*), published in 1938, centres on class struggle and is written in the typical Soviet fiction style of its time. A mixture of Soviet ideology, Maxim Gorky and Victor Hugo, it tells of the life of a mother and her two sons in Baku during the early 1920s. Falling foul of the obligatory repressive local landowner, the two sons are forced to flee. The older of the two siblings ends up as one of the early Bolshevik workers and becomes a heroic revolutionary, while the younger brother, thrown out by his employer, freezes to death. Meanwhile, embarking on a quest for her missing sons, the mother finds herself inevitably getting embroiled in revolutionary activities.

With the outbreak of World War II, Moscow began to employ raw propaganda to drum up support for the war effort. In the same way that religious leaders were called on to help get the message across, the power of Azeri literature was also harnessed by the authorities. Particularly favoured for this purpose were books that emphasized brave battles of the Azeris against foreign invaders. Yet following the war, a process of re-evaluation began and the conflict came to be viewed in a more sombre light. Now seen as a source of death and grief, it proved fertile ground for a philosophical examination of human nature and the effects of war on human psychology. Good examples of such literature are *Buz Heykel* (*Ice Statue*) by Anvar Mammadkhanli and *Insan* (*Human Being*) by Samad Vurgun.

## 'Allegory and symbols'

Following Stalin's death in 1953, the stifling atmosphere relaxed markedly, allowing for a fundamental shift in Azeri literature with writers even emboldened enough to begin questioning the effects of Soviet rule on Azeri society. Although still under the constraints of censorship, by using symbols, metaphors, parables and allegories that were accessible only to those familiar with the culture, they found ways of expressing their criticism of contemporary social conditions and their objection to attacks on the Azeri national character.

Anar Rzayev (*b.*1938), one of Azerbaijan's most prominent contemporary authors and president of the Writers' Union of Azerbaijan, summed up the predicament in which Azeri writers now found themselves:

> We grew up surrounded by hypocrisy, falsifications, lies, ignorance, and misunderstandings in a state where any independent thought could be subject to death. We breathed: more accurately, we tried to breathe. We tried to express our thoughts, and feelings indirectly, between the lines, by way of allegory and symbols.[7]

Historical fiction became an especially powerful medium by which to explore the possibilities of a post-Soviet nation. By focusing on distant past invasions, both real and imaginary, and periods of occupation of Azerbaijan by foreign powers, along with corresponding heroic tales of Azeri resistance, writers were able to provide critical commentaries and offer the reader a glimpse of a future free from Soviet domination.[8]

Another peculiarity of the period was the *meykhane* ('tavern') genre, a derivative of the *ashug* style (see the following chapter 'Spirit of the Ashugs') which was developed in the early 19th century. Performed with the accompaniment of a musical instrument, it was a form of poetry that could be used as a vehicle for nationalist, political and anti-establishment satire.

The pioneering journal *Gobustan* was published during this period. It spearheaded a revival of national consciousness and provided an outlet for increasingly incisive political commentary. Writers from this period include Samad Vurgun's sons Vagif (*b.*1939) and Yusif (1935-98), Mirza Ibrahimov (1911-93), along with Rasul Rza (Mammadkhanli), editor-in-chief of the first Azerbaijani translation of the *Great Soviet Encyclopedia* (published in Baku) and the first Azeri poet to use free verse in his poetry.

Another writer who deserves special mention is Ismayil Shikhli (1919-95), one of Azerbaijan's most talented authors who is deeply respected as a champion of freedom and independence. Beginning his literary career after World War II, he is best remembered for his novels *Ayrilan Yollar* (*Forked Roads*, 1957) and *Dali Kur* (*The Turbulent Kura*, 1957-67), along with hundreds of short stories, which tackled subjects such injustice, ignorance, poverty and despair in the Soviet system.

During the 1950s and 1960s, when Moscow embraced the cause of the Afro-Asian nationalist movements against Western imperialism and colonialism, Azeri writers drew parallels between Azerbaijan's own experience of imperialism at the hands of the Soviets. For example, in the verse-drama *Zanjinin Arzulari* (*Dreams of a Black Man*, 1949-52) by Samad Vurgun, what at face value appears to be an account of the liberation of the book's black protagonist is in fact a device to highlight the plight of Azerbaijan. Similarly, one of the most loved of all Azeri poets, Bakhtiyar Vahabzade (*b.*1925), used Algeria as a similar pretext in his long poem entitled *Yollar, Oghullar* (*Paths and Sons*). A fervent defender of the use of native language, he penned the following provocative lines:

*'Men azadam, müstagilem' sözlerini*
*Öz dilinde demeye de*
*İhtiyarın yohsa eger*
*De kim sene azad deyer?*

If, in your mother tongue,
You cannot say 'I am free,
I am independent!'
Who would believe that you are?[9]

In the 1980s, the repression of the Stalinist era became the subject of much investigation and writers felt confident enough to re-examine their more recent history in order to shed new light on contemporary social issues in Azerbaijan. Novels that proved of special interest at the time and helped boost the growing nationalistic spirit were Farman Karimzade's *Khudafarin Korpusu* (*Khudafarin Bridge*, 1983), Alisa Nijat's *Gizilbashlar* (*The Qizilbashes*, 1983), and Aziza Jafarzade's *Baku 1501* (1981), all allegories of the situation in Azerbaijan which took as their subject Shah Ismail Khatayi, the 16th-century founder of the Safavid dynasty in Iran.

Explaining the importance of history in literature, Nizameddin Mustafa writes:

> One of the functions of literature is to draw on social circumstances as a source of narrative and to analyze the facts about our past and present. That is why today we seem to be asking the general question: Where have we come from and where are we going? What is shared in the literary texts [...] is an attempt to find an answer for this very question in one way or another and to find what the recent past, present and future is of this belligerent nation [Azerbaijan] that occupies such a small space on the global map.[10]

A good example of literary works reflecting the critical spirit of the era is *Olum Hokmu* (*Death Sentence*, 1989), by the highly influential author Elchin Ilyas Oghlu Efendiyev (*b.*1943), which focuses on two time

***Menim Anam (My Mother)***
by Bakhtiyar Vahabzade, 1967[1]

| | |
|---|---|
| *Menim Anam* | My Mother |
| *Savadsizdir,* | She is illiterate. |
| *Adını da yazabilmir* | She cannot write her name— |
| *Menim anam…* | My mother… |
| *Say öğredip,* | But she taught me how to count. |
| *Ay öğredip;* | She taught me the names of |
| *İl öğredip;* | The months and years, |
| *En vacibi:* | And most of all, |
| *Dil öğredip,* | She taught me language, |
| *Menim anam…* | My mother… |
| *Bu dil ile tanışmışam* | With this language I tasted |
| *Hem sevinci* | Every joy and |
| *Hem de gamı…* | Every sadness… |
| *Bu dil ile yaratmışam* | With this language I created |
| *Her şi'irimi,* | Every poem of mine |
| *Her nağmemi.* | And every melody. |
| *Yoh men heçem,* | For without it I am nobody, |
| *Men yalanam,* | I am a lie, |
| *Kitap-kitap Sözlerimin* | And the creator of my words in |
| *Müellifi: menim anam!* | Their many tomes is my mother! |

periods—the era of repression and terror under Stalin and the years of stagnation and corruption under Brezhnev. The background and family history of many of the characters helps to establish concrete cause and effect between the past and present. The work reflects an Azeri society which is divided and polarized between Russian-speaking collaborators, who follow the ideology of the Moscow regime and identify closely with Russian culture, and the ordinary people who, though repressed and controlled by that ideology, manage to put up a resistance by preserving their own culture, language and religion.

Amongst the first Azeri poets to explore and compare Azerbaijan's ethnic, linguistic and historical ties with Turkey and the Turkic-speaking Central Asian republics—a particularly sensitive subject for the Soviet authorities who feared anything that even resembled pan-Turkism—was Sabir Rustamkhanli (*b.*1946). Travelling to republics such as Kyrgyzstan, he witnessed many of the same Turkic customs and traditions seen in his native country and, despite the risks involved, incorporated these impressions into his poems. In 'Written in Frunze' (1982), he declares:

> Whether I have lived here or not
> Is too difficult to determine;
> Somehow, though, this land seems familiar to me![11]

Other subjects tackled by authors of the 1980s included family life—especially with regard to its repressive aspects and the lack of personal and sexual freedom. A good example is Anar's *Besh Martabali Evin Altinji Martabasi* (*The Sixth Floor of a Five-Storey Building*), a novel that explores the problems faced by the middle classes in Baku. The story was filmed and televised in 1992.

The novel *Qatl Gunu* (*Execution Day*) was written and published in Baku in early 1990s by Yusif Samedoglu (*d.*1996). Using an unusual format, he wove together two tales set in different time periods: one about an 18th-century poet executed in Shusha by the Shah (a reference to Molla Penah Vagif, who was grand vizier to the khan of Karabakh and later executed by Shah Muhammad Khan Qajar of Iran), the surrealistic second is about a poet who is possibly the same man yet living in another time not dissimilar to the Stalin era. This modern or Soviet-period poet is not executed—he somehow survives, although he is banned from writing his poems of freedom and eventually dies of a heart attack. The writer's conclusion however is (according to literary critics) that the second death was also an execution. The novel contains an intriguing character, Kirlikir, a rat who lives in rubbish bins but has unparalleled access to the KGB archives. It is Kirlikir who tells the poet that he is to die soon.

Mention should also be made of the role of literary journals during this period of Azerbaijan's literary history. The Writers' Union of Azerbaijan's monthly review *Azerbaijan* published a large number of articles on the influence of Russian literature and culture on Azerbaijan, as well as thought-provoking pieces that tapped into the growing quest for national identity and solidarity. Along with *Gobustan* and the weekly *Adabiyyat ve Injesanat* (*Literature and Art*), it carried serialized historical novels, articles on historical epics, as well as increasingly frank and substantive discussions on cultural and intellectual issues. During the Gorbachev era, *Azerbaijan* had a relatively freer hand than its Russian equivalent *Azerbaijan Kommunisti* in criticizing the regime.

## War and Independence

Soon after the reforms of the Gorbachev era, the conflict between Azerbaijan and Armenia over the disputed region of Karabakh, which belied the cosy myth of the 'friendship of the nationalities', gave rise to major social movements. In the face of Armenian claims, the Azeri literati and historians set to work to establish conclusively the 'Azeri-ness' of Karabakh—an undertaking that began the cultural rebirth of Azerbaijan and sent worrying signals to the Soviet regime that pan-Turkism was again at large.

Nevertheless, despite the intensity of feeling over the war with Armenia, the events of Black January (1990) and the Khojali Massacre (1992), Azeri literature has not become obsessed with recrimination or hatred towards Russians or Armenians. Literary works instead attempt to explore the human tragedy involved in such events. An example is Sabir Ahmadli's surrealistic *Danizdan Galan Sas* (*The Voice from the Sea*, 1990), in which a son, murdered on a chaotic night of that fateful January, describes the events that surround his death as if he were writing his mother a letter. All the while, his corpse, which had been thrown into the Caspian Sea, floats around in the water along with other corpses, surreally surrounded by swimming Caspian seals. Ahmadli wrote a series of short stories about Black January, which first appeared in *Adabiyyat ve Injesanat* and were subsequently published as a collection of twenty short stories entitled *Yanvar Hekayalari* (*January Stories*, Baku 1992).[12]

In another case of parallel narratives, Isi Malikzade's short novel *Girmizi Sheytan* (*The Red Satan*, 1991) presents the reader with two time periods: that of 1920, when the Bolshevik army took over the independent First Republic of Azerbaijan (founded in 1918) and the events of the independence movements of the late 1980s which culminated in the Soviet attack of 1990. In order 'to make direct connections between the two events and emphasize the continuity of colonial invasion and domination, the author makes the characters involved in the independence movement of the 1990s the grandchildren of the characters from the 1920s, representing both groups as victims of colonial oppression.'[13]

In contemporary literature the hardship of a life in an unstable environment and with an uncertain future is a dominant theme, one that is reflected in the works of Sara Nazirova, Mehriban Vazir and many others. The short stories collected in Anar's *Otel Otagi* (*Hotel Room*, 1995) delve into issues relating to the migration of Azeris to other countries, while Sabir Ahmadli's book, *Akhirat Sevdasi* (*Love of Heaven*, 2003), is based on the events surrounding the death of his son Mahammad, who died in 1993 during the Karabakh war.

Three poets of the present-day republic deserve special mention. Firstly, Khalil Reza Uluturk, who was arrested on January 26, 1990, as a leader of the Azerbaijani National Movement against the Soviet Union and imprisoned for eight months. He went on to be named National Poet in 1992 and in 1995 was posthumously awarded the Istiglal Order (or Order of Independence). Secondly there is Vaqif Samadoglu, named National Poet in 2000—his father Samad Vurgun had been 45 years earlier the first to win the award. Finally, Ramiz Rovshan (*b.*1946) has juggled successful careers as scriptwriter, short story writer and poet. His politically charged poems are filled with darkly evocative imagery such as the nationalistic yet surreal collection *Goy Uzu Dash Sakhlamaz* (*The Sky Cannot Hold a Stone*).

Since 1990, there have been great efforts to re-examine the literary works of the past, a key player being *Adabiyyat va Injesanat*. Various books and pamphlets have been published that are devoted to the literary analysis of individual authors and their works, while the Academy of Sciences of Azerbaijan, for its part, has undertaken work on literary histories and anthologies. Despite the economic difficulties and the problems related to the process of transition to democracy, the contemporary literary scene continues to thrive in Azerbaijan.

*

# Spirit of the Ashugs: Art, Music, Theatre and Film

Phil Gibby & Zulfugar Rufatoglu

## Miniature art in Southern Azerbaijan

Azerbaijan's tradition of miniature painting is amongst the finest to be seen anywhere in the history of the genre. Beginning in the Middle Ages as a form of manuscript illustration, the development of the art is closely linked to the oriental poetry of such poets as Ferdowsi (940-1020), Nizami Ganjavi (1141-1209) and Muhammad Fizuli (1498-1556). It was also a sphere of the fine arts that enjoyed a certain degree of tolerance in the Islamic world.

Miniature art drew its boldness directly from the text. Great poems such as Nizami's *Khosrow and Shirin* and his epic *Iskander-nameh* (about Alexander the Great) provided artists with the context and inspiration to push the bounds of representational art to the limits of acceptability. The poets became adept at avoiding the censorship of the religious establishment, using allegory and other devices to conceal open sentiments of romantic love. In Azeri classical poetry, for example, it was common to compare the object of the poet's love to certain animals, for instance a deer, gazelle, pigeon or swan. Few were more daring than the 18th-century Azeri poet Molla Penah Vagif, who became known for his highly charged and blatantly erotic poems. Artists seized upon the opportunity to transform such works into visual feasts, imbuing their creations with a depth of human expression that could hardly fail to move the viewer.

Azeri miniatures were prized by royals almost as much as the finest wine and across the palaces of the East the demand for such art created a steady flow of masterpieces. The genre reached its apogee during the middle of the 16th century, a period that saw Sultan Muhammad and Kemaleddin Behzad create some particularly impressive examples of work.

Historians believe that Azerbaijani miniature art originated in the cities of Maraghe and Tabriz (today both in the Iranian province of Southern Azerbaijan) at the palaces of the first rulers of the Mongol Il-Khan dynasty. Tabriz in particular was home to the finest artists of the time, attracting painters, gilders and poets from around the Islamic world. The vast workshops and libraries located in the suburbs of Gazaniye and Rashidiye were especially important artistic centres.

Early examples of Azerbaijani miniature artwork are considered to be evidence of the formation of a complete artistic school. These include illustrations of manuscripts of Masihi's epic poem *Varga and Gulsha* by the 13th-century Azeri artist Abdul Momin Muhammed al-Khoy (now in the Topkapi Museum, Istanbul), *Manafi-al-Hayvan* (*The Uses of Animals*, 1298) and Rashidaddin's *Jame al-Tavarikh* (*Universal History*, 1306-1318). The latter was begun when Rashidaddin was still alive and depicts numerous mythological plots, battles, storms and sieges as well as other scenes of a domestic nature.

The Tabriz school of miniature art would become what the German art expert F. Shultz referred to as the 'alma mater of Central Asian and Eastern miniature art'. Various aspects of the school eventually merged with those of East Turkestan (now the Uyghur territories of Xinjiang in modern-day China) and Arab Mesopotamia (or Baghdad), a fact that is explained by the city's position on the Silk Road. Whereas, for example, the Baghdad style prevails in *Varga and Gulsha*, in the illustrations of *Manafi al-Hayvan* the style tends more towards the graphic painting typical of the Chinese Uyghur style.

In the middle of the 14th century, the Tabriz school developed a completely new and original painting style, as exemplified by the *Shah-nameh* miniatures created between 1330 and 1340, the majority of which were the work of the accomplished artist Shamsaddin. The main themes of the miniatures of *Shah-nameh* are devoted to the deeds of Rustam, Bahram, Iskander and others, featuring scenes such as 'Bahram Killing the Dragon' or 'Iskander Fighting a Monster'. Another group of miniatures is attributed to Shamsaddin's student Abdul Hay, a major artist of the late 14th century who was taken by the great Mongol emperor Timur to work at his new capital Samarkand (in today's Uzbekistan). In the 15th century many prominent artists and craftsmen skilled in the art of bookbinding were invited, or, if necessary, forced, to work at the Timurid palace in Herat (Afghanistan). Among them were dazzling artists such as Pir Seyyid Ahmed, Hoja Ali Musavvir, Gavamaddin and Giyasaddin.

The Golden Age of Tabriz miniature art blossomed in the mid-16th century, a period during which the poetry of Ferdowsi, Nizami, Saadi, Hafez, Jami and Nava'i among others, were especially favoured. Two

Scene from Sultan Muhammad's masterpiece, the *Shah-nameh.*

prominent masterpieces are the *Shah-nameh* (Ferdowsi's epic composed between 980 and 1010) of 1527-1537 and a very well-known copy of Nizami's *Khamse* (1539-1543), both of which were illustrated by Sultan Muhammad and his assistants. These miniature works plunge the viewer into a vivid world of visual poetry where human figures, especially those of the Shah and members of the aristocracy, are rendered with an exceptionally stylish elegance while the beauty of nature is brought alive through wonderfully vibrant colours. The beauty and majesty, for example, of 'At Keyumarse's Party' from the *Shah-nameh* was such that the master calligrapher Dust Muhammad was forced to concede admiringly that 'its success in art circles was so great that other artists of the Shah's library grieved from envy and the shame made them bow their heads'.

Sultan Muhammad's work, which also includes miniatures such as 'The Party at Sam Mirza's Palace', 'In the Meyhane' from the manuscript of Hafez's *Divan* (*Collection*), and the diptych 'The Royal Hunt' (based on a work by Jami) epitomize the Tabriz school of the 16th century. The artist's elegance of style and wonderful use of colour had such an impact on miniature art, that long after his death even the finest artists were unable to break free from his influence. In 'The Royal Hunt', the viewer is presented with a complex and fantastic mixture of rocky mountains, lawns, royal hunters and animals. Meanwhile, 'In the Meyhane' features a riotous assembly of drinkers each painted with individual, even grotesque, features—a rare sight in the miniature art of the Middle East and Central Asia.

Sultan Muhammed had numerous students and followers, among whom Mirza Ali and his son Mir Said Ali are the best known (examples of their work can be seen in the museums and collections of Cambridge, London and Boston). These artists played a key role in the formation of the Mughal miniature school in India, heading the resident artists at the palaces of Humayun and Akbar between 1549 and 1570, where they took an active part in compiling four of the twelve volumes of *Dastan-e Amir Hamze* (*The Romance of Amir Hamza*).

During the 17th and 18th centuries, Azeri cultural development went into decline and miniature art fell by the wayside. In the midst of successive upheavals and defeats at the alternate hands of the Ottomans, Russians and Afghans, the strong Safavid centralized state began to weaken and Azeri artists were no longer able to count on the generous state funds that had hitherto been channelled into the arts.

By the first half of the 18th century, Northern Azerbaijan itself had disintegrated into small and semi-independent khanates and ceased to be an integral part of the Iranian empire. In the 19th century, Russia

Detail of Tripolskaya's monument in Baku to the 26 Commissars.

swallowed up the khanates and set about importing European culture and art into the region and so, given the massive influx of foreign influences and artisans, it is difficult to identify any kind of art that is representative of Azeri culture during this period.

## 20th-century sculpture in the Republic

With the collapse of the Russian empire and the establishment of Communist rule, new art forms began to develop in Azerbaijan, although, for much of the Soviet period, quality and true vision were mostly

Statue of poet Nizami Ganjavi, designed by Fuad Abdurahmanov, in Baku.

sacrificed to the demands of state ideology throughout the republics that made up the USSR.

Baku in the 1920s became home to a number of Russian sculptors, one of whom, S. Gorodetsky, founded the republic's first workshop for sculpture. In 1923 the sculptor Y. Tripolskaya produced a monument to the 26 Commissars of Baku, a piece that depicts a muscular worker at the centre resting on a stele inscribed with the number 26 and holding the eternal flame, the symbol of revolution forever remembered. Like a mini Mount Rushmore, the surrounding relief wall is carved with the images of the commissars. Two subsequent modifications of note have been made to the work: the nude figure of the Russian Fioleto has been modified for modesty's sake, while the figure of the Armenian Shaumian was removed.

During the 1920s and 1930s, the Azeri sculptor S. P. Sabsai (1893-1980) played a prominent role in the design of monuments of that came be seen as typical of the period. His monument, for example, to the great Azeri writer and thinker Mirza Fatali Akhundov (1812-1878), father of the modern Azeri language, was erected in 1930 in the Baku square that bears his name. It depicts its subject deep in thought over a book and conveys a very real sense of intimacy and spirituality. An interesting feature is the subject's name carved on the pedestal in the Latin alphabet he created—Akhundov had dedicated considerable time and effort to creating an accepted Latin-based alphabet for his people.

After 1945, the development of sculpture, such as that seen in squares and public places, was highly influenced by monumental works created by the likes of Fuad Abdurahmanov (1915-71) and J. M. Garyaghdy

(1914-2001). During Abdurahmanov's comparatively short life he left behind a catalogue of well-known works, including the 1949 statue of the Azeri poet Nizami Ganjavi—portrayed with a scroll in his hand and grandly dressed in a robe that sweeps to the ground—which stands in Nizami Square, Baku.

Statue of the poet and thinker Fizuli by Omar Eldarov and Tokay Mamedov.

A statue of Lenin (1954) at the Soviet-built Government House in Baku, was considered a major work by the highly influential sculptor J. M. Garyaghdy. His overall concept was determined by the rather unforgiving architecture that surrounded it. Placed on a pedestal set in the centre of the building's courtyard, the figure was designed so that its silhouette could be easily seen against the imposing background. Garyaghdy's creative style is displayed in such works as 'Farhad Cutting the Behustun Rocks', in the depictions of the women war veterans Ziba Ganiyeva and Adilya Gouliyeva, or his compositional portraits from the 1960s ('Tar-player', 'Singer' and 'Keman-player'). Garyaghdy's portraits may be considered the turning point in the development of the genre in Azeri art, bringing to the fore the intensity of human character.

The monuments designed by the sculptor O. G. Eldarov (b.1927) are also distinguished by their intimacy and lyricism. His statue of the 19th-century poetess Khurshud-Banu Natavan (1960) in Baku has the appearance of a highly private portrait, with the subject captured in momentary thought as she rests on a chair.

Between the 1930s and 1950s, sculpture, as with all other art forms in the Soviet Union, became heavily politicised. Yet while the new art was expected to feature the Communists, labourers, collective farmers and other heroes of the Soviet age, Azeri sculptors tried bring to their work a certain national colour and character and a more timeless quality. For example, in his sculpture entitled 'Azadliq' ('Freedom'), also known in Azerbaijan as 'Azad Qadin' ('The Liberated Woman'), Abdurahmanov reveals popular characteristics of the Azeri national character. A woman in national costume is shown with the wind blowing the hijab from her head—Turkic women traditionally never covered their heads.

By the 1960s and 1970s sculptors were trying their hand at complex compositions in thematic sculpture, using materials such as wood, marble and granite. In the sculptural work 'Lovers' (1962, in wood), by G. G. Abdullayev the world of contemporary feelings is expressed through the use of restrained plastic form. Meanwhile the 'Female Torso' (1972) by F. E. Salayev (*b.*1943) reveals a superb mastery of the rules of classical sculpture.

## Traditional and popular music

'Work' folk songs are considered to be among the most ancient forms of song in Azerbaijan. Still found today, these chant-like songs take their themes from the agricultural cycle, such as ploughing or harvest time, and the activities of shepherds, cattle-breeders or craftsmen, with titles such as 'Shum Negmesi' ('Plough Song'), 'Bichinchi Negmesi' ('Song of the Reaper') and 'Hesiri Basma' ('Keep Off the Threshing Mat'). The most sophisticated of these songs are *hollavar*, ritualistic chants that extol the spirit of hard work.

Closely related are *sayachi* songs. Though the origin of the term is obscure some experts believe that it has the sense of 'good', 'generosity' and 'benevolence'. *Sayachi* performers would visit villagers' homes (usually in the autumn time) wishing them 'all good things', abundance and fertility. The singers were invariably peasants and usually shepherds.

Also common were seasonal ritual songs, including *ovsun* or spell songs. The most popular of the genre are those devoted to spring or Novruz, the traditional New Year in March, which heralds the arrival of spring after the cold winter months. As in other parts of the Middle East and Iran, the festival is frequently celebrated in a theatrical way, accompanied by songs and plays. This is a time when people organise galloping contests or light huge bonfires and jump over them to incantations.

Another important group of Azeri folk songs is represented by domestic or family songs for weddings and funerals. The former were more widespread and included touching songs of farewell and admonition, usually performed by the mother of the bride or groom, or the matchmaker. There were also upbeat songs of congratulation performed by the relatives and friends of the newly married couple. An essential part of the ceremony was taken up by praise songs devoted to the bride and groom and their forebears. There are quite a number of songs of this type connected to rituals such as *hena yakhdi*, the ceremony of decorating women's hands with henna.

In Azeri weddings, song and dance are inseparable, a fact reflected in *halay* songs, ancient songs that are believed to have been first performed in a rural context because they show clear connections with their agricultural counterparts. Later, due to their rhythmic and light-hearted content, they were adopted for wedding ceremonies. *Halay* songs are usually performed by two female chorus teams, each consisting of six or more singers, who accompany their singing with dances accompanied by tamborine and hand claps.

Music also had a place in funerals. According to historical sources, the *yugh* was a burial ceremony that was accompanied by singing. The old meaning of the word is 'mourning' and the ceremony was originally a form of street play in which mimes, dancers, singers and reciters took part. The participants could be either professional players or members of the audience, and, on occasion, professional mourners were invited to join in. The most popular form was the *marsya*, or lament, which was so important a genre that many well-known poets wrote lengthy poems in this style. The *marsya* was usually dedicated to those who had died by violent means and there was also a variant traditionally recited only by the wife or relatives of the deceased. Although sad, these laments were also intended to be uplifting to the spirits of those who listen. The *marsya* also forms a key part of the *shabih* or religious passion plays performed during Ashura, the Shi'ite festival to honour Husein and Hassan, the sons of Imam Ali, who were killed by their political rivals in Iraq during the seventh century.

An important place in Azeri folk culture belongs to the epic—historical or heroic songs that praise past folk heroes or peasant warriors and their struggle for the motherland. Heroes such as Koroglu, Qachaq Nabi ('Fugitive Nabi') and Qatir Mammad (the leader of a major peasants' revolt) are the best characters for the genre. The scope and structure of these epics also gives us the chance, frequently in comic language, to see how the greed and vanity of the rich landlords and rulers is pitted against the noble spirit and honesty of the common folk.

Traditional Azeri musical instruments (above and opposite) include the stringed tar (played with a plectrum), saz (lute), balaban (bagpipes), the kamanche (spiked fiddle played on the knee), garmon (button accordion), double-reed duduk (like a shawm), zurna (larger than a duduk), shvi (recorder), utek (whistle flute), naghara (cylindrical drum), ghaval (frame drum) and dhol (double-sided drum played with the fingers).

As in the rest of the world, love is a favourite topic in Azeri folk music. The main motifs of love songs include the pain of separation from a loved one, praise of her beauty and the sorrows and joys of life. In these songs we see the anthropomorphising of nature, where the flowers become beauty, the stars twinkle for lonely hearts, lakes became loved one's eyes, the thunder her anger and the sunshine her compassion.

Technically, folk love songs are strictly metric: the lines are exactly rhymed. Textually they are usually composed on the basis of such poetic forms as *bayati* (seven syllables in each line) or *goshma* (11 syllables). In most cases, whatever the metre, there are invariably four lines in each couplet. Love songs characteristically include exclamations such as *'balam ey!'*, *'ay aman!'* or *'ay, balam!'* These are quite distinctive and generally act as syllable fillers and can be translated into English as the classic pop song tag 'oh baby!'

## Ashugs

Also found especially in Turkey and Armenia, *ashugs* or bards are still extremely popular in Azerbaijan, where they accompany themselves on the *kobuz* (short-stringed lute), improvising songs or reciting the national epics.

The origin of the word *ashug* comes from Arabic, meaning 'lover'. In different periods of history *ashugs* were often called differently. In Azerbaijan's quintessential Turkic epic *Dada Gorgud* (or *Dede Korkut*), bards were called *ozans*, while in other sources they are known as *varsaqs* (a word of unknown origin). In some districts of Azerbaijan, where tightly-knit indigenous Caucasian populations might be less accepting of the bards' art, it seems that *ashugs* were known as *yanshags*. The term is evident today when people exclaim '*Yanshaglama!*' ('Don't be a *yanshag*!') in order to express disapproval at someone talking too much. Another *ashug*-inspired remonstration can be found in the verb *dastanlamag* (literally 'to deliver lengthy speeches')—used to express boredom with another's longwinded conversation, such as in the exclamation '*Dastanlama!*'—'Don't tell me epics!'

*Ashugs* played a fundamental role in the development of Azeri poetry. While their songs were mainly about love, they also tackled themes of heroism and the homeland, as well as aiming satirical attacks on wealthy rulers known for their greed or brutality—a habit that made Azeri bards common targets for repression by the secular and religious authorities alike—and they generally fell into one of three categories. First there was the universal *ashug*, also known as the *usta ashug* or 'master *ashug*'. He was a mix of composer, singer, instrumentalist and sometimes poet and dancer. Then there was the instrumentalist *ashug* who neither wrote or composed, but instead performed songs written by other *ashugs*. The third category was the *ashug*-poet, who did not compose music but wrote the lyrics or poems that were adapted by the master or instrumentalist *ashugs*—it was these *ashugs* who played a hugely influential role in the early development of poetry in the Azeri language.

*Ashugs* performed lengthy *dastans* or heroic epics, such as *Shah Ismayil* and *Ashug Kerib*. During the performance of these long poems, the *ashug* would periodically interrupt his singing with a spoken narration of the story. Many songs also incorporated morality lessons and were termed *ustadnames* or 'master poems'. Another interesting tradition was the *deyishme* contest. The word '*deyishme*' can be translated into English as 'battle of words', where two *ashugs* stood opposite each other and tried to outplay the other. Usually they resorted to songs with riddles that required the opponent to respond with the correct answer using the same melody. This continued until one of the players failed to come up

## Popular music

There is a wide range of modern popular music in Azerbaijan and Iran that has a distinctive Azeri flavour and the following musicians are fine examples of the quite diverse styles to be found.

Baku-born (1969) Aziza Mustafa Zadeh, or simply 'Aziza', is a jazz pianist and scat singer whose unique fusion style blends the improvisational elements found in *mugam* (which itself has been likened to a form of traditional jazz). Classically trained, she is influenced by her father Vagif Mustafa Zadeh (who died in 1979 at the early age of 39), also a pianist and who was one of the pioneers of the Azerbaijani *mugam* jazz movement in the late 1960s. Since her self-titled first album was released in 1991, Aziza has released a string of albums that have been acclaimed worldwide and performs regularly.

An interesting phenomenon in neighbouring Iran is the growing popularity of Azeri folk-based music. A leading light is Rahim Shahriari, a garmon (button accordion) player, and his group, the Araz Ensemble, which frequently boasts a line-up of more than 20 musicians and dancers. Born in Tabriz in 1971 and based in Tehran, Rahim is an Iranian Azeri who not only plays and sings but is also a prolific composer, arranging melodies to lyrics by some of Iran's top poets such as Dashgin (Ali Huseynzade) and Valeh (Mahmud Dastpish). The fact that the lyrics to tracks like *Bayaz Gejalar* (*White Nights*) and *Aghlama!* (*Don't Cry!*) are in Azeri is no barrier to the rest of the country who speak Farsi (or Persian) or other national languages. Thanks to Rahim's influence, Los Angeles-based Iranian diva Zoya Sabet, though not ethnically an Azeri, now regularly features Azeri songs in her albums and concerts, even producing a CD entitled *Yasha Azerbayejan!* (*Long Live Azerbaijan!*) after one of Rahim's best-selling songs.

The more traditional side of Azeri music is just as popular. Father and son *tar* players, Ramiz and Ayyub Guliyev, are supremely gifted performers whose blend of virtuosity and scholarship has made them deserved leaders in their field. Ramiz was born in 1947, in the Karabakh town of Aghdam. The duo perform just as easily with a full Western-style orchestra as in a folk ensemble, guesting with orchestras such as the Gara Garayev Chamber Orchestra—they were even invited to play at the jubilee concert held in Baku in 1997 by world-renowned cellist Mstislav Rostropovich (who was born in the Baku). Ramiz and Ayyub are avid musicologists, doing all they can to bring traditional *mugam* to public ears as well as promoting new works—there are currently more than 20 classical concertos for the *tar*—and Ramiz is especially proud of his three-volume set for *tar* and piano which includes 100 pieces by Azerbaijani composers.

Mostly founded in the Soviet period, Azerbaijan's many dance companies continue to keep alive traditional dance and music.

with an answer. There were also contests where the competing *ashugs* sang an unfinished stanza, challenging the other to find an acceptable rhyme to complete it.

The commercialisation of the *ashug* tradition, for so long praised and respected as the focus of any folk gathering, became the source of some contention. By taking payment for his services, the *ashug* was seen to be devaluing the art form—giving rise to the humorous yet somewhat cynical Azeri saying: 'You pay ten roubles to an *ashug* to sing, then you have to pay him another ten to shut him up!'

## *Mugam*

Many *ashugs* in Azerbaijan started to adopt elements of *mugam* in their performances and its influence on both modern and traditional music grew rapidly during the 20th century. *Mugam* (also spelt *mugham*) is a musical form where a simple melody is repeated in cycles, guided by rules that allow for its perpetual renewal and evolution. Despite its strict frame and forms, it maintains its origins as a traditional oral folk art.

It avoids chordal structures and is therefore freed up to follow microtonal nuances across 84 micro-intervals. It is also metre-free, meaning that it follows no fixed time signature. Like a sort of folk jazz, the result gives a dreamy, almost mystical and uplifting effect. The style is particularly developed in Azerbaijan but is also found in many parts of the Middle East, Iran and Central Asia.

In Azerbaijan *mugam* is usually performed by a trio of *sazandes* (from the Persian for 'musician'), playing the tar, the kemancha and tambourine. Traditionally the tambourine player is also the vocalist. Vocal-instrumental *mugam* music performed by such a trio is called *destgah* (from the Persian for 'compilation'). In *destgah*, improvised instrumental passages (*reng* or 'colour') are interchanged with clear-cut vocal sections (*tesnif* or 'song').

*Zerbi-mugam* is a distinctive style of vocal-instrumental Azeri *mugam*, distinguished by the way the vocalist is accompanied. One of the instruments will detach itself from the melody played by the ensemble to track or imitate the singer's melodies note for note, nuance for nuance.

*Mugam* is very much the product of the general musical expression of Middle Eastern or, more precisely, Arab-Persian culture and philosophy. However, from the time when poets started writing the first *ghazal* verses in Azeri around the 10th-12th centuries, there also emerged a specifically Azeri *mugam*, paralleling the formation of classic Azeri poetry based on the Arabic and Persian forms.

## Birth of the dramatic arts

The development of Baku as the world's first oil capital in the second half of the 19th century and early 20th century saw a huge cultural renaissance in every aspect of the arts and the media. The process continued, albeit with different emphasis, during the Soviet period (which saw increasing Russification) and into the modern post-Soviet republic. The renaissance is particularly impressive since it actively drew on the region's Golden Age of the 11th to the 13th centuries and mixed this not only with Russian influences but also, thanks to direct links as a result of the oil trade, with the exciting ideas and movements flowing out of Western Europe. Azerbaijan's artistic independence and flowering inspired Turkic

Muslims throughout the Russian Empire and abroad, and brought about a string of cultural landmarks, such as the establishment of some of the Muslim world's first theatres and opera houses.

Azeri theatre effectively began in 1883, when the Baku-born oil baron Zeinal Abidin Taghiyev financed the building of the city's first theatre, named the Taghiyev Music Comedy Theatre (among many other acts of supporting the arts, Taghiyev also sponsored new writers in the Azeri language through printing presses that he owned). During riots in 1909, the theatre was burned to the ground, but Taghiyev lost no time in ordering it to be rebuilt. A large number of theatres and concert halls have since been built in the capital, including the Azerbaijan State Theatre of Opera and Ballet, which opened in 1910.

First and foremost among the playwrights of Azerbaijan is Mirza Fatali Akhundov (1812-78), who deliberately made a break with the literary Azeri language and wrote in language that reflected the way people spoke. His plays, particularly his comedies, created a truly popular national theatre, and continue to have widespread appeal.

Azerbaijan can also boast the Islamic world's first opera—an adaptation of Fizuli's *Leyli ve Majnun* (*Layla and Majnoon*) by the composer Uzeyir Hajibeyov (1885-1948), then only twenty-two years old, which was first staged in 1908 at the Taghiyev Theatre. Probably the most inspirational love story in the Middle East and Central Asia, *Leyli ve Majnun* is a powerful tragedy based on an original epic that predates Shakespeare's Romeo and Juliet by hundreds of years. The classical poets Nizami, Jami and Fizuli each in the own way wrote definitive versions of the love story. Fuzuli, uniquely among the great poets, left us three *divans*, or collections, of his poetry: one each in Persian, Arabic and Azeri Turkish. It is upon his Turkish version of *Layli ve Majnun* that Hajibeyov based his opera's libretto, written with his brother Jeyhun.

The opera tells the story of Majnun who is driven mad by his love for Leyli—their union is forbidden by the constraints of society. Having lost his sanity, Majnum (*'majnun'* is Arabic for 'the mad one') wanders in the desert but manages to find salvation in poetry and the wild animals that become his companions. The lovers finally meet once more, but it is too much for their tortured hearts and they die together. Hajibeyov not only introduced traditional themes in his classical music compositions, but also the innovation of using traditional instruments and choirs. Leyli and Majnun, for example, mixes the poetic emotion of Azeri *mugam* music and the lyrical singing that accompanies it with Western arrangements to create a musical palette filled with drama and emotion.

A Baku concert poster from the 1920s.

Hajibeyov went on to write a string of equally popular hits, such as the 1913 comic operetta *Arshin Mal Alan* (*The Cloth Pedlar*) and his last stage work *Koroghlu* (*The Blind Man's Son*), a heroic opera with lyrics written by the novelist Mammad Sayid Ordubadi (1872-1950), with the famous tenor Bul Bul ('Nightingale'; Murtuza Mammadov 1891-1961) taking the lead role. *Koroghlu* was based on a local legend that supported the Soviet emphasis on accounts of the peasants and workers rising up against the landowners and industrialists. Reputedly one of Stalin's favourite operas, the overture subsequently became an unofficial anthem for the Azeri people and, ironically, was memorably played in the streets during the nationalist demonstrations against the Soviet state between 1988 and 1991. To this day, it remains a popular opening for concerts.

Gara Garayev (1918-1992) and Fikrat Amirov (1922-1984) were key composers who followed in Hajibeyov's footsteps in the post-World War II period. Garayev based a symphonic piece on Nizami's version of *Leyli ve Majnun*, although musically this was inspired by the work of his mentor Dmitri Shostakovich rather than traditional Azeri models.

Meanwhile, Amirov is most remembered for his opera *Sevil*, based on the play of the same name by the dramatist Jafar Jabbarli (1899-1934). Dealing with the tale of a free-thinking woman who decides to discard her chador or veil, when it was originally staged in 1928, women were reported to have thrown off their own veils on leaving the theatre. It is popularly asserted that by the end of the run of Jabbali's play, the veil was no longer worn in Baku.

Scenes from the heyday of Soviet Azeri theatre.

The main platform for performances was the Azerbaijan State Opera, founded in Soviet times, which was designed to reflect the different traditions celebrated in Hajibeyov's work. It operated three separate companies: one performing the works of traditional *mugam*, another the works of Azeri composers such as Hajibeyov that combined *mugam* and the Western operatic tradition, and a third dedicated to the works of the Western repertory, mainly Russian operas.

Initially under Soviet rule, Azeri cultural expression was encouraged, but it was not long before a programme dedicated to imposing Russian culture and language was vigorously implemented. Stalin's purges during the Terror Years of the 1930s resulted in the imprisonment, exile or murder of thousands of Azerbaijan's creative artists and evidence of their lives and work was cynically wiped from the historical record.

Some respite came during the 1950s under the Khrushchev regime, a time in which many who had been victims of Stalin's

Uzeyir Hajibeyov's 1913 musical *Arshin Mal Alan* (*The Cloth Pedlar* or *Arshin Takes a Wife*), recreated and directed by Reza Takhmasib in 1945.

purges were posthumously rehabilitated and their works performed or republished. During *glasnost* under Gorbachev in the 1980s, a process of rediscovery and the restitution of Azerbaijan's not-so-distant creative past began —a process that has continued to gather momentum after independence.

## Film

Cinema arrived early in Azerbaijan, thanks to the Russian-born Frenchman, A. H. Mishon who arrived in Baku in 1879. After working as a photographer, he used his French connections to bring over one of the new cameras developed by the Lumieres in Paris. In 1898, he premiered a series of short films showing everyday life in the streets of Baku as well as scenes from other parts of the Caucasus and Central Asia. Their titles were appropriately evocative: *Fire Resulting from an Oil Gusher at Bibi-Heybat Oilfield*, *The Departure Ceremony of His Excellency Amir of Bukhara on the Steamship 'Grand Duke Alexei'*, *Folk Dance of the Caucasus*, and scenes from a dramatic comedy *So You Got Caught!*, filmed in one of Baku's many parks. These pioneering movies were destined for the

Afrasiyab Mammadov in the title role of Husein Seyidzade's epic *Koroglu* (1960).

International Paris Exhibition of the same year, where they made as much of an impact as they had with the Azeri public.

Mishon's mantle was taken on by a Georgian, the film-maker Vasili Amashukeli (who had already produced one of the world's first feature-length documentaries in 1912, *Akaki Tsereteli in Racha-Lechkhumi*), and two Belgian brothers by the name of Pirone. The latter arrived from France in 1915 and set up the first film production laboratory in Baku, to be followed five years later by the region's first film studio. The Pirones brought the Russian director M. Svetlov to Azerbaijan, and it was his

A scene from *O Olmasin, Bu Olsun* (*If Not This One, That One*; also called *Mashadi Ibad*), based on Uzeyir Hajibeyov's 1911 musical and directed by Husein Seyidzade (1946).

work—notably *The Woman*, *An Hour Before His Death* and *An Old Story in a New Manner*—that truly established an Azeri film culture while also consolidating the reputation of the country's most famous actors of his generation, Husein Arablinski.

Although enthusiasm for the genre was evident from early on, it took the Soviet era to provide the organisation and structure that the Azeri film industry required (under Communist rule, each of the 15 Soviet republics went on to develop its own distinct film industry). In Azerbaijan during the 1920s, the republic's leader Nariman Narimanov nationalised the film industry, so creating the first formal studios, and also set up a national film institute, which controlled the cinemas and distribution agencies.

However, this consolidation came at the expense of artistic freedom, a state of affairs that would continue for the next seven decades. Films articulating folk culture in a context that suited the propagandists of Moscow were encouraged and films—silent and talkies—were produced in both Azeri and Russian-language versions. Movies more typical of the era included Abbas Mirza Sharifzade's *Bismillah* (*In the Name of God*) in 1925, an exposé of criminal acts conducted by fake clergy, which dovetailed ideally with the prevailing Soviet ideology of the times. Even more recent films, such as Tofig Ismayilov's *Azabli Yollar* (*Painful Roads*, 1982) and Eldar Guliyev's 1979 epic *Babek* continued to typify the Soviet

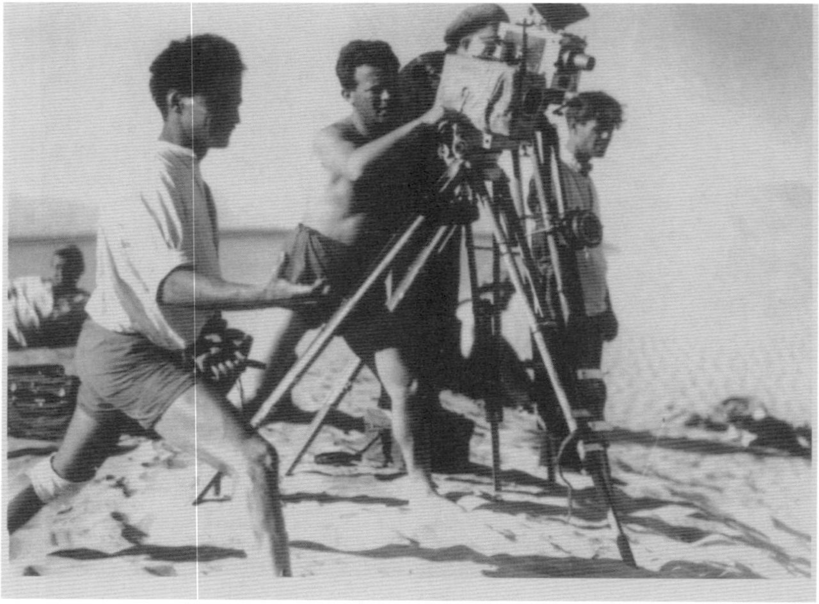

The pioneering director Nikolai Shengelaia shooting *26 Baki Komisari* (*The 26 Commissars*) in Azerbaijan.

tradition, outlining stories of heroic national defence against the Arab invaders.

The stifling artistic climate imposed by the Soviet authorities came to an end in 1991, allowing a new wave of Azeri filmmakers to emerge. However, the industry found itself ill-suited to the fast-paced and flexible world of international contemporary cinema. Only three years after independence, the AzerFilm headquarters, inherited from the Soviet era, was closed down in a dispute over non-payment of water and heating bills. Slowly, however, it has built itself up again, reinforced by the leaps and bounds made by the television industry.

Part of Azeri cinema's richness lies in its position at the crossroads of three very contrasting cinematic cultures—those of Iran, Russia and Turkey. It is a cosmopolitan mix that has been successfully harnessed in the past, notably by the iconic Sergo Paradjanov. Although a filmmaker of the old Soviet school, as an Armenian born in Georgia who was repeatedly imprisoned by the authorities, he had real feeling for the Caucasian style. While he made distinctively Armenian and Georgian films, *Ashik Kerib* proved to be a landmark

*Telefonchu Giz* (*Telephone Girl*), directed by Hasan Seyidbeyli (1962).

Azeri film. Released in 1988, through Paradjanov's trademark vignettes and sumptuous imagery, it tells the tale of an Azeri *ashug* minstrel who falls for a rich merchant's daughter. Rejected by her father, he is sent to wander for a thousand and one nights, but not before making his beloved promise not to marry till his return.

Outside of the republic, Azeri culture has also been the inspiration behind more recent films such as Iran's Persian-language *Tavalod-e Yek Parvane* (*Birth of a Butterfly*, 1998), directed by Mojtaba Raie. An international award-winner, it presents an allegorical glimpse of the impact that modern life has on a rural village in Iran.

A guiding figure in Azeri cinema is the scriptwriter and director, Rustam Ibrahimbeyov. His work on Russian director Nikita Mikhalkov's Russian-language film *Utomlyonnye Solntsem* (*Burnt by the Sun*) took the honours at the 1994 Cannes Film Festival and landed an Oscar for best foreign film a year later. Set in Soviet Russia in 1936, the film deals with the policies and paranoia of Stalin by exploring the effect on a holidaying hero of the Revolution and his family of an unexpected visitor, his wife's former lover. Like Paradjanov, the Soviet system played an important part in shaping Ibrahimbeyov's career yet like the former, he was also to embrace the the greater artistic freedom of the post-Communist years and, in so doing, to find a means of expressing himself fully.

Today, the greatest challenge facing aspiring Azeri filmmakers is to be able to find the resources to translate their ideas to celluloid. Another area that is also in need of development is to attract international producers to film in a country that has a remarkable range of natural locations as well as technical know-how. A notable boost came when the 19th James Bond film *The World is Not Enough* (1999), starring Pierce Brosnan, featured the Caucasus in its plot, including locations such as Baku and the Oil Rocks. In an era where international media and communications have experienced an unprecedented boom and where Azeri culture is resurgent, the film industry in this remarkable corner of the Caucasus may yet, as it follows a journey of rediscovery, prove to be one of Azerbaijan's cultural jewels once more.

*

# Sacred Flames: A History of Religion in Azerbaijan

Nicholas Awde & Fred James Hill

THREE GREAT religions—Zoroastrianism, Christianity, and Islam—have loomed large in the history of Azerbaijan. Of the three, it is Islam that has survived as the faith of the overwhelming majority of Azeris. In a world in which Sunnis account for four-fifths of Muslims, the Republic of Azerbaijan is rare in that the majority of its population adheres to the Shi'ite interpretation of Islam—the only other Shi'ite majority states of the world are Iran, Iraq and Bahrain. Shi'ites make up around 70 per cent of the Republic's Muslim population, the rest being mostly Sunnis along with a small minority of Ali Allahis and Bahais.

While Shi'ism sets Azerbaijan apart from the other former Islamic (Sunni majority) Soviet Republics, a common Turkic heritage has done much to help maintain strong bonds between them all in their newly-found independence—around 80 percent of Muslims of the former Soviet Union are, like the Azeris, of Turkic origin and speak one of the Turkic languages.

There is also a small yet significant presence of Christians in Azerbaijan belonging to the Russian and Armenian Orthodox Churches (around 5.6 and 2.5 per cent of the population respectively). Two other communities, tiny in numbers yet with a long-standing and historically important presence in the Caucasus, are the Christian Udins and the Mountain Jews.

For centuries Islam has profoundly influenced Azeri social traditions and customs as well as its literature and art. Given the systematic attempts on the part of the Christian Russian Empire and the subsequent atheist Soviet Union to eradicate the religion from the region, the fact that Islam continues to thrive in present-day Azerbaijan amply testifies to its continuing spiritual and cultural appeal for the population.

While Muslim values still have an important part to play in modern Azeri society, there are few outward signs of religious strictness. In a country that prizes spiritual and intellectual freedom, religion is viewed by many as a matter of personal conscience and choice. This is reflected in the country's constitution, which identifies no official state religion and extends freedom of worship to all faiths. The Azeris' progressive attitude towards religion and society is not a new phenomenon. The short-lived First Republic of Azerbaijan, which existed between 1918 and 1920, can be considered the first modern Islamic democratic parliamentary state in history and one that gave Muslim women the unprecedented right to vote. Interestingly, Azerbaijan can also boast the world's first Islamic opera—an adaptation of Fizuli's *Leyli ve Majnun* by the composer Uzeyr Hajibeyov (1885-1948), then only twenty-two years old, which was first staged in Baku on January 12, 1908.

## Early beliefs and Zoroastrianism

The region of Northern and Southern Azerbaijan, i.e. the territory that today roughly corresponds to the Republic of Azerbaijan and Northwestern Iran, with its history tied to the fortunes of the various Persian empires, is closely identified with the major religion of Zoroastrianism. From the time of the Median Empire in the seventh century BC to the violent death of the last Sassanian ruler of Persia at the hands of the Arabs in 651 AD, the faith exerted a profound influence on the great empires centred in Iran, seeping into all aspects of Persian culture.

The religion has its roots in the traditions of the early inhabitants of the land. Amongst these were the Indo-European nomadic tribes that perpetually wandered across the Caucasus and Persia, worshipping forces and elements found in nature, such as the sun, moon, fire, water, earth and wind. Over time, some of the descendants of these nomads began to settle in agricultural communities and, drawing on their past religious traditions, they developed a powerful belief system that underpinned the sedentary life they now led. Named after its great prophet Zoroaster (or Zarathustra), the religion tended towards monotheism by fusing the old gods into a single deity named Ahura-Mazda, the 'Wise Lord'. It taught that people possessed free will to choose the right path in a world in which a cosmic battle between good and bad was being fought—the reward for which was Heaven or Hell. A major feature of Zoroastrianism is the central role of fire in its sacred rituals, representing the ultimate symbol of justice and immortality as well as the purity of Ahura-Mazda.

Key players in the history of the spread of Zoroastrianism were the Magi (members of whom were the 'Three Kings' of the Bible), a priestly class belonging to the tribes of the Medes who occupied part of Iran, the

### The survival of ancient religious traditions

None of the major monotheistic religions ever succeeded in entirely eradicating the ancient symbolism and associated rituals that have their origins in the distant prehistoric past. Festivals such as Novruz (New Year), while being part of the local Islamic culture also exhibit distinctive Zoroastrian influences, which in turn suggest even older pagan influences.

The ancient tradition of venerating natural objects and places has also proved enduring in the region of Azerbaijan, coexisting alongside more orthodox religious rituals. Such places are known as pirs ('pir' is a word of Persian origin meaning 'saint' or 'elder'), examples of which are trees (such as oaks), rocks, rivers and streams. Age-old cults focusing on the sun and moon have also survived. Pirs can also include the tombs of holy people and a number of sites in Azerbaijan have been major pilgrim sites for many centuries. Perhaps unsurprisingly in a region that was so long a bastion of Zoroastrianism, Muslims, Christians and Mountain Jews alike have kept alive fire cults until recent times.

Pirs may be visited for spiritual assistance in matters relating to family problems or physical complaints ranging from specific illnesses to general aches and pains or fertility problems. In some areas, bathing in sanctified streams may be practised in order to communicate with the spirits of the departed. Pilgrims arrive bearing offerings, including money, cloth and certain types of food. A pir at Buzovna, near Baku, known as Ali Ayaghi ('Ali's Foot'), features an impression in a rock that is popularly believed to be the footprint of the Prophet Muhammad's cousin and son-in-law, Ali. Animals are traditionally ritually slaughtered at the shrine and other offerings made. A familiar sight at pirs is the abundance of strips of coloured cloth tied by believers to bushes, rails, fences or any other suitable place. This ancient practice is not restricted to Azerbaijan but is common to other parts of the Caucasus, Middle East and Asia.

most northerly of which was territory in the region of Southern Azerbaijan. The Magi claimed that their native Azerbaijan was the home of Zoroaster—a tradition that proved enduring and would later be maintained by the powerful Sassanian dynasty that ruled over Persia from the third to seventh centuries AD. In reality, such claims have little or no historical basis[1]—it is more likely the religion's founder hailed from somewhere in the region of eastern Persia or northern Afghanistan. Nevertheless, the impact of the religion has ensured that the name Azerbaijan will always be identified with the fire temples of old. Indeed the very term 'Azerbaijan' has been traced back to the ancient Median word *Âtrpât(ak)âna* meaning 'Place of Tending the Sacred Fire(s)'.[2] The Ancient Greeks also knew the region with the similar name of 'Media Atropatene'.

No region other than Baku and the Apsheron Peninsula could have provided such a perfect setting for a religion such as Zorastrianism. The flames rising from the earth there, a result of natural gas emissions catching fire, and the copious quantities of oil that were collected easily from the ground stimulated the imaginations of Zoroastrianians and provided a fitting location for fire temple complexes in which to worship.

For centuries, priests and pilgrims from far-flung ancient kingdoms felt compelled to travel to the region and worship in the 'Land of Eternal Flames'.

Zoroastrianism was strengthened in Persia by Darius I, one of the greatest rulers of the vast Persian Achaemenid Empire (545 to 331 BC), which included territory in both Northern and Southern Azerbaijan. Elevating the faith to official state religion, the Achaemenids declared their realm to have been bestowed on them by no less a deity than the supreme god Ahura-Mazda.[3] Despite such lofty claims, the realm of the Achaemenids remained culturally highly diverse. Its rulers extended a great deal of tolerance and respect for other religions in the empire and, as a result, the degree to which Zoroastrianism was absorbed by the various subject peoples in the numerous provinces is unknown. The continuation of obscure ancient religious beliefs and practices was certainly the case, along with a good degree of syncretism as these mingled with Zoroastrianism.

Under the ruler Atropates, Southern Azerbaijan became a bastion of Zoroastrianism. Atropates had formerly been a satrap (governor) of the region in the service of the Achaemenids. Yet, as a reward for siding with Alexander the Great (the man responsible for the destruction of the Achaemenids in 331 BC and who paved the way for Greek Seleucid rule in Persia), he was declared ruler of the province. For a while at least, Atropatena, as his kingdom was known, had the distinction of being the only former Achaemenid territory to be ruled by a Zoroastrian dynasty. It roughly corresponded to the region of present-day Iranian Azerbaijan and reached up to the River Aras (Arax) incorporating the southeast of the present-day Republic of Azerbaijan. Following the Macedonian destruction of the holy city of Raga (usually equated with medieval Rayy near Teheran), the Atropatenian city of Ganzak, situated near Lake Urumia (in Iranian Azerbaijan), became the new home of the immensely important holy fire of Adur Gushnasp.[4]

Under the Sassanians Zoroastrianism took on a more intrusive role as the official state religion. The Sassanians were zealous adherents of the faith, their clergy teaching that the kingdom and the 'true' religion were 'twins'. Power and legitimacy were now maintained at the expense of religious tolerance and frequently violent campaigns to force conversion are well documented. The destruction of the Sassanian Empire by the Arabs in the middle of the seventh century and the subsequent rise of Islam marked the decline of Zoroastrianism. The Zoroastrians, who had their own scripture, initially fared reasonably well under their Muslim overlords who associated them with the Christians and Jews who were

## Novruz

Novruz Bayrami is a major festival in Azerbaijan which coincides with the spring equinox on March 21. Novruz (meaning 'New Day' in Persian), traditionally marked the first day of the calendar in Azerbaijan until it was replaced by January 1 as a result of Soviet influence.

Novruz is also celebrated in other countries, including Iran, Tajikistan and Afghanistan, as well as by people such as the Kurds. Despite being celebrated by many Muslims, the festival has pre-Islamic origins that can be traced back to Babylon in Ancient Mesopotamia, where New Year was celebrated on the 21st day of the month of Nissanu (corresponding to March and April). It symbolised the victory of good over evil as things began to grow again after winter. Adopted by the Zoroastrians, it also came to include the veneration of the four cosmic elements of Water, Fire, Earth and Air and the day of the ascent of the Sun (considered the Divine Star) to the throne, where it retains its power and governs the world until September 21, the autumnal equinox.

Traditionally, celebrations begin four weeks before the actual day of Novruz. The Wednesday of each week is devoted to one of the four elements: *Su Charshambesi* (Water Wednesday), *Odlu Charshambesi* (Fire Wednesday), *Torpaq Charshambesi* (Earth Wednesday), and *Akhir Charshambesi* (Last Wednesday) or *Yel Charshambesi* (Air Wednesday)—water thaws and flows again, fire brings the sun, the earth awakens, and the air warms up.

During Sassanian times, twelve pillars of mud bricks, each dedicated to one month of the year, were erected in the royal court. Seeds such as wheat, barley, lentils and beans were sown on top of each pillar and sprouted by New Year's Day itself, when the king received his subjects and declared amnesties.

The days leading up to Novruz are spent spring-cleaning and making all types of special foods for the festivities. The mystical number seven is a regular element in Novruz rites, notably the *yeddi lovun* ('seven things') where seven things—salt, bread, a dyed egg, grain, a piece of coal and a mirror—are put in a copper tray onto the holiday table and left for 12 days. These were originally an offering to the sun. The traditional New Year feast includes at least seven items that start with the Persian letters *sîn* (س) or *sâ* (ث), including *sabzi* (sprouted grain), *sib* (apple), *serke* (vinegar), *somakh* (a lemon-flavored spice), *sir* (garlic), *sonbol* (hyacinth), *senjed* (a date-like fruit), *saat* (clock) and *sekke* (coins).

Unsurprisingly for a country which has such a rich history of fire veneration, Azerbaijan also has many Novruz traditions that are associated with the Zoroastrian concept of the purifying properties of the element. Holding bonfires in the streets, roofs or tops of hills is common and on Akhir Charshambesi everyone of all ages takes part in jumping once over seven small fires or seven times over a single one. Another tradition involves children knocking on their neighbours' doors and asking for candy and other treats.

'Peoples of the Book' as mentioned in the Quran (see page 142). In time, however, they came to face sustained oppression and marginalisation.

The religion has long since died out in Northern Azerbaijan although it has managed to survive in Iran, especially in the vicinity of the central Iranian city of Yazd, where there are estimated to be as many as 30,000 followers. In the same city, at the temple of Ateshkade, there is a holy flame which is said to have been burning since the fifth century. Meanwhile, another surviving group of Zoroastrians are the Parsees

The Atashgah ('Place of Fire') temple in Surakhani, near Baku.

(meaning 'from Persia'), whose descendants originally left Persia in search of a more hospitable environment after the Arab conquest and settled in India in the eighth century. The Parsees continue to practise Zoroastrianism and today thrive not only in India but other parts of the world.

A potent symbol of Northern Azerbaijan's close identification with the cult of fire is the Atashgah temple (meaning 'place of fire'), which still stands in Surakhani near Baku. Although the temple itself was built in the 17th century (long after Zoroastrianism had been abandoned by the Azeri population), the vicinity has a history of fire cults going back some 2,500 years. In plan, the complex is reminiscent of a caravanserai, with cells arranged around an irregular pentagonal courtyard and a perimeter wall with merlons (tops of battlements) and gates with fortified towers. The fire temple is situated at the centre of the courtyard and is a square-shaped pavilion with semicircular arches crowned by a cupola. The temple was maintained and modified up to the mid-19th century by pilgrims and ascetics who lived in tiny cells and devoted themselves to the cult of fire. Sanskrit and Hindi inscriptions on the walls testify to the fact that these believers were in fact of Indian origin. The last in the line of priests to tend the fire at the temple died in 1879.

The following is a first-hand account written by a visitor to the temple when it was still in use in 1845:

> At the eastern termination of the Caucasian range, ten miles from Baku, and near the village of Surakhani, jets of inflammable gas issue from the porous shelly limestone. In the daytime, these fires are not particularly striking, but at night, when they illuminate the gloomy and deserted neighbourhood, the picture changes, and behold, the simple temple of fire-worshippers becomes a fairy castle. Multi-coloured tongues of fire dance weirdly in the winds. Tongues of fire are carried away by the breeze, but at the points which they leave there spring up flames of greater brilliancy.[5]

The 19th-century French novelist Alexander Dumas travelled widely in the Caucasus and wrote vividly of the impending demise of the temple:

> With the exception of Frenchmen who rarely travel, the whole world is aware of the Atashgah in Baku. My compatriots who want to see the fire-worshippers must be quick because already there are so few left in the temple, just one old man and two younger ones about 30 to 35 years old.

Dumas also described the temple:

> We went inside the temple through the gates, which were entirely enveloped in flames. The prayer room with the cupola is erected in the middle of a large quadrangular court; the eternal fire is ablaze right in the middle of the prayer room.

The potent mix of mystery, fire and oil made the temple an irresistible image for the oil magnates Robert and Ludvig Nobel, who used it, complete with flames, as their company logo.

## Christianity

The adoption of Christianity by the ancient Albanian kingdom, a state that covered a sizeable portion of the territory of the present-day Republic of Azerbaijan, gave rise to a long-lived Christian heritage in the region. At a time when Zoroastrianism was the official religion of the Sassanian Empire, the existence of a local Christian state has been used to strengthen claims of the existence of an early Azeri nation—one with a culture that is distinct from that of mainstream Persia.

The original inhabitants of Albania, which began to assert itself around the fourth century BC, most likely belonged to a number of non-Indo-European Caucasian tribes whose eventual union evolved into a feudal society complete with its own language—one that belonged to the indigenous Eastern Caucasian linguistic family. Little is actually known

## Caucasian Albania

Albania of the ancient Caucasus has no connection with the Albania of Eastern Europe. The Albanians were an indigenous people of the region whose state occupied a good deal of the territory that today comprises the Republic of Azerbaijan. The founding of the Kingdom of Albania is generally placed at around the late fourth century BC and, like neighbouring kingdoms, its capitals and frontiers shifted constantly. In particular, there was a constant struggle with the Armenian empire over the territory that lay on their common borders.

It was during the fourth and fifth centuries that Christianity gained a strong hold in the Caucasus and, one after the other, the three kingdoms of Albania, Armenia and Iberia (Georgia) converted to the new faith. In Albania, King Urnayr led the conversion. Each kingdom was given its own unique script, specially created at the time to record the Bible, liturgy and other literature. While the Armenian and Georgian alphabets are still used today, Albanian has survived in written form in only a few inscriptions and manuscripts, including some recently discovered in 1996 at the Orthodox monastery of St Katherine's in Sinai. A form of the Albanian language is still spoken today by the minority Udin or Udi people, who live in the villages of Nij and Oghuz in Azerbaijan, and Zinobiani in Georgia. It is interesting to note that the Roman historian Pliny the Elder had long ago associated the 'Albani' with the 'Udini'.

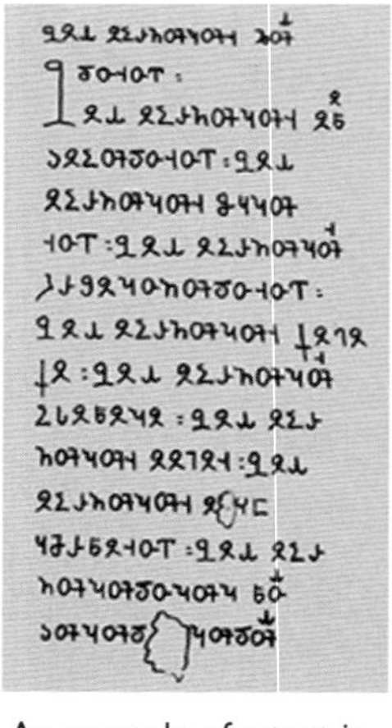

An example of a text in the Albanian script from the tenth century.

Christianity brought a dramatic shift in the regional balance of power as Albania, along with its neighbours, shifted its allegiance to the empire of Christian Byzantium in the west instead of paying tribute to Zoroastrian Persia in the southeast. The ruling Persian Sassanids sought to re-impose their influence and so marched on the recalcitrant Caucasus. The allied armies of the Albanians, Armenians and Georgians were defeated by the superior forces of the Persians at the Battle of Avarayr in 451. With the Albanian kingdom left in tatters, the nobility and church leaders took refuge in the mountainous parts of Albania, particularly modern-day Nagorno-Karabakh. It was here that the council of Aluen (Aghuen), held in 498, justified their church's theological position (see below) and therefore the battered state's independence.

The political demise of Albania came with the arrival of the Arabs, who conquered much of the Caucasus during the seventh and eighth centuries in the name of the Caliphate in Damascus (later Baghdad) and who incorporated the region into the Islamic Empire. However, Albania survived in the form of the petty kingdoms that sprang up in the eastern Caucasus, such as Arran (the Arab name for Albania), Khachin and Shirvan, which lasted for many centuries to come, even thriving at times.

The fate of a unified Albanian culture was similarly sealed. The link between church and state may have been a source of strength for Albania but it was also to prove its undoing. The Albanians were diophysites, meaning that they believed in the dual nature of Christ, being both human and divine. This exposed them to intense pressure from the Armenians, who were monophysites, believing that Christ was divine but not human in nature, and who used the adoption of this doctrine as a way of absorbing the Albanian heartland. And so, from 720 onwards the Albanian Church and its people were gradually assimilated into that of its larger monophysite neighbour.

about the early pre-Christian religious beliefs of the Albanians. The Classical historian Strabo claimed that their leading deity was the moon and that their priesthood exerted a great deal of power, being subordinate only to the king.

The exact process by which Christianity arrived in the Caucasus is hazy. Yet the it had clearly taken a firm hold by the time of the conversion of the Armenian king Tiridates by Saint Gregory in around 300 AD. The sovereign subsequently declared his newfound faith the religion of his realm, making Armenia the first country in history to adopt Christianity as the official religion of the state. Albania and Iberia (Georgia) eventually followed suit, founding their own churches in the fourth century. The Albanian king Vache II (*r.c.*451-*c.*463) is known to have renounced Zoroastrianism and proclaimed Christianity the official religion of his kingdom during the mid-fifth century.

Life for the Christian states in the Caucasus was precarious. Armenia was divided in 428 AD between the Christian Byzantine Empire and Persia, the latter ruled by the Sassanians. Resting their legitimacy firmly on the Zoroastrian faith, the Sassanians were eager to prevent any bonding between the Caucasian and Byzantine Christians. To this effect, they targeted the Armenians living under their rule, unleashing a major campaign to eradicate Christianity and to convert the Armenian leadership. A dramatic showdown, involving Christians from all over the Caucasus, including the Albanians, eventually took place in 451 at the Battle of Avarayr (in the region of present-day Nakhchivan). With no help forthcoming from Byzantium, the Caucasian Christians were defeated at the battle. Nevertheless, in an ensuing peace treaty, a more conciliatory Sassanian leadership agreed to restore freedom of Christian worship in the region and to abolish the fire temples it had established. The Armenian and Albanian Christians managed to weather the remainder of the Sassanian period, despite periodic upheavals.

New challenges for Christians came with the arrival of Islam. During the seventh and eighth centuries, the entire region of Azerbaijan, along with the rest of the South Caucasus, was incorporated into the Islamic empire. Nevertheless, Christians were not subject to state-sponsored religious intolerance. In exchange for the payment of a special tax, known as *jizya*, Christians were able to practise their religion in relative freedom. However, in time much of the Christian Albanian population came to adopt Islam.

The Albanian Church was officially merged with the Armenian Church in the early ninth century with the approval of the Caliphate in Baghdad.[6] However, descendants of the Albanian Mihranid dynasty restored the Albanian kingdom in Karabakh and an Albanian catholicos

## Christian churches and monasteries

Ancient Albanian churches and monastery complexes can be found throughout Azerbaijan, a testimony to the region's rich Christian heritage. Evidence suggests that Christian places of worship were often built on sites held sacred in pagan times. The origins of one of Azerbaijan's famous churches (*pictured below*), which still stands at Kish (near Sheki), are shrouded in mystery—it has been celebrated as the country's oldest church with oral tradition placing its construction in the first century AD—although recent carbon dating places its construction considerably later, perhaps even as late as the 12th century. Neverthless, the discovery of a sample of Kur-Araz pottery that dates to the 3rd century BC was found underneath the altar of the church and there is evidence to suggest the site had been used by religious cults as far back as 5,000 years ago.

A favoured site for the siting of monasteries was up mountains, where steep and craggy rocks, mountain rivers and ravines provided a natural defence from the outside world. Such difficult access was not merely to protect the monks themselves from enemy invasions, but also to provide a refuge for the inhabitants of nearby villages and towns. In later times, when the very survival of Christianity was at stake, the monasteries became the bastion of the Faith. Faced with increasingly difficult times, wealthy local members of the aristocracy and religious dynasties became ever more pragmatic, moving themselves and their families to monasteries and becoming permanent 'tenants'. The complexes became bustling self-contained communities with schools, libraries (the monasteries played a major role collecting and archiving precious manuscripts), and workshops for craftsmen who likewise had moved to the relative security of the religious fortresses.

During the 13th century, important architectural projects were undertaken at the Gandzasar monastery complex (*pictured opposite*), which lies in the Agderin region of Nagorno-Karabakh. The complex was the residence of the head of the Albanian Church and contained the family burial vault of the Jalalid Albanian princes, members of the last Albanian dynasty. While the Jalalids may have lacked real political power, they played a key role as the spiritual guardians of the Albanian Christians. The hand of the Jalalids in building the magnificent Gandzasar cathedral is recorded there on an inscription of 1240. Ordered by Hasan Jalal (*r.c.*1240-*c.*1261), who went by the official

title of prince of Syunik and Albania, it declared: 'My father before his death entrusted my mother Hurisha and myself with the task of building a church in Gandzasar—the place of our fathers…'

The 13th century coincided with devastating attacks by the Mongols and, in a desperate attempt to reduce the threat to their community, the artists of the Gandzasar monastery even resorted to adding Mongoloid features to the face of their stone statue representing Christ's crucifixion.

managed to survive into the 11th century at Ganja until the city was seized by the Seljuk Turks under their leader Togrul in 1054.

The Albanian Church subsequently lived on in the principality of Khachen, which lay in the mountainous region of Karabakh. Under the rule of Hassan Jalal (*r.c.*1240-*c.*1261), important religious architectural projects were undertaken, especially at the famous Gandzasar monastery complex (in the Agderin region of Nagorno-Karabakh). The Jalalid clan eventually disintegrated, leaving in its wake a handful of smaller units, or melikdoms. An autonomous patriarch-catholicos survived, however, until as late as 1836, well into the period of Russian tsarist occupation, at which point the Russian authorities merged it with the Armenian Church. To this day a few thousand remaining Udins (or Udis), direct descendants of the Albanian Christians and who speak a related language, continue to be closely identified with two Azeri villages, Nij (Nic) and Oghuz (Varashen) and one Georgian, Zinobiani. However, many Udins fled Oghuz in the early 1990s as a result of ethnic tensions arising during the war with Armenia.

## The Mountain Jews

Azerbaijan is home to small communities of Mountain Jews, a people who have inhabited the Caucasus for many centuries. Worldwide, the number of Mountain Jews may be in excess of 100,000. In the Caucasus there are presently around 40,000, the majority living in Daghestan (Derbent, Kaitag and Makhachkala). Present-day numbers in Azerbaijan are critically low. The collapse of the Soviet Union prompted many thousands to emigrate to Israel (already a principal destination for Mountain Jews since the 1950s) and Russia. While failing to distinguish between different types of Jews, an official census carried out in 1999 illustrated the dramatic decline of Judaism in Azerbaijan: that year the number of Jews was estimated at a mere 8,900, down from 35,500 and 30,800 in 1979 and 1989 respectively.

The origin of the Mountain Jews is shrouded in mystery. According to one theory, they are descendants of substantial numbers of Jews who once lived in Southern Azerbaijan and spoke Tat—a Persian-derived language still spoken not only by Mountain Jews but also by the Muslim Tat people of Azerbaijan and neighbouring Daghestan.

Others hold the Mountain Jews to be descendants of the Khazars, a Turkic people who were originally nomadic shamanists, perhaps related to the Uighurs of Central Asia and China, who established a presence in the North Caucasus. They converted en masse to Judaism in the eighth century and their kingdom managed to resist the Muslim Arabs as they rapidly expanded their new Islamic empire. Eventually, however, the Khazars succumbed to later invasions by the Pechenegs and the 'Viking' Rus of Kiev.

After most of the Caucasus eventually fell under Islamic rule, Jews in Azerbaijan lived under similar conditions as the Christians, paying the *jizya* tax to the Islamic authorities, which secured them the right to continue practising their faith (see the section on Islam below). This status quo continued into the period of tsarist occupation during the 19th century, but after the Soviet establishment of power the Mountain Jews fell foul of Communist intolerance towards all forms of religion. The Soviets banned Hebrew, the Jewish liturgical language, and ordered synagogues to be destroyed. Overnight, the identity of the Mountain Jews officially disappeared by simply considering them to be ethnically identical to the region's other Tat speakers.

While the Mountain Jews have, over time, come to share a good many aspects of everyday life with their non-Jewish neighbours, they have also managed to retain their distinctive religious practices and community way of life. Deprived of Hebrew books, prayers have been handed down orally, but with little or no understanding of the meaning of the words. Like Muslims, the Mountain Jews remove their shoes before entering the synagogue.

The all-Jewish town of Krasnaya Slobodam is seen as the 'capital' of the Mountain Jews. Located across the river Gudialchai at Quba in the very north of Azerbaijan, the town numbers around 5,500. The synagogues (only two of the town's original eleven synagogues survived the Communist period) are decorated with distinctive and beautiful Caucasian carpets. Other concentrations of Mountain Jews are to be found in Oghuz (Vartashen) and Baku.

With such a long history in the region, it is not surprising that many Mountain Jews feel the Caucasus to be their proper home. Indeed, some of those who emigrated to Israel have chosen to return. Yet, it remains to be seen how long they can retain their unique culture and way of life in the face of a rapidly changing world.

## The development of Islam in Azerbaijan

Islam arrived in the region of Northern and Southern Azerbaijan at an early date in the religion's history. Booty-seeking Muslim Arab armies began entering Persia as early as 633 AD. The following decade they defeated the Persian Empire of the Sassanians and, extending their influence into the region of the South Caucasus, soon brought Atropatena (Southern Azerbaijan), Albania, Armenian and Georgia under the sway of their Islamic empire, ruled by the Damascus-based Umayyad dynasty.

Conversion of the population to Islam was by no means immediate. Firstly, Christians and Jews were under no obligation to convert—the Quran saw to this. Under Islamic law Christians and Jews were considered to be 'Peoples of the Book' (in Arabic '*Ahl al-Kitaab*') on account of their common scriptures and belief in a single God, and they were accordingly granted special status within the Islamic state system. Known as *dhimmis*, they were entitled to practise their religion and receive the protection of the Muslim community in return for paying the special *jizya* tax. While Zoroastrians, also known as 'Magi' or 'Magians', are not specifically identified by the Quran as one of the 'Peoples of the Book', they nevertheless came to be considered as such (although in time they would face increasing marginalisation).[7]

The Arabs were more interested in exacting tribute from their newly conquered territories rather than finding new converts. Having ensured local rulers acknowledged their suzerainty, they merely allowed things to continue as they were, using the existing administration to ensure they received what was due. Governors sent by the caliphs (the rulers of the Islamic Empire) generally limited themselves to the collection and payment of tribute and taxes and to making sure the armies were paid.

The authority of the Islamic Caliphate was by no means universally accepted and challenges to its rule came from Muslim and non-Muslim quarters alike. The Abbasid caliphs, who ruled at Baghdad from the mid-eighth century onwards, faced numerous revolts as they struggled to retain power over their huge empire.

It was in Azerbaijan, during the ninth century, that one of the most celebrated uprisings took place. Staged by the Khurramite leader Babek, it had its roots firmly in religious faith. The term 'Khurramite' loosely covers various revolutionary movements of the time that opposed the caliphate and whose ideologies were suffused with traditional Persian religious beliefs. Amongst these groups were the neo-Mazdakites, to whom Babek belonged. Neo-Mazdakites adhered to a variant form of Manichaeism, a dualistic religion founded in Persia that has been described as a Christian heresy but which owed more to the Zoroastrian tradition.[8] A religion of popular appeal, Mazdakism had, 300 years previously, temporarily supplanted Zoroastrianism as the religion of the Sassanian state. Aiming to do away with social inequalities by abolishing private property and holding all things in common (a principal the men even extended to their womenfolk), it had threatened the very fabric of the Persian Empire. Babek's own popular revolt was ruthlessly quashed but his stance against the authorities would become legendary, symbolizing the Azeri spirit of resistance.

Under the relative stability brought by the Seljuks, an Oghuz Turkic dynasty that had seized the reins of power from the Abbasid dynasty in Baghdad in the 11th century, Islam gained a greater hold over the population of Azerbaijan. There is little architectural evidence of Islam's presence in Northern Azerbaijan prior to the Seljuk period. Azeris often converted Christian churches or chapels into mosques, which involved little more than removing the altar, putting in a mihrab (a small central niche marking the wall nearest to Mecca), and adding a minbar (a pulpit from which the Quran is read).

The Seljuks pumped a new lease of life into the cultural and social life of the region and it was a time that saw major developments in Islamic architecture. No longer was it necessary for Islamic towns to be fortified behind natural mountain defences to ensure their survival, such as had happened with the Azeri Christian strongholds. Under the relative stability of the Seljuks, settlements on the caravan routes or Silk Route were able to flourish, and therefore in Azerbaijan what were once small and unimportant villages became transformed into important urban centres of trade. As with many other developed towns of the Middle East, those of Azerbaijan were planned along the lines of a citadel or 'inner town' (*shahristan* in Persian), surrounded by the 'outer town' (or *rabad*, an Arabic word that is also the origin of the name of Rabat, the capital of modern-day Morocco).

The 13th century saw widespread death and destruction at the hands of the Mongols. Hulegu (1217-1265), the grandson of the great Mongol general Jengis Khan, was responsible for destroying Baghdad and putting an end to its central role in the Islamic world. Neverthless, the Mongol Il-Khanate state that came to rule Persia from the Southern Azeri city of Tabriz eventually converted to Islam and helped to rectify some of the damage inflicted by its predecessors.

## The rise of Shi'ism under the Safavids

The most famous and influential rulers to emerge from Azerbaijan belonged to the Safavid family, who had their origins in Ardabil (Southern Azerbaijan). The dominance of Shi'ite Islam in Iran and Republic of Azerbaijan today is directly attributable to this dynamic and influential Azeri Turkish-speaking dynasty, which ruled Persia between 1501 and the 1720s. It was the first Safavid shah, Ismail (*r.*1501-1524), who launched the campaign to replace 'orthodox' Sunnism with Shi'ism in the Persian Empire (to which Azerbaijan and much of the South Caucasus belonged).

The deep and divisive rift between the Shi'ite and Sunni interpretations of Islam goes back to the formative years of the religion.

## Islamic memorial buildings

One of the most interesting architectural features of Azerbaijan is its tower tombs, also known as Seljuk mausoleums, which became especially popular during the 11th and 12th centuries. These were built across Azerbaijan, Iran and Anatolia and referred to in written sources as *gunbez*, meaning 'dome'.

Historians believe the tower mausoleums may have evolved from Turkic or nomadic yurt-shaped burial mounds. The tower tombs played a role similar to that of monuments in Western Europe, yet deliberately avoided the use of sculpted figures of living creatures, in keeping with Islamic norms. The burial vaults of such tombs (which could be round, square or polygonal in shape) were placed underground, while the upper part of the construction could reach as high as 30 metres—a highly visual way of immortalizing the deceased.

Two mausoleums in Harrakane, between Hamadan and Qazvin (Iran)—known as the 'Twin Imams'—are masterpieces built by Muhammad Abul Maali, who hailed from Zenjan (in historical Southern Azerbaijan). The brick constructions, which were built in 1067 and 1093 for the Turkoman beks (local princes), are octagonal in shape, with cylindrical turrets punctuating the corners.

The 12th-century tower mausoleum in Maragha called the Girmizi Gunbez ('Red Dome'), which followed a square plan, was innovative for its decorative use of glazed brick. It was built by Bekir Muhammad, who belonged to at least three generations of architects.

The patriarch of Azerbaijani architecture is considered to be Ajemi, who was responsible for the Mausoleum of Momine Khatun (*pictured opposite*), which still stands today in Nakhchivan City. The monument is distinguished from its predecessors by its huge proportions and the complex form of its design. Ajemi was born in Nakhchivan, then part of the Atabeks of Azerbaijan, under the rule of the Arab Caliphate. His influential style can easily be detected in the works of other architects of the Middle East. According to a 13th-century source, he had the title of 'Sheikh-ul-Muhandisi' ('Sheikh of Engineers'). He left the following words on the interior walls of the mausoleum:

> The world is transient.
> We all shall pass,
> The world will remain.
> We shall die,
> But this building will remain.
> So dear Lord deliver us
> From the Evil Eye...

The Momine Khatun mausoleum is the only building by Ajemi known to have survived the ravages of war and time—his other magnificent buildings have either vanished or lie in ruins.

Blue-tiled tomb of Jehan Kudi Khatun, 14th century, Karabaglar, Nakhchivan.

The problem stemmed from the fact that the Prophet Muhammad left no declared successor, a fact that led to the establishment of rival lineages. After Muhammad's death, four of his closest followers—Abu Bakr (*r.*632-4), Umar (*r.*634-644), Uthman (*r.*644-56) and Ali (*r.*656-61)—were successively elected as 'caliphs', a term signifying a successor or deputy of the Messenger (i.e. the Prophet Muhammad) of God. This period is known by the Sunni Muslims as the Golden Age of the 'rightly guided' caliphs. In addition to subscribing to the legitimacy of the rightly guided caliphs, the Sunni majority generally supported the Umayyad and later Abbasid caliphs, who ruled from Damascus and Baghdad respectively.

Meanwhile, there were those who believed that only the descendants of Ali (Muhammad's cousin) and his wife Fatima (Muhammad's daughter) were the legitimate leaders of the Muslim community. These followers became known as Shi'ites—from *Shiat Ali* meaning 'Ali's party' (or 'sect'). Their leaders, starting with Ali, became known as imams, who are highly revered and looked upon as infallible sources of divine guidance. Mainstream 'Twelver' Shi'ism supports a succession of twelve Shi'ite imams in total. The final imam mysteriously disappeared in 873 and is believed to have remained in a state of 'occultation' or hiding. The Twelvers subsequently began a long wait, believing he would return as the Mahdi (or Messiah) who would right the wrongs perpetrated by the Sunni majority and restore justice in the prelude to the Day of the Last Judgement.

Shah Ismail was a direct descendant of Safi a-Din of Ardabil (1252-1334), an enormously charismatic and popular ascetic Sufi from whom Safavid dynasty took its name. It was claimed that Safi ad-Din could work miracles and make prophecies, and he established an enduring Sufi order in 1301 which went on to enjoy widespread support, especially among the Turkic tribes of the region. His order even gained support from the Mongols, possibly even from Timur Leng (Tamerlane), whose military genius established the Timurid Empire.[9] By the end of the 15th century, the order had grown into an important military and political force whose influence was felt across western Persia and Eastern Turkey. Significantly too, the Safavids who now ruled the region underwent a doctrinal transformation, exchanging their Sunni teachings for those of Shi'ism—although they would still remain popular with many Sunnis. With their newfound militantism, the Safavids launched a jihad in the Caucasus against the Christian Georgians.

The Safavid shahs claimed to be true representives of the line of imams and, like Safi ad-Din, were seen to play an active and vital role in God's plan for the world. Ismail was considered by his followers to be paving the way for the coming of the Mahdi in the prelude to the Day of Judgement. He claimed to be descended from the seventh imam, a bearer of the divine fire that was passed down from generation to generation. Furthermore:

> Ismail, leaning on religious syncretisms of almost two centuries of Sufi movements in northwestern Iran and Anatolia, and combining diverse religious influences including Shi'ism, Sunni messianism, Buddhism and Zoroastrianism, also proclaimed himself the incarnation of Khidr, the bearer of ancient wisdom and the spirit of Jesus.[10]

Ultimately, Shi'ism provided Persia with a strong sense of unity which it had not enjoyed since the days of the Sassanians, creating a strong sense of identity and a popular banner behind which the state was able to rally the population. Shi'ite and Sunni tensions became an important

The ceremony of *shaksi-vaksi*, during the great Shi'ite festival of Ashura (see page 150), around the turn of the 19th century. The writer and traveller J. D. Henry described seeing groups of men in street processions repeatedly whipping their own backs with chains to the beat of a steady drum, drawing blood in the process. Amidst the frenzied wailing of the crowd, others staggered around, or had to be carried off, blood-soaked and dizzy after repeatedly striking the tops of the heads with *kinjals* (daggers). He was informed that in some cases wealthy Muslims paid others to undergo the ordeal on their behalf in order to expiate their sins.

characteristic of the wars between the Safavid and (Sunni) Ottoman Empires during the 16th and 17th centuries. In Northern Azerbaijan conversion to Shi'ism proved slower and, in fact, was never so effective as to ensure a majority during the Safavid era—this would only finally come about during the 19th century as a result of Russian imperial policies in the region.

## Islam in imperial and Soviet Russia

In the early 19th century, Russia launched a major campaign in the South Caucasus which culminated in the successful annexation of practically the entire region, primarily at the expense of Persia. Apart from Christian Georgia, the South Caucasus at the time was home to a mosaic of Muslim khanates that had emerged after the disintegration of the Safavid Empire the previous century and which enjoyed various degrees of autonomy. While the population was predominantly Muslim, Christian and Jewish communities still continued to thrive in the region:

> Non-Muslims lived under certain disadvantages, notably a higher rate of taxation, but they do not seem to have been actively persecuted... Christians and Jews lived in their own villages and enjoyed certain advantages, especially the local governance of their co-religionists... 'Peoples of The Book' [i.e. Christians and Jews] were able to maintain

Imamzade tomb, Nakhchivan—built for Abu Muzaffar Badhur Khan, ruler of Nakhchivan (1722-1732).

their houses of worship, obtain religious literature, and employ the clergy of their faith for their congregations.[11]

The treaties of Gulistan (1813) and Turkmanchai (1828) between Russia and Persia sealed the fate of the khanates, which were gradually absorbed into the Russian imperial administrative system—a process that was part of an official policy designed to facilitate the Russification and (Russian Orthodox) Christianization of all subjugated peoples within the tsar's empire. Muslim populations in the region would now find themselves subject to discriminatory practices designed to weaken the bonds of their religion.

Antagonism of the Russian authorities towards Muslims living under their rule was not a new phenomenon. At various times in the past, Muslims living in Russian territory had faced policies of forceful conversion, closure of mosques, the seizure of *waqf* (religious charitable foundation) properties and even the risk of the death penalty for preaching Islam.[12] It was Catherine the Great (*r.*1762-1796), who, faced with growing unrest throughout the Russian Empire, had seen fit to moderate the state's treatment of Muslims.

Now, in an attempt to control Islam in the Caucasus, ecclesiastical boards were set up. Headed by a (Shi'ite) 'sheikh al-Islam' and a (Sunni) 'mufti'—both positions represented the highest Islamic authorities and were appointed by the state—the boards conducted their business under the watchful eye of the Ministry of Internal Affairs.[13] The Russian government now had a means by which to undermine the authority of the *ulema* (the collective name for Muslim religious leaders and scholars), perceived to be the most obvious threat to Russian rule. Not only were they the bastion of Islamic values, but many of the highly influential mullahs had also been educated in Turkey or Iran, a worrying situation for the Russian authorities who were keen to keep the Caucasus from sliding back into the Islamic world.

Sharia law was deliberately eroded as mullahs and *qadis* (Islamic judges) were excluded from involvement in civil and criminal law (now reserved entirely for the state courts) and restricted to matters relating to family law, such as marriage, divorce and inheritance. Clerics, who were required to pledge loyalty to the tsar, were rewarded by receiving privileges of rank, such as exemption from taxes and corporal punishment. Many such privileges were also extended to their children. Meanwhile, Islamic literature was subject to tsarist censorship and Muslim religious land liable to confiscation. Furthermore, in terms of representation, by the end of the 19th century, Muslims in Azerbaijan found themselves increasingly marginalised as tsarist discriminatory practices deliberately led to overrepresentation of Armenian Christians in the civil service.

Russian imperialism was also responsible for the rise to majority of the Shi'ites in Northern Azerbaijan. Although Shah Ismail had initiated an official policy of conversion to Shi'ism in Persia during the 16th century, the process had been less successful in Northern Azerbaijan, where until the mid-19th century, the numerical balance between the two forms of Islam was more or less equal. Yet Sunnis found themselves marginalized when tsarist wars against the (Sunni) Ottoman Empire erupted. While Shi'ite volunteers were enlisted by the tsarist regime to fight against the Ottomans, Sunnis faced a host of repressive measures, which included total exclusion from holding official posts and the expropriation of all clerical land. By the 1860s, Sunni numbers had fallen significantly, with many having emigrated to Turkey, leaving Shi'ites a two-to-one majority.

An unusual *juma* mosque in Quba, built in the 19th century. In most of the larger towns, in addition to smaller local mosques there were also larger mosques, known as *juma meschids* ('Friday mosques'), which were designed to accommodate larger numbers of worshippers for the collective Friday prayers. Many people from surrounding villages who came to the towns to shop or trade would attend Friday prayers in these mosques.

Ultimately, Russian attempts to persuade the Azeris to give up Islam would never be successful. Islamic identity and traditions stood firm and public expressions of faith were evident to travellers such as J. D. Henry, who visited Baku in the early 1900s.[14] There he was able to witness first hand the public displays of self-flagellation (*'shaksi-vaksi'*) during Ashura, the major festival of atonement in the Shi'ite calendar, which commemorates the martyrdom of Husein (the third imam, son of Ali and grandson of the Prophet Muhammad) at the hands of the Ummayad caliph Yazid at the Battle of Karbala (680 AD). Despite driving a wedge between the Shi'ites and Sunnis, the repressive attitude towards Islam by the state eventually unwittingly helped to foster close relations between the two factions.

The crisis of the Russian Revolution of 1905 marked a new phase in the social and political life of Muslims in Russia. The first of several Muslim congresses was held secretly in August 1905 in the Russian city of Nizhny-Novogord. Bringing together Muslim activists and thinkers from around the empire, the congress demanded that Muslims be given the same rights as Russians. To this end, it approved the creation of a new political party, Ittefaq-ul-Muslimin (Muslim Union), which embraced 'Muslims of all sectors and regions of Russia'.[15]

In subsequent congresses, there were differences of opinion over whom the Muslims should ally themselves. The prevailing view was to co-operate with the new Russian Constitutional Democratic Party, on account of its aims to see a democratic form of government adopted in Russia and because it was perceived to be sympathetic to the Muslim plight.[16] However, a small number of Socialists held that the future lay with the Marxist Social Democratic Party (which was to later become the Communist Party) and distanced themselves from Ittefaq-ul-Muslimin.

A key player in the congress and in defending the rights of Muslims was the Azeri Ali Marden Topchubashi (1862-1934), a law graduate from the University of St Petersburg who became editor of the Baku newspaper *Caspian*. He was elected to the short-lived First State Duma in the Russian capital in May 1906 as a Transcaucasian (South Caucasus) representative and became an important spokesman for Muslim interests. After the dissolution of the Duma, his continued high-profile advocacy of political and social freedoms earned him a spell of imprisonment. Nevertheless, he would emerge to become the first minister for foreign affairs and speaker of parliament during the short-lived First Republic of Azerbaijan and also represented his country at the Paris Peace Conference and subsequent Treaty of Versailles that immediately followed World War I.

There were attempts to maintain Islamic unity after the outbreak of the new Russian Revolution in March 1917. A Muslim congress was held in Moscow on May 1, with 900 Muslim representatives. Yet there was little overall consensus as to whether it best served Muslim interests to have a central government that guaranteed cultural freedom for the Muslim regions or a federal system that permitted a good deal of political autonomy.[17] A subsequent Muslim congress, held in Kazan, appeared to make some progress and approved, amongst other things, the formation of a military council (*harbi shura*) to create a Muslim Army and a National Muslim Board, yet the seizure of power in November 1917 by Lenin and the Bolsheviks irrevocably changed the political landscape.

May 28, 1918 saw the creation of the First Republic of Azerbaijan. It was during this brief spell of independence that the word 'Azerbaijan' was first concretely adopted, both as a political name for the territory of Northern Azerbaijan and the word 'Azerbaijani' or 'Azeri' officially used for its citizens, who had formerly been referred to by the Russian regime as 'Transcaucasian Muslims', 'Caucasian Tatars' or simply 'Turks'. While the new state was distinctly secular in terms of its constitution, Islamic culture clearly united the Azerbaijanis and differentiated them from their Christian Georgian and Armenian neighbours. Bonds were strengthened with the Turkish Ottomans, and it was to them that the embryonic nationalist government, with its capital in Ganja, had appealed to help wrest Baku from the hands of the Bolsheviks. The Turkish army had been only too eager to help, aided by a volunteer army made up principally of Azeris and dubbed the 'Army of Islam'.

## Islam during the Soviet years

From April 1920, Azerbaijan was once again under Russian rule, this time as a socialist republic of the newly formed Soviet Union, and Islam was to face its harshest test. For the next seven decades, atheism would remain the official policy of the Soviet state. In the early years, as part of what was seen as a secularising and modernising process, the authorities curbed the activities of Islamic civil courts and nationalized the *waqfs*. However, Stalin soon launched a more intense attack on Islam in an attempt to destroy its core institutions. Mosques and *madrasas* (Quranic schools) were targeted, practices such as polygamy and the wearing of veils, a highly visible manifestation of Islam, were banned. As Stalin's purges intensified, outward expressions of faith brought very real dangers. Any state official exhibiting religious sympathies was liable to be branded a pan-Islamicist and hauled before the courts as an enemy of the state, the consequence of which could be fatal.

Of the estimated 2,000 mosques in Azerbaijan at the beginning of Soviet rule, by the 1980s only 14 Shi'ite and two Sunni officially registered mosques remained. Unsurprisingly, public daily prayers were no longer observed. Meanwhile, the number of registered clerics had dwindled to no more than 70.

Although the Bolsheviks had effectively destroyed the Ecclesiastical Boards set up the previous century, these were revived in 1943-4 as World War II raged on. Representing Muslims throughout the Soviet Union, the four boards were placed under the control of the Council of the Affairs of Religious Cults. Their real purpose was for propaganda purposes, primarily aimed at drumming up support for the war effort and not, as may be imagined, to promote religion. The Muslim Board of Transcaucasia (South Caucasus) was based in Baku. It was responsible not only for the Shi'ite and Sunni Muslims living in Azerbaijan, Armenia and Georgia, but also for Shi'ite communities throughout the rest of the USSR. (The other three Muslim Boards were those of Kazakhstan and Central Asia, the Russian Federation and Siberia, and the North Caucasus, all of which were headed by Soviet-appointed Sunnin muftis.) The board became the sole outward manifestation of organised Islam, and its role was strictly limited to spiritual, not social or political, concerns.

In the post-war years, despite a relaxation of the widespread persecution of the 1930s, there was no real change to the status of religion. During the late 1940s and 1950s, carefully chosen Islamic leaders were sent abroad to attend congresses and other religious events and only a select few were permitted to make the *hajj* pilgrimage to Mecca—which had been banned by the Soviet authorities in 1935 but theoretically revived in 1944. Yet the trips had more to do with foreign policy considerations: there was political mileage, not to mention lucrative weapons deals, to be gained from showing a more presentable face to the Islamic world, especially when it came to Russia's image in the strategically important region of the Middle East. The decision to officially permit a number of students to study to become *ulema* was similarly exceptional and marked no change in official Soviet policy.

Discouraging Islam continued to be an official concern right up until the final years of the Soviet Union. Atheism was disseminated with ideological fervour across academic institutions and in Azerbaijan, as in other Muslim regions of the Soviet Union, a steady stream of anti-Islamic books and pamphlets were published. Meanwhile, Azerbaijan was deliberately isolated from its traditional spiritual and teaching centres in Iran and Iraq (namely Qom and Najaf respectively)—a situation that would continue until the collapse of the Soviet regime.

Such treatment inadvertently led to unprecedented co-operation between Shi'ite and Sunni communities, as they searched for ways to express and practice their religion away from the reaches of the repressive state. Over the years, clandestine structures developed, leading to a system of 'parallel' Islam in which designated houses around the country became secret prayer centres for the faithful. Faced with such conditions and with a desperate shortage of clerics, Shi'ites and Sunnis would worship shoulder to shoulder as the same cleric performed the two different rites. (This is not to say that differences were not respected. Marriage between Shi'ites and Sunnis was not the norm and other traditions, such as burying the dead in separate cemeteries, were upheld.) Another survival strategy was the code of *taqiya* or *ketman*, which made it morally defensible in times of trouble for believers to conceal their faith—a device the Shi'ites had effectively employed in their struggle for self-preservation amidst persecution at the hands of the Sunnis.

Overall, the practice of unofficial Islam was of tremendous significance. It ensured that Islam remained a functioning religion right up to independence, despite the machinations of a state whose ideology was fundamentally antagonistic towards such beliefs and which had intentionally set up an inadequate official structure to purportedly administer spiritual concerns.

Despite anti-religious policies in the Soviet Union, popular traditions relating to faith were by no means entirely banished from the public eye. Pilgrims, for example, continued to visit the shrines of Muslim saints and this was especially so in Azerbaijan. While the other Muslim boards, informed by Sunni beliefs, viewed the practice in a negative light and branded it superstitious, there was no attempt to discourage pilgrims by the Transcaucasian Board—in Shi'ism, the veneration of Imam's shrines is a respected centuries-old tradition. In the post-war years under the supervision of the Baku-based board, the popular shrine known as Qoy Imam, a centuries-old mausoleum situated near Ganja, became the focus of an officially recognized pilgrimage that attracted considerable numbers. From the 1950s onwards, the sacred shrine at Nardaran, outside Baku, also became a key pilgrimage site, again with the full approval of the board.

## Developments in Post-Soviet Azerbaijan

When Azerbaijan finally shook off its Soviet shackles and gained independence in 1991, religion came filtering back into the clear light of day. The fledgling republic adopted a constitution that guaranteed freedom of worship for all faiths and designated none the official state religion. Upon becoming president of Azerbaijan in 1992, Abulfaz Elchibey declared that the reforms in the newly independent state would be based on democracy, Turkism and Islam. Yet, in keeping with the mood of the great majority of the population, the heavy-handed proselytising of Islam was not part of his vision.

Battered, but by no means broken, Islam had survived the relentless physical and ideological attacks meted out by the Communist Party's blind faithful. Yet in terms of organization it was in poor shape. There was a serious shortage of reputable theologians and literature to complement the spate of mosques and Islamic schools that had begun to appear across the country.

The Bibi Heybat mosque in Baku: built by Shi'ites between 1264-1266, dynamited by the Soviets in 1934, and rebuilt in 1998.

Soon links and agreements were established with the international Muslim community and many looked towards Iran for help in re-establishing the formal aspects of their faith. This seemed only natural given the common heritage of the two countries, not only with regard to Shi'ism but also the shared Azeri Turkic bond (Azeri Turks in Iranian Azerbaijan form the largest ethnic minority in Iran). Before long, projects were set up allowing for the training of Azeri clerical students in Iranian *madrasas*. Nevertheless, optimism was tempered by concerns that hard-line religious trends might also be imported from Islamic revolutionary Iran. When it came to the secular development of a newly emerging predominantly Muslim state such as Azerbaijan, many found Turkey, not Iran, to be a more convincing role model.

During Heydar Aliyev's presidency, from 1993 to 2003, Islam was presented as a national, culturally defining tradition. International Islam and differences between Sunnis and Shi'ites were downplayed. The key body representing Islamic concerns in Azerbaijan was, and remains, the South Caucasus Board of Muslims. Established in the late 1980s, its leadership is directly elected by the Muslim community.

Although opposition to the government along religious lines was generally not seen as a serious threat, a number of Islamic fundamentalist groups were in existence by the mid-1990s. Of these, only one, the Islamic Party of Azerbaijan, was officially registered. These parties typically had small membership and little sense of unity with each other. Yet, in 1996 the state felt sufficiently threatened by the spectre of fundamentalism to have many of the Islamic Party's leaders imprisoned and hundreds of Iranians around the country arrested and deported on suspicion of aiding Shi'ite Azeri fundamentalists. Meanwhile, to the north of the country, small pockets of Sunni fundamentalists became involved in aiding conflicts in neighbouring regions such as Daghestan and Chechnya—areas that are susceptible to extremist ideologies on account of remoteness, poverty and, in the latter case, a continued state of war.

The perceived threat of religious extremism has since become less prominent, reflecting the confidence of a modern society that also continues to observe many religious practices and rituals, especially those relating to death, in accordance with Islamic tradition. However, Western or secular practices are always evident. At typical weddings, for example, alcohol in the form of vodka and wine is consumed liberally. With regard to women, there is no visible form of public segregation and the tradition of covering one's head and face with veils, often seen in other Muslim countries, is rare (although in more traditional and rural areas women can be seen wearing hijabs, scarves that leave their faces uncovered).

Traditional Muslim holidays and festivals are still celebrated in every town and village. These are based on the Islamic lunar calendar, although the country usually uses the Western (Gregorian) calendar. Important national holidays are Ramazan Bayrami or Uraza Bayrami (Id al-Fitr, which marks the end of Ramadan, the Islamic month of fasting), Gurban Bayrami (Id al-Adha, the day of sacrifice celebrated 70 days after Ramazan Bayrami), and Ashura, also called Maharamlik (the Shi'ite 'Month of Mourning'). Meanwhile, European influence has made New Year (December 31/January 1) one of the country's major festivals, while Novruz Bayrami, the ancient New Year or Spring Festival on March 21 (and on the 22nd in some rural areas), is celebrated by everyone regardless of their religion. The official state calendar continues therefore to be a reminder of the remarkable history of religion in Azerbaijan.

*

# Cycles of life: Traditional Culture

Zulfugar Rufatoglu

## The family

Large families were commonplace in Azerbaijan up until the beginning of the 20th century. This was primarily for economic reasons since in rural areas the family functioned as a working or production unit. The Azeri family was (and in some areas still is) hierarchically structured, with the father being the absolute head, while the youngest member was accorded the least privileges, although held in great affection and called *sonbeshik*, the 'last cradle'.

Male children would remain in their father's home until the end of their days. Female members of the family, however, were generally less privileged and were expected to work, usually doing more than their male counterparts. In farming they had their own particular tasks, ranging from selecting seeds for sowing to milking the cattle or even, in the event of a lack of males in the family, pulling ploughs in place of bulls. At harvest time a woman's life was particularly hard.

The abolition and ultimate demise of the feudal structure and the launch of the Cultural Revolution by the Soviets in the 1920s ushered in a new era. As the traditionally large Azeri family began to lose its economic importance, the new generations sought to have their own homes and to have fewer children. And so by the mid-1960s the average number of the children in a family had shrunk to three, while today two or even one child has become quite normal. By 1999, for the first time in recorded Azeri history, population growth had shrunk to zero.

## Pregnancy

Young families are likened to young trees, the best wish for them is to 'have as many branches as possible' in order to keep the family name alive. There are customs where a bride is given a child to put on her lap and her wedding veil placed on a fruit tree as a way of guaranteeing fertility. Another custom involved placing a baby on the bed of a newly-wed couple as a wish that they might soon have their own child.

When a woman therefore breaks the news of her pregnancy, the family's reaction is one of great happiness and relief. A small celebratory party is thrown and the mother-to-be is given presents from both sides of the family. Gifts could include dresses, gold and jewellery. However, there might be a degree of competition between the in-laws: the expectant woman's parents will tend to give more expensive presents in an effort to increase the respect their daughter receives in the home of her in-laws. Despite their joy at the good news, the immediate family will keep the news to themselves. It is believed that by not publicizing the pregnancy until it has become obvious, the mother-to-be will be protected from the 'evil eyes' of ill-wishers and their spells and sorcery. The family panders to the woman's cravings, a period known as *yerikleme* since it is believed that to ignore her desires will affect the future child's strength.

The pregnant woman is obliged to observe a number of rules intended as safeguards to protect her child's physical and psychological well-being. Many of these have ancient origins that pre-date Islam and include the avoiding of fortune-tellers, funerals and graveyards. Instead the pregnant woman is encouraged to contemplate peaceful things such as the moon, the sun, flowers and clear running water. A family might even try to prevent people they consider to be ugly from entering their home.

There is an abundance of other traditional beliefs relating to this period. For example, if a pregnant woman eats fish or does so much as look at one, it is believed that there is the danger that her baby will start to speak late or not at all. If a baby moves in its mother's womb in the presence of another, its own face will look like the face of that person. If a woman spends a geat deal of time looking in the mirror, her baby will be good-looking. If she has a craving for pomegranates, her baby will be beautiful, but if she wants watermelons then the child will grow cold and indifferent to its home and parents.

People have always tried to predict the sex of an unborn child and it was believed that one way of doing this was to divide the top part of a watermelon into quarters and throw the slices onto the ground. The way they landed determined whether it would be a boy or girl. Another way was to trick a pregnant mother into looking at her hand by asking unexpectedly: "What happened to your hand?" If she looked at her palm, the baby would be a girl, while if she looked at the back of her hand it meant that she would have a boy. And if a woman saw an apple in a dream, this predicted that she would have a girl.

## Infertility

Since the child is the most sacred element of the family, somewhat cruel attitudes continue to prevail even in modern Azeri society towards childless women, who are considered to be the unhappiest members of any family. They can face insults, reproach and other forms of criticism or even intimidation from their extended family, especially the mothers of their husbands. Father-in-laws, however, rarely become involved even if they are unhappy with the situation. As for the husband himself, his attitude is dependent upon the traditions, culture and education of the family in which he has been brought up. In rural areas, childlessness can often end in separation, despite the fact that the problem of infertility might come from the husband.

Prior to medical advances in fertility, people looked for answers in the spiritual realm. Infertility was often attributed to the evil eye. Thus Azeris would say that childless women had been struck by the evil eye (*goz deymek* or *bad nazar*) or that they had fallen under a *chille* or curse. The remedy for such a condition was for the infertile woman to drink the first milk from another woman who had just given birth. It was also believed that if a young mother shook a tablecloth over the head of an infertile woman or if the latter saw an egg in her dreams then she would become pregnant.

A women afflicted by a *chille* could get rid of it in a number of ways. One was to pass it on to a pregnant cat by looking at the animal and declaring loudly that she was giving it the curse. Another was *chille kesme*, or 'cutting the *chille*', which involved tying the woman's thumbs and toes with white thread and singing the following song:

*By the passion of the Prophet Solomon,*
*By the power of Jinn Marjana's daughter,*
*By beast or by human,*
*Jinn or Satan or running water,*
*By the deep valley's tree with roots*
*At the cross of seven roads,*
*No matter whose chilla it may be,*
*I cut that chille away!*

—quoted from Bahlul Abdulla's
*Azeri Ritual Folklore and Its Poetry*,
Baku, 1990

## Childbirth

Nowadays, the majority of women in Azerbaijan have the opportunity to give birth in a hospital. However, until the mid-1950s the majority of women in rural areas had to deliver at home under the care of a midwife. The midwife would restrict the number of people in the delivery room since it was believed that an evil spirit might take advantage of such a crowded room and enter wearing another person's face. Other rituals during labour included the pregnant woman crossing the threshold of the house several times to get rid of the pain, or stepping over pots filled with water—the water was thought to have a magical power to purify her. If labour still proved difficult, all the covered items in the house such as chests and jars would be opened up. These rituals were accompanied by chants invoking the names of important religious figures.

With the baby safely delivered, the umbilical cord was cut either by the midwife or an elderly and respected female relative and then placed at the doorway to the house. If the child at a future date took the cord down, this was taken to be a good sign. The water of the baby's first bath always had salt added in the belief that it would bring strength. The power attributed to salt is immortalized in the famous Azeri epic of *Koroglu* when, after the hero Koroglu is struck by the sword of the treacherous Gajar Ali, he declares: "You are not to blame, O Gajar! It is the midwife who is to blame, she who washed you in unsalted water!"

The birth was officially announced first to the father who would give the bearer of the news a gift of money, known as *mushtuluq*. Considered to be at her most vulnerable during this time, the woman who had just given birth was given the special title of *zahi* and needed immediate protection to save her from the visitations of the malicious spirit Albasti. A mythological entity known to all Turkic peoples, Albasti usually appeared before the mother in the form of a woman with long white hair and sagging breasts. She would try to seize the mother's liver and wash it in water, so bringing about her demise. Gunshots fired by male members of the family were used as a way of warding off the unwelcome spirit.

A baby's facial and bodily features were believed to hold clues to its future temperament. If the baby's forehead, for example, was covered with hair, it was thought that he or she would grow to be cruel. A large head was an indication of wisdom. If a baby happened to be born with teeth, a lamb had to be sacrificed in order to prevent the death of someone in the family. The time of the birth could be of significance: a baby born in the morning might be lucky in life, while things could prove to be harder for one born in the evening.

Throughout the night after the birth itself, the bedroom of the mother and child was kept lit with candles and lamps. Objects including a knife, sword, plate and mirror were placed under the mother's pillow, while a pair of scissors and a plate with an onion, believed to have magical powers to ward off the devil, were placed at the doorway.

## First days of infancy

During the three days after birth, the mother was given *guymaq*, a special meal of flour and granulated sugar. For forty days after the birth anyone visiting the mother was expected to bring a gift. The baby was kept in a separate room to which only the closest relatives had access—a measure intended to protect the infant from the evil eye or the spells of ill-wishers. Even foods such as eggs or meat were not allowed in the room.

There were different ways of protecting the newborn baby from being stricken by a *chille*. One was for the mother to take her child to the local cemetery, place the baby on a grave and declare: "I do not need a child with a *chille*, so please take him/her away!" Having tied threads of seven different colours to her baby's legs, she would then take him to the village mill where the threads would be removed and the baby's head sprinkled with flour.

In order to discover if the child had been given the evil eye, a piece of coal was put into a jar filled with spring water. If the coal sank, the baby was afflicted and would need to be washed in the water. Another way to remove the chille was to take a lamb, circle it around the baby's head and then sacrifice it. The meat was eaten by the family and the skin and bones taken to the cemetery and buried.

The fortieth day, known as *girkh tokmek* or 'washing away the forty', was an important event since this was the day the baby was named and given a ceremonial bath. Early in the morning, forty handfuls of water, known as *girkh suyu*' (literally 'forty waters') were taken from a nearby spring and poured onto the heads of both mother and child.

Other customs marked a baby's developmental stages. When a baby's teeth first appeared, the family cooked a special meal called *hedik* that was prepared from seven different types of grain. This was believed to ease the pain of teething. When the baby reached the age of one, his or her hair and nails were cut for the first time. It was considered unlucky to throw the cuttings away so these were wrapped up in a clean cloth and placed in the crack of a wall. There was always the possibility a bird might carry the cuttings away to its nest, in which case the child was destined to suffer from constant headaches. This practice is believed to have its origins in the ancient Avesta, the holy book of the Zoroastrians.

## Naming your child

Names of Arabic origin were first introduced into the region following the arrival of the Arabs and Islam from the seventh century onwards. Prior to this it was common for people to have two names: one that was native to the Caucasus, the other from the Bible. Azeris, Georgians and Armenians bore variants of the same names such as those still seen today, such as Bahram (Azeri)/Bagram (Georgian)/Vahgram (Armenian).

During the Soviet era the Communists portrayed the Arabs as invaders who had imposed Islam by force of the sword while the Quran itself became a target for the atheist authorities. Under Stalin's iron rule, Azeri history was rewritten from a strictly Caucasian perspective. Therefore it came as no surprise that Javanshir, the name of the Christian Albanian king responsible for a sustained campaign against the Arabs, was now adopted as a favourite name, as was Babek, the Azeri leader who famously later resisted Muslim rule. Ancient Turkic names, however, were pointedly frowned upon by the authorities.

There were also attempts to create new Sovietized Azeri names, especially by Azeri writers. It proved quite a successful undertaking and names created in the 1940s, 50s and 60s have become the most popular names in Azerbaijan. The Azeri dramatist Jafar Jabbarly was especially inventive, creating some 50 new names such as Aydin (boy, 'clear, intelligent'), Solmaz (girl, 'one who never fades'), Yashar (boy, 'who lives long') and Dönmez (boy, 'one who never changes his mind').

Some names for girls reflected the deep-rooted prejudices commonly found in many traditional societies. The following names refer to the disappointment felt at having one or more girls born into the same family: Kifayet (Arabic), Tamam (Arabic/Azeri), Yeter (Azeri), Besdi (unknown origin). All of them mean 'enough' or 'that's enough'.

Traditional and modern Azeri names also reflect the natural world:

***Nature***

Ruzgar (girl)—wind
Shafag (girl)—dawn
Gursel (boy)—flood
Ildrim (boy)—lightning
Bulud (boy)—cloud

***Months***

Yanvar (boy)—January
Fevral (girl)—February
Ramazan, Safar, Muharrem—from the lunar Arabic calendar

Bahman, Isfandiyar—from the Zoroastrian calendar

***Planets and stars***
Aykhan (boy)—master of the moon
Gunesh (girl)—sun
Zohrah (girl)—Venus
Ulker (girl)—star

The names of strong and wild creatures are given to boys while those that are gentle and peaceful are given to girls. Some examples are:

Aslan (boy)—lion
Bebir (boy)—panther
Shahin (boy)—falcon
Jeyran (girl)—antelope
Maral (girl)—deer
Goyerchin (girl)—dove
Tovuz (girl)—peacock

The names of flowers and trees as well as precious stones are usually given to girls:

Chinar—plane tree
Lale—tulip
Chichek—flower
Nargiz—narcissus
Benovsha—violet
Yagut—ruby
Almaz—diamond
Zumrud—emerald

## The wedding feast

Wedding receptions are, for practical purposes, traditionally held in large tents with long tables and benches designed to accommodate the numerous guests, hence the name *palatka toyu* (literally 'wedding party under the tent', from the Russian *palatka* meaning 'tent' and Azeri '*toy*' 'wedding party'). However, Baku tent weddings tend to be smaller, only catering for 20 to 30 people at a time—as a result, guests arrive and leave at different times in a kind of shift pattern. Similarly in Baku, eating and dancing do not take place in the same tent. After guests have eaten their *bozbash* (kofte in soup) and drunk their vodka they will make their way to a specially erected dancing *palatka*, where traditional music is played. This is the only event in a Baku wedding to which children are invited. In more conservative regions of Azerbaijan the sexes are segregated, with women on one side of the tent and men on the other.

The most popular choice of dress at modern Azeri weddings is a smart Western-style suit and tie for the groom and a white dress for the bride. At the reception the bride and groom sit in the centre of the tent. Placed on their table are a mirror and two candles. The groom is accompanied by a male friend or relative called a *saghdish* (literally 'one who sits on the right side'), whose role is to mind him and offer advice on intimate matters, such as those relating to the first night. Similarly, the bride has a married female companion called a *yenge*. The *saghdish* and *yenge* have the additional responsibility of verifying that the bride is indeed a virgin.

Keeping a watchful eye over the proceedings is the *toy beyi* (literally: 'chief of the party'). It is up to him to ensure people's needs are met, to keep noisy children away and to curb any rowdy and drunken behaviour. He is also given the important responsibility of guarding the vodka. If he deems anyone to be the worse for drink he will turn down their requests for more alcohol. Despite their Islamic heritage, Azeris have a relaxed attitude towards alcohol. Indeed, drinking and eating at the Azeri table are intricately linked and alcohol is happily indulged in at celebrations such as weddings. However, an ability to hold one's drink is expected and outward signs of drunkenness are frowned upon. The favoured drink is neat Russian vodka, no ice, while food enjoyed at weddings includes a variety of kebabs, including *lule kebab* (barbecued minced meat), *tike kebab* (diced lamb), and *baliq kebab* (sturgeon) as well as *pilav* rice (Iranian style). Tea, coffee and ice cream are served at the end.

A major feature of celebratory meals, whatever the size, is toasting. Generally speaking, Azeri toasts are not as long as those in neighbouring Georgia but certainly ample praise will be given to the person or persons in whose honour any party is thrown. At wedding receptions the first toast is dedicated to the bride and groom, the second to their parents, the third to their uncles and aunts, followed by their brothers and sisters, friends and so on.

Every party has its 'tamada' or toast-master, whose job it is to introduce guests to each other, to make speeches and toasts as well as to encourage other guests, particularly the important ones, to make their own speeches and toasts. Until recently, people chose a tamada from their own circle, but it has now become popular to hire poets or professional actors to take on the role. The tamada is expected to have excellent speaking skills and plays a central role at a wedding since it is only with his express permission that a person can make a toast. Breaching the rules could result in the tamada ordering the transgressor to drink an extra glass of vodka or wine by way of atonement. The tamada is also the person who invites the guests to dance.

At about 11.30 p.m. the bride and groom leave the wedding party and make their way to their own home, if they have one at this stage, or to that of the groom's parents. They are accompanied by the *saghdish* and *yenge* along with an entourage of close relatives. It was traditionally believed that a bride's honour was dependent on her virginity—an attitude that still persists in rural areas. In the more conservative regions, especially those in the south, if a bride was found not to be a virgin she risked being sent back immediately to her parents, often accompanied by a barrage of verbal or even physical abuse. Often the unfortunate woman would find herself unwelcome in her own home and have little choice but to leave the village—in extreme cases this could even lead to suicide.

Once at home, the bride and groom retire to their specially prepared room, known as the *bey otaghi* (literally 'groom's room') where they consummate their marriage. Traditionally, it was the job of the *saghdish* and *yenge* to sit outside and wait until the groom emerged to declare that his wife was indeed a virgin on her wedding night. The *saghdish* then fired three rifle shots into the air to spread the news to the other villagers. Meanwhile, the *yenge* would enter the room and take the sheet stained with blood—proof of the bride's virginity—and present it to the groom's mother. Satisfied with her daughter-in-law's honour, the matriarch would then make the evidence available to the other female relatives on both sides of the family. In Baku and other big cities the role of the *saghdish* and *yenge* have become symbolic and the inspection of the sheet is no longer practised.

## Death and burial

The period of mourning following a death lasts forty days, but Azeri tradition demands that the dead be buried immediately after the confirmation of death. There is a belief that the spirit of the dead can become agitated if there is undue delay in taking the body to the grave.

The sex of those preparing the body depends on that of the deceased. Sharia law dictates that it is washed, an act that is carried out for a fee by a *murdashir* (from the Persian, meaning 'one who washes the dead'). The specially prepared and covered place where the washing is carried out is called a *yuat* (from the Azeri *yu* 'wash'). The body is then wrapped in a five-metre long white cotton shroud known as a *kefen*. The body is never left alone, a precaution taken to prevent Satan or some other malicious entity from interfering and preventing the spirit's passage to paradise. Rituals are carried out to protect the body from malign forces, including putting scissors, a knife or mirror on the coffin.

Women weep loudly and in some areas scratch their faces with their nails in grief—an ancient custom all over the Caucasus. In many Azeri villages and towns there are women who specialize in mourning. Only men attend the actual burial—women are not allowed to visit the grave until the fortieth day. A stone is placed on the coffin as it is taken from the house in the belief that it will prevent the death of other family members. As the coffin is put down at the graveside, the mullah recites an extract from the Quran. He then opens the coffin slightly and whispers further verses from the Quran into it.

Although they prepare the food for the wake, the women do not join in the meal on this particular day, but will do so on subsequent commemorative days. After a reading by the mullah from the Quran, two or three kinds of hot meals are served such as *dolma* (vine leaves stuffed with minced meat) and lamb *pilav*. In the poorer rural areas, *yakhni*, a simple dish of beef boiled in water, is prepared. Unlike other celebrations in Azerbaijan, no alcohol is consumed. Tea is served after the meal and relatives and close friends of the deceased will typically remain until late into the evening. The mullah becomes the focus of attention, recounting the lives of the prophets and saints and reciting religious verses.

Although Islam traditionally holds that there should be no sign indicating that there is a grave, Azeris create stone tombs in memory of the deceased. Richer familes construct large pavilions over graves, turning them into large mausoleums. Another custom often practised—one which similarly does not sit easily with accepted Islamic practice—is that of placing photographs of the deceased on the headstone. The headstones are generally made from red or brown granite, black marble (imported from Georgia) or, as was popular in the past, sandstone, and face the *qibla* or direction of Mecca. Women's graves might feature images of flowers, glass beads, sewing needles, pots and pans, while men's have horses, guns, swords and other typically male objects. In some regions such as Shemakhi, the headstones are coloured with oil paints. Rich people typically build statues of loved ones over their tombs.

Azeris visit the grave of a loved one on the anniversary of their death, birthday and the day before a major festival. Unlike the funeral rituals, female relatives and friends participate fully. Flowers are typically placed on graves and some gently tap the headstone with a small stone to let the deceased know of their visit. Thursday is the traditional weekday for visiting graves in Azerbaijan.

## Costume

The wearing of traditional Azeri costumes has, by and large, become a thing of the past, having died out at the beginning of the 20th century. Outside of exhibitions and museums, they can still be seen at public displays and functions featuring traditional dance and song. A familiar image is that of groups of young women in national costumes regaling visiting heads of states with flowers, bread and salt while they are greeted by the Azeri president at the airport—a custom that is more of a Soviet-Russian invention since in traditional Azeri society women would never be the ones to greet strangers.

Nowadays, Azeris uniformly adopt Western-style dress and, although elderly men may don traditional caps, these are rarely worn by young people. During the 16th century, however, the Azeris were dubbed the Qizilbash or 'red-heads', owing to their *chalma* (headdress or turban), decorated with twelve purple stripes in honour of the Twelve Shi'ite Imams. These turbans were mainly worn by the higher classes, while the ordinary people would wear simple white *chalmas* or felt caps called *gulakh* (literally 'ear'). Women wore hats and headscarves with colourful lappets (side flaps), kerchiefs with ornaments, and crowns in the form of tiaras or embroidered skullcaps. The most popular male attire of this period was the *aba*, a long shirt which had narrow sleeves. Those belonging to the highest classes wore the *khalat* and *faraj*—garments with heavily decorated shoulders and chest—on top of the *aba*.

Around the 18th century, the most popular form of dress consisted of the *ust koyneyi* (outer shirt), an *arkhaliq* (long jacket) and trousers. *Arkhaliq*s could be single or double-breasted and made of silk, cashmere, satin, or other cloth. Women also wore *arkhaliqs*, the main difference being length—a man's reached the calves while a woman's reached the hips. Hers was also far more richly embroidered on the collars and sleeves. A typical winter garment for men was the *kyurk*, a collared sheepskin coat with fur on the inside and without buttons. The characteristic headwear of the time was a conical fur cap that varied in length—in rural areas men wore the modest *motal-papakhs* made of sheepskin. Men might also wear the *araqchin*, a decorated skullcap.

Other items of women's clothing were the *tuman* (skirt), the *chutbalaq* (a double skirt) and *chakhchur* (belt and trousers). In the larger towns women going out in public would wear the *tuman* over the *chakhchur*.

There were several types of hood or headdress for women. The *chadra*, or veil, was more characteristic of Baku and the surrounding area where the influence of Sharia dress codes was stronger. Azeri women living in rural areas to the west and in neighbouring Georgia and Armenia, where Islamic dress codes were more relaxed, went around without headdresses, earning them the nickname of *achiqbash* ('bareheaded').

## Cuisine

Azeri cooking has much in common with other countries in the region especially Turkey and Iran. Nevertheless, many of the country's national dishes remain highly distinctive and reflect the abundance of fresh local produce. Mutton and beef are popular meats and typical vegetables include aubergines, tomatoes, red beet, radish, beans and cabbage. Spices used to flavour dishes include saffron, paprika, caraway seeds, aniseed, mint and dill. Other ingredients commonly used are pomegranate juice, dried fruits (such as apricots, lemons, quince, and plums). It is not unusual to mix sweet and tangy flavours. Chestnuts are used to garnish meat and pomegranate seeds to decorate plates and bowls.

Starters are considered to be an important part of the meal. Favourites include salads, cold stuffed omelettes, pickled mixed vegetables, cow's tongue and other cold meat, to name but a few. Soups are popular and can be served as a starter or as a main course. They are often made with large amounts of butter or sheep fat. It is common to remove the meat and vegetables intended for the main course and serve the remaining broth as a starter. Pilav dishes are very popular and there are dozens of versions. They are typically boiled rice with a topping. Common toppings are mutton (*govurma*), mutton with vegetables (*sabza kaurmali*), meat with dried fruit (*shirin*). Saffron can be used to colour the rice.

Perhaps the most well-known Azeri dish is the kebab. There are actually two types depending on the style of cooking: kebabs (various barbecued or roasted meats) and shashliks (skewered meat, roasted on a spit). Both can be served with vegetable kebabs, which are typically barbecued tomatoes, aubergines and peppers. A popular dish is dolma (steamed or roasted stuffed leaves). Depending on the season, the leaves, which can be vine, cabbage or quince, are stuffed with minced lamb or vegetables (especially aubergines, peppers and tomatoes), pinenuts, currants, rice and herbs (such as coriander, dill, mint).

With access to the Caspian Sea the quality and assortment of fish in Azerbaijan has always been excellent, and there are many superb dishes. The most popular is fish kebab, especially from sturgeon.

Children in traditional costume.

Meanwhile, Azerbaijan's most famous food export is caviar, made from the roe of the sturgeon. The country produces some of the finest quality in the world.

Of course, taking into account the innumerable regional variants, there is a huge number of common dishes in Azerbaijan. However, to give a flavour, here is a small selection of typical recipes:

***Dushbara (dumplings in soup).*** *Ingredients:* 100g mutton, 40g wheat flour, 1/2 onion chopped, 1 egg, 1 tablespoon chopped fresh coriander, 1/2 teaspoon dried mint, a few splashes vinegar, seasoning. *Method:* Make a broth from the mutton bones. Mix onions, herbs and minced meat. Add the egg to the flour to make dough. Roll the dough to the thinness

## Art of the carpet

Carpets have always been integral to Azeri life and are prized by their owners as well as collectors the world over. In addition to keeping the house warm, carpets can also be gifts for guests or dowries for brides.

More practical uses include the pileless *mafrash*, *khurjun* and *kheiba* (saddlebags), *chuval* (sacks), *chul* (coverlet), *yakhar ustu* (saddle cover) and *namazlig* (prayer rug). Pileless carpets (or rugs) include the simply woven *palas* and *kilim*, and the intricate *sumakh*, *zili*, *shadde* and *vemi*, while piled carpets include the exquisitely patterned *khalcha*.

Azeri carpets are divided into four types: Quba-Shirvan (with manufacturing centres in Quba, Shirvan and Baku); Ganja-Qazakh (with manufacturing centres in Ganja and Qazakh); Karabakh (manufacturing in Karabakh, Shusha and Jabrail), and Tabriz inIran (manufacturing in Tabriz and Ardabil). Well worth a visit is Baku's Azerbaijan State Museum of Carpets and Applied Art, which houses the world's largest collection of Azeri carpets.

of a pancake (about 1 mm). Cut into squares. Put a spoonful of meat filling into middle of squares and fold in half, pressing the edges together. Boil in the broth for 5 minutes until they float to the surface. Serve sprinkled with coriander or dried mint.

***Gutab (patties).*** *Ingredients:* 100g mutton, 1/2 chopped onion, 1 egg, 1 teaspoon pomegranate seeds, 100g wheat flour, knob of melted butter, pinch salt and pepper, pinch of sumak (a squeeze of lemon juice can be used instead). *Method:* Make the dough by mixing the flour, egg and salt. Knead and then roll to the thinness of a pancake (about 1 mm). Cut out plate-sized circles. Meanwhile, mix the mutton, onions, salt and pepper and pomegranate seeds. Spoon the mixture onto the dough circles. Fold the dough over and mould to make a crescent shape. Press the edges and fry each side of the patty in butter. Sprinkle with sumak.

***Goy gutab (vegetarian patty).*** *Ingredients:* 150g spinach, 150g sorrel, 6 spring onions, 1 teaspoon each of dill and coriander, 150g wheat flour, 50g natural yoghurt, 1 egg, seasoning. *Method:* Make dough by mixing the flour, egg and salt. Knead and then roll to the thinness of a pancake (about 1 mm). Cut out plate-sized circles. Meanwhile, chop and cook the spinach and spring onions. Add the herbs and mix thoroughly. Spoon the mixture onto the dough circles. Fold the dough over and mould to make a crescent shape. Fry both sides in butter. Serve topped with butter and with yogurt at the side.

***Suzme khangal.*** *Ingredients:* 160g mutton, 100g wheat flour, 1 egg, 1 chopped onion, knob of butter, 15g feta cheese, 50g natural yogurt, 1 clove of garlic, chopped, a pinch of saffron. *Method:* Fry the chopped meat with the onions, salt and pepper. Add saffron. Next make dough (see previous recipes) and roll out into 5 diamond-shaped pieces. Cook the dough in boiling water and drain. Place the meat mixture on top of the dough shapes and pour on melted butter. Crumble the feta cheese onto the yogurt mixed with garlic and serve separately.

***Lule kebab.*** *Ingredients:* 330g mutton, 20g butter, 1 onion, 4 spring onions, 1 teaspoon each of parsley and basil, 45g wheat flour, salt and pepper to taste, pinch of sumak. *Method:* Mix the onions and minced mutton and season with pinch of salt and pepper. Leave in the fridge for 20 minutes to chill. Roll the mixture into a sausage shape and place on a skewer. Cook on a barbecue or grill. Serve in pitta bread, garnished with barbecued onions.

***Pilav rice.*** *Ingredients:* 200g mutton, 150g rice, 50g yogurt, 30g raisins, 30g dried apricots, 50g peeled chestnuts, 1 onion, pinch of saffron, wheat flour, salt and pepper to taste, 500 ml stock. *Method:* Chop and fry the onion. Add the chestnuts, apricots and a small amount of stock. Add the meat and stew until cooked. Typically, long grain rice is steamed with saffron on top and a layer of golden crust called *qazmaq* on the bottom. Boil the rice until half-cooked and then sieve it. Prepare *qazmaq* by mixing flour, egg, butter and yogurt, rolling it into a thin dough then placing it at the bottom of a pan. Add the rice, pour melted butter on top and steam for half an hour. Place the meat mixture on top of the boiled rice. Cut the crusty *qazmaq* into diamond shapes and place on top of dish.

***Green kuku (vegetarian omelette).*** *Ingredients:* 2 eggs, 4 chopped spring onions, 1/2 teaspoon each of coriander and dill, 30g spinach, 30g melted butter, pepper, salt. *Method:* Shred the dill, spinach and spring onions finely, add the pepper, salt, eggs, and beat thoroughly. Some cooks may add finely crumbled white bread or a teaspoon of flour. Heat up the butter in the frying pan and pour in the mixture. When cooked, cut the omelette into four pieces and turn over to brown. Pour on melted butter when serving. To accompany, sour milk is served separately.

## Fishing

Archeological finds testify to well-established fishing practices on the Azeri shores of the Caspian Sea and the fish-rich waters of the Kura and Aras rivers during the Stone Age. Historians from Classical times wrote about the fishing of sturgeon in the territory of Caspiana (another name for Azerbaijan in Greek sources) while others reported how the Caspians salted it, and sent it on camels to Ecbatana (now Hamadan, Iran). They were also reported to have made fish glue.

According to later Arab historians, the inhabitants of Albania, the ancient kingdom of Northen Azerbaijan that survived into the early Islamic era, produced dried and salted fish that was popular across the Middle East. Meanwhile, during the Middle Ages, European and Russian diplomats reported that the Azeris caught salmon and sturgeon and used their caviar for gastronomic purposes. Incorporation into the Russia Empire and then the Soviet Union had the result of boosting the Azeri fishing industry and ensured that the Volga and Kura rivers became Europe's leading source of caviar.

Prior to the introduction of motor-driven boats, Azerbaijan's main source of fish was its rivers. Large-scale sea fishing began to develop in the 1930s and it was only in the 1950s that the first proper Azeri Caspian fleet came into being. However, fish stocks plummeted as a result not only of over-fishing but also the disastrous ecological effects of Soviet oil production. In 2000, a new organization, Azerbalyg, was established to manage the Azeri fishing industry (including factories and shops). The private fishing of sturgeon was banned and heavy sanctions introduced to prevent illegal sales of this and other fish. Today, with the legal status of the Caspian Sea so hotly debated by the surrounding states, a question mark hangs over the future of fishing in the region.

Since the eating of scaleless fish is not recommended in Islam, some Azeris have some reservations about eating fish such as sturgeon and catfish, especially in the more religiously conservative areas to the south. Generally speaking, the most popular types of fish are the kutum (Caspian roach), khasham (Caspian asp) and Caspian salmon. However, many Azeris and international visitors consider sturgeon kebabs to be the ultimate national dish. Sturgeon also tops the list of smoked fish—a delicacy known to the Russians as *balyk*, from the Azeri for 'fish'.

## Caviar

The Caspian region is unquestionably the top producer of caviar—a delicacy that has become synonymous with luxury and wealth the world over. The Caspian Sea is home to around ninety per cent of the planet's population of sturgeon, from whose roe caviar is made. Almost all caviar is produced from three types of sturgeon, known by their Russian names as beluga, osetr and sevruga.

The beluga sturgeon (from the Russian meaning 'white fish', Azeri: *aghbalik*, also meaning 'white fish'), is the largest member of the sturgeon family. Its scarcity means increasingly few are caught annually. With a length of around four metres, it can weigh more than 1,000 kg (2,200 lb). The weight of the roe can be as much as fifteen percent of its total body weight. The colour of the roe ranges from light to dark gray with an eye, or target-like, pattern in the middle.

The osetr (Azeri: *nara*) is a medium-sized sturgeon which is more numerous than the beluga. It is two metres long and weighs up to 200 kg (440 lb). The colour of its roe, which has a taste reminiscent of hazel nuts, ranges from dark brown to gray, often with a gold hue.

The sevruga (Azeri: *uzum burun*, 'long nose') is the smallest of the sturgeon family, with an average length of 1.5 metres. Its roe, which is the most common, ranges from light to dark gray.

The sturgeon is caught with large nets and landed by ship. The belly

Fisherman on the Caspian shore with a catch of sturgeon.

is carefully cut open and the roe removed. Eggs are rinsed, checked for damage, then sorted according to size and colour. There are three grades of colour: 'ooo', the lightest caviar; 'oo', medium; and 'o', the darkest caviar.

The eggs are are then salted—the Kura river delta provides some of the purest and best salt for this purpose. The finest quality caviar, and therefore the most expensive, contains the least salt—a factor that shortens its shelf life. Caviar can be pasteurized to extend its shelf life, but most agree that this method compromises the taste. Eggs that are physically damaged or overripe are processed differently and sold as *payusnaya* ('pressed caviar'). Resembling jam in appearance, this caviar is especially popular in Russia and Greece.

Azeri caviar was an important export for the Soviet Union.

## Honey

Another delicacy the Azeris have always prized is honey or *bal*—both for its taste and its practical uses. Traditionally it was viewed as a sacred food, dubbed 'God's sweet dew'. Details of honey production, such as the number of bee families, hives and the quantity of honey, were closely guarded by beekeepers in order to protect the bees from the evil eye. This explains the practice of placing special fences of interlaced rush around hives.

The behaviour of bees could be used to forecast the weather. Bees working on cloudy days would be taken as a sign that there would be no rain, while bees finishing earlier in the evening meant a downpour was imminent. For newly-wed couples, honey has traditionally been considered to be a gift that will bring happiness and peace. During weddings, when the bride arrives at her husband's house, she is met with a bowl of honey. Both she and her mother-in-law place a spoonful of honey in each other's mouth as a symbol of their harmonious future relationship.

According to an Azeri saying, honey is a cure for a thousand and one diseases. It has been used in the treatment of slow healing wounds (often mixed with cod-liver oil) and diseases of the liver, stomach and heart. It was popularly believed to increase vitality, improve eyesight and also featured in folk remedies to combat rheumatism and aid the healing of broken bones.

## Hunting

With the huge and sometimes unique diversity of terrain and wildlife throughout the Caucasus, hunting was an important part of life for many sections of Azeri society. Not only did the activity provide food for the family but it also became a part of their folklore and customs.

Animals typically hunted in Azerbaijan included wild boar, bears, goats, deer and numerous types of bird. The latter were especially popular in the southern coastal area of the country, a region that has long been a wintering ground for hundreds of species of birds. Nowadays there are restrictions on hunting and several nature reserves have outright bans.

Hunting with birds of prey remained popular up until the mid-19th century. Under the reign of the later Safavid rulers, who themselves kept large numbers of royal hunting birds, falcons were even included on the list of taxes received by the royal coffers. However, owing to their near extinction the practice has all but died out. From the 19th century onwards, the gun became the main choice of weapon used by hunters for all types of prey. Locally made hunting rifles tended to be of poor quality and were seldom accurate. Better and more accurate were those made in Russia and these (in single and double-barrelled form) began to replace local ones from the late-19th century onwards.

The hunter in Azeri folklore is often portrayed as a figure who likes to joke and spin a yarn (mainly in the form of exaggerating the details of a recent hunting expedition), thus the popular proverb *ovchu gopchu!*—'A hunter, a liar!' Nevertheless, the character Pirim, who figures large in Azeri hunting folk tales, symbolizes heroism, wisdom and mystery. There are many hunting songs in Azeri folklore, the singing of which was believed to protect the hunter and make his hunting successful. Evocative, philosophical and witty, in many ways they sum up the Azeri national spirit:

*The bird's name was Ekil-Bekil,*
*It landed on a tree branch.*
*I climbed up to catch it,*

*But it caught me instead*
*And jailed me in the square!*
*The trees in the square are lofty*
*Where the birds peck their fruit.*
*There I found myself trapped*
*But soon found a way out*
*When a rose thorn snagged me,*
*Then my grandmother came to help*
*So off I fled empty-handed without even a flower!*

Another song goes:

*Hey hunter,*
*Happy hunting!*
*And let your prey*
*Be a deer or a bird!*
*So draw your bow*
*And let your target be*
*An evil one's evil eye.*
*On the peaks, in the valleys*
*Let the wolves fear you!*
*And let God protect you*
*From the evil-eyed one,*
*From the sinister one*
*From the fearful one—*
*By them never you'll be waylaid!*

*

# Politics and Revolution in Iranian Azerbaijan

Nicholas Awde & Fred James Hill

UNTIL THE Russo-Persian wars of the early 19th century, the peoples in the present-day regions of the Republic of ('Northern') Azerbaijan and Iranian ('Southern') Azerbaijan, lived in territories that had long been subject to the power of the Persian Empire. However, the 1828 Treaty of Turkmanchai between warring Russia and Iran favoured the Russians and cemented their dominance over the South Caucasus—it also saw the imposition of a permanent international border dividing Azerbaijan. Those to the north of the border, who had been living in a collection of khanates, were integrated into the Russian Empire, while those to the south continued to be ruled by the Iranian Qajar Dynasty (1797-1925). Today there remain two Azerbaijans: the Republic of Azerbaijan, founded after the collapse of the Soviet Union; and Azerbaijan in Iran, consisting of the three provinces of Western Azerbaijan, Eastern Azerbaijan and Ardabil.

However, from its creation, the border proved highly porous, allowing for a continuity of relations between northern and southern Azeris. Well-developed lines of communication between the two regions, especially the bustling hubs of Baku and Tabriz, reinforced co-operation between the Azeris and nurtured a shared sense of identity and purpose that gave impetus to their respective struggles against unsympathetic regimes.

## The seeds of discontent

Following the 1828 defeat at the hands of the Russians, Iran not only relinquished its claims to a large area of territory, but was also forced to make a whole range of highly favourable economic concessions to Russia, which were subsequently extended to Britain and other European powers. As the 19th century progressed, Iran steadily lost control of its foreign trade and by the early 20th century most of it lay in European hands.[1] Foreign competition and monopolies choked local industry. Cheap European manufactured goods, now widely available on the international market, flooded Iran, competing with, and often replacing, those made locally. Worryingly, Iranian textiles faced particularly strong competition from European exports—up until the early 19th century, the country had still enjoyed a longstanding reputation as a major centre of production. According to the British advernturer and diplomat Sir John Malcolm, visiting Iran in 1801:

> The manufactures of Persia that are in demand all over that Empire, are silks of various kinds, coarse cotton cloths, plain and coloured nummuds [felts], cotton cloths, Kirmaun shawls, gold cloths, etc.'[2]

Such textiles were not restricted to Iranian consumption, but found their way to important trade centres such as Turkey and Egypt from where they found their way into Europe. However, according to Lord Curzon, Viceroy of India, by the 1890s the situation in Iran had changed to the point that 'the humble peasant' was now being 'clothed from Manchester or Moscow; the indigo that dyes the hood which his wife [wears] has been shipped from Bombay [i.e. the British Empire]'. Curzon went on to declare that Persia 'from the highest to the lowest grade, is absolutely dependent upon the West'.[3] Meanwhile, although there were early private and government attempts to develop successful Iranian enterprises in order to compete with imported textiles, they were ultimately doomed to failure on account of 'mismanagement and political intrigues'.[4]

At the same time, Iranian goods, especially silk and textiles, were deprived of their export markets—a rare exception was the carpet industry which managed to survive on account of its not being in competition with colonial production.[5] The result was a dramatic 'decline of Iranian production, guilds, and merchantry'.[6]

Azerbaijan itself was accutely affected by the economic upheaval. Iran's major commercial centre was Tabriz, which acounted for around half the national total of Iran's trade during the mid-19th century.[7] Along with Esfahan and Mashhad, the city was also a major manufacturer of textiles and carpets while nearby Qaradagh boasted one of Iran's most productive mining zones of the 19th century. The Russian traveller L. Berezin, who visited Iran in 1842, noted the dramatic economic shift that was taking place in Azerbaijan:

> The trade of Tabriz... falls into two sharply defined periods: until 1837 the Persians themselves were predominant and after that date foreign merchants, including Russian, were preponderant.[8]

The Azeri provinces of Iran today: West Azerbaijan (with its capital at Orumiye/Urumia), East Azerbaijan (its capital at Tabriz) and Ardabil (its capital also called Ardabil).

Merchants in Iran could expect no protection from the government. On the contrary, compared to their European counterparts, they were not only 'far less secure in their property', they also shouldered the burden of higher taxes.[9] A despatch from the British consul in Tabriz in 1851 detailed that 'whereas a European merchant paid 5 per cent on his imports, an Iranian paid 7½ on textiles and 14 per cent on sugar and, in addition, was subject to *rahdarlik* (road tax) every time his goods passed through an Iranian town.'[10] In Tabriz, as early as 1840, merchants took their plight to the Shah, hoping to redress the devastating effects wrought by foreign domination of the city's commerce by restricting the import of European goods, but such appeals fell on deaf ears.[11]

Meanwhile, peasants fared no better. While conditions had often been hard for them in the early part of the 19th century, subject as they were to high taxes and the whims of oppressive governors, by the mid-19th century their lot had worsened markedly. As rising taxes became unbearable, so too did the tyrannical means of collecting them. As imports of manufactured goods increased, exports of cash crops, such as raw cotton, increased. Peasants, now no longer producing crops for themselves, found their fortunes precariously tied to the pitiless fluctuations of world prices, and for the peasant, there was no state aid or intervention that might stave off or cushion the blow of financial ruin. Added to the list of woes of peasants and merchants alike was the new threat of unemployment, a direct result of the 'disintegration of the traditional, self-contained village economy and the integration of Iran into the world market'.[12]

A major consequence of Iran's severe economic conditions was economic migration. As conditions became ever more difficult, a steady flow of workers from Iran made their way to the Caucasus and Central Asia, encouraged by Russian demand for cheap labour and faciliated by the systematic issuing of visas on the part of obliging Russian consulates. For the large numbers of Azeris who left their homes to find work, the principal destination was Baku, which by the end of the 19th century had turned into a thriving industrial centre thanks to its vast oil deposits and use of cutting edge methods in extraction and distribution. The influx of migrant workers was noted by General E. Gordon, who wrote:

> Baku swarms with Persians, resident and migratory. They are seen everywhere—as shopkeepers, mechanics, masons, carpenters, coachmen, carters and labourers.[13]

## Azerbaijan and the Constitutional Revolution

When revolution erupted in Iran during the early 1900s, the progressive city of Tabriz, second only to Tehran in terms of political development and activity, took a leading role in shaping the politics of the day. The Iranian Constitutional Revolution of 1906-1911, a landmark event in the history of Iran, arose in response to the difficult economic conditions and the accompanying ineptitude of a weak and corrupt regime. The latest in the line of the nation's monarch, Mozzafar-al-Din Shah (*r.*1896-1907), had personally given away major concessions to foreign powers and taken out huge loans to feed an extravagant lifestyle. Yet events finally conspired against him. In 1906, a series of major demonstrations erupted, involving protestors from all sections of Iranian society keen to see the establishment of the rule of law and an end to overbearing foreign influence on the country, most notably Russia. Forced to make concessions, in December of that year, the Shah signed the 'Fundamental Laws' of a new Iranian constitutional monarchy, drawn up by an elected assembly, which set strict limits on the powers of the shah and provided for an elected majlis, or parliament.

However, Mozzafar-al-Din Shah died within a few days of signing the new constitutional laws and his successor, Muhammad Ali, threw himself into the task of liquidating the constitutionalist gains. In reality, the new monarch amounted to little more than a Russian puppet who relied on the Persian Cossack Brigade, led by Russian officers, to keep him on the throne. After failing to seize total control in an attempted coup in December 1907, his relations with the majlis became irreparable. On June 23, 1908, Muhammad Ali ordered his personal brigade of cossacks, under the command of the Russian Colonel Liakhov, to bombard the majlis. Having reduced the Iranian parliament to rubble, the Shah immediately had leading constitutionalists rounded up and executed and launched a ruthless campaign to quell opposition across the country.

In July 1908, while the whole of Iran was subdued by the ferocity of the repressive regime, Tabriz rallied and launched a popular and well organised armed resistance under the leadership of Sattar Khan. Since the early days of the Constitutional Revolution, the city's anjuman, a council made up of local representatives, had coalesced into a powerful, organised body of opposition. Anjumans had been established throughout Iran in January 1907 and were charged with the task of supervising elections and investigating irregularites,[14] yet they soon overstepped the limits of their original remit. By the time of the rebellion against Muhammad Ali, the Tabriz anjuman had all but taken over the governing of the province, ignoring the central government and becoming a dominant force in the majlis. Now, headed by Sattar Khan, the city's popular guard seized control of the city 'in the name of the Tabriz anjuman, and replaced the Iranian flag with the flag of the Tabriz anjuman'.[15]

Rejecting the sovereignty of the Shah, Sattar Khan declared 'Tabriz the temporary capital of Iran'.[16] In a telegram sent to other anjumans across the country on July 14, 1908, the leadership in Tabriz called for a revolution against the 'iniquitous government' in Teheran and urged all to demand a republic on the grounds that no understanding with the Shah could be deemed popular.[17]

Around Iran, there was a groundswell of support for the Tabriz rebels and by November other provinces had taken up arms. Tabriz was effectively besieged by the Shah's forces throughout the winter of 1908-09 and eventually fell in late April. Yet far from spelling the end of the revolution, the defeat of Tabriz galvanised revolutionary forces elsewhere in the country. In May 1909, the beleaguered Shah was forced to restore the constitution, yet it was too late to save him. By July, Teheran was occupied by two revolutionary armies from Gilan and Esfahan. Muhammad Ali was immediately ousted, replaced by his 12-year-old son Ahmad Mirza and forced into exile in Russia. In November, the second majlis was inaugurated after national elections. Despite Sattar Khan's role as a hero, he fell foul of the government in 1910 after refusing a government order to disarm and disband his forces, and was shot and wounded. Quietly pensioned off, he lived the last few years of his life in the capital and died in 1914.

Sattar Khan.

## Links of Azerbaijan to the Transcaucasus

Azerbaijan's close links to the neighbouring Turkish-speaking areas of the Russian Transcaucasus and the Ottoman Empire, forged by a common language and continuous travel and emigration, played a critical role in the province taking the lead in the Constitutional Revolution. In both the Ottoman and Russian Empires revolutionary movements were continually striving to limit the powers of unpopular, and ultimately doomed, monarchies. In the 1870s the Young Ottomans had temporarily forced the Sultan in Turkey to respect a constitutional monarchy, while the Young Turks were set to launch their own revolution in 1908, which would inaugurate a second constitutional era, hasten the downfall of the Sultanate and see the ultimate creation of the Turkish Republic in 1922.

Meanwhile, the Transcaucasus had been caught up in the empire-wide struggle against royal absolutism which culminated in the 1905 Russian Revolution, in which the tsar was also forced to permit the establishment of a parliament—the later revolution of 1917 would see the tsarist regime come to a final and bloody end. Across the Transcaucasus there was a rapidly growing political awareness amongst the population, inspired by new Socialist ideas. Baku, with its ever expanding army of workers employed in the oil sector, was an especially fertile ground for political activists—it was a magnet for Bolsheviks and Mensheviks, playing a formative role in the careers of numerous influential revolutionaries, including Joseph Stalin, who later helped dismantle Tsarist Russia and founded the Soviet Union. For Azeris, the Caspian city was especially important, providing a cosmopolitan venue for Muslim intellectuals from both Northern and Iranian Azerbaijan to sit together and explore, or even put into practice, new ideas. Seasonal workers, who faced hardship and expoitation in Baku, returned to Iranian Azerbaijan having witnessed the new political climate, where highly active labour organisation and strikes held out the hope for a less fraught existence. Tabriz, in turn, became an energetic transmitter of the revolutionary new thinking, disseminating revolutionary thinking and activism beyond itself to the rest of Iran.

An important organization that was active amongst workers in the oilfield of Baku was the Social Democratic party Ferqe-ye Ejtema'iyun Amiyun Mojahed (FEAM). Founded around 1905 in the Transcaucasus by Iranian emigrants it also established a branch in Tabriz, as well in other parts of Iran. Placing action above doctrine,[18] FEAM members played an active and influential role in the Tabriz anjuman and also helped to lay the foundations of the socialist movement in Iran. It is interesting to note that Lenin, who was then living in exile in Western Europe, had set his hopes on Tabriz for the 'rise of the East', hailing the 'Iranian resistance leaders, especially Sattar Khan, as the torchbearers of the oppressed nations'.[19]

FEAM was closely associated with Hummat, a Marxist-inspired party that had close ties to the Russian Workers' Social Democratic Party (RSDWP). The party had emerged in Baku around 1904-5 and championed the cause of the Muslim population in the Caucasus. One of Hummat's leading figures, Nariman Narimanov, also played a key role in directing the Iranian Social Democrats and drew up their ideological strategy[20]—Nariman would later go on to become the first leader of Soviet Azerbaijan following the collapse of the First Republic of Azerbaijan in 1920. After translating the RSDWP programme from Russian into Azeri for Hummat, he then adapted it for FEAM, well aware of the religious sensitivites of the population he was attempting to galvanise into action, as his own words testify:

> The question of religion is so important in the Muslim's life that, in 1906, I had to omit from the programme those clauses pertaining to the separation of church and state, and to the separation of schools from church. This was the time when, as the leader of the Iranian Social Democratic party, I had to send agitators to Iran with the programme of our party... I may have

> committed a crime but nonetheless we threw off the throne the most foolish hangman of the world, the Shah Muhammad Ali.[21]

Amongst the demands in the programme were 'an eight-hour workday for all laborers; guaranteed government social security for all women, children, and old men; low-cost housing for the poor; free schools for orphaned children; progressive taxation; government subsidies of sugar, tea, kerosene, and other essential commodities through the decrease of customs import duties levied on the them'.[22]

FEAM, proving a little too radical for the Tabriz anjuman, also advocated redistribution of land to the peasants, calling for an end to 'the bondage imposed [upon them] by landlords and their *mobashers* (bailiffs), and from the need for a great number among them to emigrate to gain the necessary loaf of bread and thereby perish as victims of hard labour in mines'.[23] FEAM was also behind organising the *mojahedin*, volunteer Muslim fighters armed and trained in the Caucasus, to cross over to fight in Iran. Hundreds of Transcaucasian *mojahedin* crossed the frontier to join Sattar Khan's forces in Tabriz while others made their way to the province of Gilan.[24] Although in the grand scheme of things their numbers were relatively low, the presence of these fighters gave a valuable boost to the morale of the revolutionary movement in Iran.

At the time of the Constitutional Revolution, there was a burst of journalistic activity which saw a flood of papers and pamphlets published in both Iran and the Caucasus. FEAM itself launched its own own publication, *Mojahed*, in Tabriz in 1907. Two highly influential papers, popular for their satirical pieces, were *Molla Nasreddin*, published in Azeri in Tbilisi, and *Musavat* (*Equality*), which was moved from Tehran to Tabriz in 1909. Another publication was the immensely influential *Iran-e No*, the organ of the Ferqe-ye Demokrat-e Iran (Democratic Party of Iran, Iran's first modern political party) which was launched in August 1909 and helped pave the way for modern European-style journalism in Iran. It openly espoused socialist ideas and sparked national debate and action.

One of the founders of both the party and the paper was the journalist and activist Mammad Amin Rasulzade (1884-1955). Rasulzade had became actively involved in Baku's burgeoning social democratic movement in the early 1900s and was a founder of the Hummat Party. Hounded by the Russian authorities, he made his way to Iran in 1909 to take part in the Constitutional Revolution. Rasulzadeh was forced to leave Iran in 1911 and eventually returned to Baku, where he participated in the creation of the First Republic of Azerbaijan and would be remembered as one its founding fathers.

## Demise of the Constitutional Revolution

Despite the successes of the constitutional forces, the experiment in Iran was ultimately doomed. Its bid to fend off foreign interference and establish a newfound independence failed: the country had failed to free itself from the heavy influence of Britain and Russia, who were able to consolidate their position following their plan, previously agreed in 1907, to divide the country into spheres of influence allowing each other to pursue their own interests freely (the former took territory in the east and south-east, the latter took from the middle to the the north including Teheran and Esfahan, while the centre was declared neutral).

In 1911, as part of the daunting task of reforming the country's financial system, the government turned its attention to exerting control over the unrulier provinces and collecting taxes from them, by force if necessary. The man who oversaw the reforms was the financial advisor Morgan Shuster, an American who was appointed precisely because he was deemed independent of the British and Russians. His proposals to enforce tax collection with a dedicated tax police force and deploy them in the Russian sphere of influence brought swift protest from the provincial elite, as well the Russians themselves. The Russians, mixing diplomacy with military threat, insisted that Shuster be removed. While the majlis rejected the ultimatum, the advance of Russian troops to Teheran was enough to persuade the Iranian cabinet to capitulate. Shuster's departure in December 1911 left the Constitutional Movement 'severely limited, if not destroyed'.[25] The result was the closure of the majlis and a suspension of the Constitution.

The Constitution would remain in effect for another decade, but, despite its achievement in helping to create a new political awareness in the country and being instrumental in bringing the country into the modern era, the Revolution would ultimately remain an unrealised dream. While a new majlis was elected in 1914, the anjumans 'were dissolved, the press was censored and power returned to a conservative cabinet under vigilant British and especially Russian control... many people reverted to apathy and cynicism when faced by the restoration of foreign and conservative controls'.[26] Weakened by the turmoil, the country drifted into further economic and political crisis.

## Further revolution in Northwestern Iran

Amidst the chaos of World War I, the central government ground to a near halt. Chaos spread throughout the country as various factions challenged the central government. In 1917-18, in the province of Gilan, a revolutionary group called the Jangalis took control under the leadership of Kuchuk Khan, a veteran of the Constitutional Revolution. Two years later, in June 1920, Kuchuk Khan founded a Soviet Socialist Republic in Gilan with the aid of the Bolsheviks who, seeking to consolidate their power in the South Caucasus, had arrived in the region in the hunt for opposing White Russian forces who were still fighting the Red Army during the Russian Civil War (1917-1923). However, the republic came to an end in September the following year after Soviet support was withdrawn and the land-owning pro-Islamic Jangalis fell to quarrelling with radical leftists.[27]

A more serious challenge came from Tabriz. Vehemently opposed to government policies that paved the way for increasing British interference in Iran as the Western power sought to protect its oil interests, Shaikh Muhammad Khiyabani, a well-respected scholar, along with members of the Democratic Party of Azerbaijan, launched a revolution and declared an new Autonomous Republic in Iranian Azerbaijan named Azadistan ('Land of Freedom') in April 1920.

Khibayani's radical views had been forged during his time spent studying in the Caucasus, yet he and his co-conspirators did not advocate an independent Azerbaijan. Instead, drawing on the spirit of both the Constitutional Revolution and Islam, they saw their rebellion as part of a wider movement to bring change to Iran. However, the experiment proved short-lived and was liquidated in September 1920 with the death of Khiyabani in Tabriz at the hands of the shah's ubiquitous Cossack force.

The troubled system of constitutional monarchy came to an end with the rule of Reza Shah Pahlavi (1925-1941). The only Iranian to have become commander of the Persian Cossack Brigade, Reza Shah took charge of re-establishing central control in Iran. In 1921 he staged a coup and, after later deposing the last Qajar monarch, installed himself as shah in 1925. His rule descended into despotism with political repression, censorship and corruption being the order of the day.

Reza Shah was forced to abdicate on September 16, 1941, as a result of his unwillingness to bow to British and Soviet pressure. Although he had declared Iran's neutrality in War War II, Britain and Russia, concerned over the shah's sympathies with the Germans, brought pressure on him to adopt measures that would bolster the country against the Nazis. The previous month, as part of a plan to ensure that key war supplies made their way unhampered between the the two sides, Russia and Britain had invaded and stationed troops in Iran.

Reza Shah Pahlavi's son and successor, Mohammad Reza Pahlavi (*r.* 1941-1979), continued to rule autocratically. Only able to retain his throne by staging a coup with the backing of the CIA, he proved as unpopular as his predecessors. By the end of his rule, prior to his dethronement and exile in 1979, he had dismantled multiparty politics in Iran and ruled through his Rastakhiz ('Resurrection') Party, to which all Iranians were expected to belong. Muhammad Reza's heavy reliance on the US, along with the record of his predecessors' dealings with the European powers, contributed to the vociferously anti-Western stance taken by the 1979 Islamic Revolution in Iran.

The outbreak of World War II, which had already directly contributed to the fall of Muhamamd Reza and the Allied occupation of Iran, led to a new political climate fuelled by the release of political prisoners who set about reviving nationalist and socialist groups. Under Soviet protection, activists from northern (Soviet) Azerbaijan were able to foster especially close relations with their counterparts in Iran during the remaining war years. Azeri resentment at this time was particularly bitter towards the Iranian government, which had not only done little to ameliorate harsh living conditions but had also committed itself to eradicating national differences in Iran, including imposing Farsi (Persian) as the sole language permitted in universities and schools.

Facing soaring prices and the ill effects of unfair food distribution, many Azeris believed that 'in the eyes of the central government, Iran meant only the capital, Tehran' while an official telegram sent from Tabriz to the government complained that:

> Since the invasion, the textile ration has only been 1.5 metres and one third of the city's inhabitants have not even received that. Furthermore, Tabrizis have not received their sugar rations for the last six months of 1943.[28]

Meanwhile, two new pro-Soviet parties, the national Tudeh Party (Hezb-e Tudeh-ye Iran, 'Party of the Iranian Masses') and the Azerbaijani Democratic Party (ADP) (Firqe-ye Dimokrat-e Azerbaijan) would take the lead in channelling popular discontent in Azerbaijan. The Tudeh party was founded in September 1941 by a group of 'mainly Marxist intellectuals', including a number who had recently been released from prison.[29] Although in the post-war years it would evolve into a Communist party, in its early form 'it resembled more closely a popular or democratic front run by Marxist intellectuals and activists, similar to those groups that were active in occupied Europe to resist Nazi rule'.[30]

Tudeh was especially active in organizing workers' protests against rising prices, low wages and food shortages. Within two years, it had coalesced into a hugely popular national movement, especially in Azerbaijan, where it became a formidable force to be reckoned with:

> With the rapid growth of the party organizations, the Tudeh party became the de facto government of Azerbaijan. As the British consul reported, its leaders exercise more power than the governor-general, its militias rivalled the city police, its rural cadres more authority than the gendarmeries, its unions ran the factories, and its programme appealed to discontented merchants as well as to workers, peasants, and intellectuals.[31]

The same British consul reported 'the contempt in which the incompetent and corrupt local government' was held by 'all classes' and the 'growing feeling of indifference of the central government to Azerbaijan', going on to declare that the Tudeh party leadership's authority was 'so obvious as to lead cynics to enquire why the Governor-General does not retire to Tehran and leave his prerogatives to Mohammad Biriya [head of the pro-Tudeh labour unions in Tabriz]'.[32]

By 1945, there was a general feeling amongst Azerbaijanis that not only had their demands for reform and change been ignored, but that the central government had now adopted an undisguised policy of repression in the province.[33] In the midst of increasing tensions leading to strikes and other forms of protest, both peaceful and violent, events took a radical turn. On September 7, 1945, the provincial committee of the Tudeh party convoked a conference, the result of which was its fusion with the newly created Azerbaijani Democratic Party.[34] Two months later, in November 1945, the ADP boldly declared the creation of the Republic of Azerbaijan in Tabriz, an 'autonomous democracy', with Azeri as its official language.

The ADP had only just been formed in September 1945 by Mir Ja'far Pishavari, an ex-political prisoner, and other leading Marxists. Pishavari was born in Khakhal in Eastern Azerbaijan in 1892 and moved to Baku in 1905 with his father who was seeking work in the oilfields.[35] In Baku he began a career in journalism and soon became involved in the creation of the short-lived Republic of Gilan.

With the aid of feda'is, or volunteer fighters, armed courtesy of the Soviet Union, the ADP engineered 'an almost bloodless revolt thoughout [Iranian] Azerbaijan'.[36] After taking key government posts throughout the region, in November the feda'is gained control of Tabriz. Convening a National Congress of Azerbaijan on November 21, the ADP set out its programme:

> 1. The People of Azerbaijan have been endowed by history with distinct national, linguistic, cultural, and traditional characteristics. These characteristics entitle Azerbaijan to freedom and autonomy, as promised to all nations by the Atlantic Charter [created in 1941 by the UK and US].

2. The Nation (*Mellat*) of Azerbaijan has no desire to separate itself from Iran or to harm the territorial integrity of Iran, for it is aware of the close cultural, educational, and political ties that exist between itself and the other provinces, and is proud of the great sacrifices it has made for the creation of modern Iran.
3. The Nation of Azerbaijan supports, with all its might, democracy, which in Iran takes the form of a constitutional government.
4. The Nation of Azerbaijan, like all citizens of Iran, will participate in the functioning of the central government by electing deputies to the Majlis and by paying taxes.
5. The Nation of Azerbaijan officially and openly declares that it has the right to form its own government, like other living nations, and to administer its internal and national affairs, observing the integrity of Iran.
6. The Nation of Azerbaijan, having made great sacrifices for freedom, is determined to base its autonomy on the firm foundation of democracy. It therefore calls for a National Congress that will elect the ministers for the Autonomous Government of Azerbaijan.
7. The Nation of Azerbaijan has a special attachment to its national and mother language. It realizes that the imposition of another language on the people of Azerbaijan has hindered their historical progress. This Congress therefore instructs its ministers to use the Azerbaijani language in schools and government offices as soon as possible.
8. This Congress, supported by 150,000 signatures, declares itself a Constituent Assembly and appoints a Commitee to adminster Azerbaijan and implement the above resolutions until the convening of a National Majlis.[37]

At meeting of the National Majlis in Tabriz on December 12, formed mostly of representatives from the ADP, the majlis reaffirmed the ADP programme.[38] Azerbaijan was not the only province in Iran to stage such a rebellion. Events were mirrored in neighbouring Kurdistan, where in Mahabad, the newly created Democratic Party of Kurdistan declared the formation of a Kurdish republic. Both republics were cushioned by the Soviet army which prevented Iranian forces from making their way into the northwestern region of Iran.

The events in northwestern Iran contributed to one of the first episodes in the Cold War. From the outset, the Soviet and British occupation of Iran was intended to be strictly temporary with both sides agreeing to evacuate Iran within six months of the termination of the war. Yet as the deadline set for March 1946 passed, Soviet troops were still in Iran, with Moscow now visibly propping up rogue regimes in the country. International pressure, led by Britain and America, soon forced the Soviet Union to withdraw, leading to the republic's collapse in November 1946. The following month, with the Russians gone, the Shah marched an army into Tabriz and unleashed a punitive bloodbath designed to put an end to all further aspirations of Azeri self-governance. Pishavari was forced to escape to the Soviet Union but died soon afterwards in a road accident.

Following the events of 1946, ethnic activists were branded as separatists or agents working in the interests of foreign powers. Linking culture with sedition, the Azeri language again came under attack from the authorities and was banned from the official sphere, including education, government offices and the media. In both Azerbaijan and Mahabad immediately after the collapse of the republics there were incidents where books in both Azeri and Kurdish were publicly burned.

## Azerbaijan in recent times

In the years following World War II, writers from both Southern and Northern Azerbaijan explored themes of separation and cultural repression among the Azeri people. A notable Azeri figure of this time was the teacher, writer and social critic Samad Behrangi (also known as Semed Emi). Born in 1939 in Tabriz, he saw the linguistic oppression of Azeri as an act of cultural oppression. A teacher who taught in rural districts of Azerbaijan during the late 1950s and 60s, he was highly critical of the Iranian education system as a whole and scathing of state text books which he deemed highly inappropriate. Unable to publish his work (which included children's stories, most famously *The Little Black Fish*, along with essays and a work on the oral history of Azerbaijan) in his native Azeri, Behranghi was only able to gain a readership by translating his works from Azeri into Farsi. In 1968, Behranghi drowned in the Aras, the very same river that physically separates the two Azerbaijans and which has been seen as a symbol of division of the Azeri people.

The lack of the Azeri language in education and media was linguistically stifling and although 'intellectuals occasionally found ways to get books that were published in Azerbaijani Perso-Arabic script from the North' (most notably by Progress Press-Moscow and Yazichi Press-Baku), it survived more as a spoken language rather than written, to the extent that 'when it comes to writing, most Iranian Azerbaijanis, no matter how highly educated, simply cannot read and write it'.[39] With no TV programmes or movies produced at home in their own language, Azeris had to content themselves with Baku radio or pirate radio stations.[40]

There was a slackening of government control immediately after the

1979 Revolution, headed by Ayatollah Ruhollah Khomeini, which saw a brief revivial of Azeri publications and even a resurgence of movements advocating autonomy for the region. Nevertheless, once the new regime had consolidated its power, Azeri nationalist sentiment was discouraged and while the teaching of the Azeri language and the study and publishing of its literature was not banned by the state, in reality its use was highly restricted, as was the case with other non-Persian languages such as Kurdish, Arabic and Turkmen. During the late 1990s under the presidency of Mohammad Khatami, which led to a relative liberalization of Iranian society, there was an increase in local newspapers carrying articles in Azeri, which were able to survive on account of their ability to generate revenue from local advertising and, therefore, were not dependent on government support.[41]

Meanwhile, Tabriz has remained a politically charged centre. During the 2000s, the city saw a series of demonstrations of a nationalist nature that involved clashes with the police and armed forces. The year 2006 saw a huge wave of Azeri protest that spread from Tabriz across to other parts of Azerbaijan, fuelled by outrage over a cartoon published in the Teheran-based state-owned newspaper *Iran* on May 19, which depicted a cockroach uttering a word in Azeri and contained captions that were seen as derogatory towards the Azeris. The protest was taken to Teheran where activists demanded recognition of Azeri as an official language and a medium of instruction in schools, along with the right to a free Azeri media and press and to be able to organize political parties and trade unions.

While issues affecting Azeris were capable of rallying massive popular protests, organizations advocating Azeri independence or autonomy, including the separatist National Liberation Movement of Southern Azerbaijan (NLMSA, founded in 1996) and the Southern Azerbaijan Awakening Movement (Guney Azerbaijan Milli Oyanish Herekati, founded in 1995), failed to gain widespread support. While their effectiveness was certainly hampered by action on the part of the Iranian government, an overall lack of consensus over the Azeri question certainly served to weaken their appeal.

Although there are those who see Azeri grievances in an ethnic context necessitating political solutions such as autonomy, independence or even unification with Northern Azerbaijan, many Azeris see them within a wider Iranian context as part of a desire for democratic change and reform—just as did many of those who participated in the Constitutional Revolution a century ago. Azeris are a considerable force to be reckoned with in Iran. Rather than seeing their history with Iran as one of enduring struggle as a repressed minority, the Azeris can identify with their own powerful role in shaping Iran. They constitute the country's largest ethnic minority, making up around 25 per cent of the country's population (other estimates put this as high as 30 per cent), and exert a major influence on the economic and political life of the country. Far from being geographically isolated in their traditional homeland, huge numbers are fully integrated in Teheran and other major Iranian cities. (It should also be noted that the Azeri provinces of Iran are home to significant communities of non-Azeris who in turn exert influence on Azerbaijan.)

While the empires of Iran exerted a powerful and sustained influence over the region, the Azeris successfully established their own cultural traditions and in turn made an enormous contribution to the Persian world, producing great leaders, poets, artists and other influential figures. The Azeri-speaking Safavids (1501-1736) ruled Iran from the Azeri city of Tabriz and although they subsequently moved the capital southwards to Esfahan, the influential dynasty never shook off its Azeri roots. The Safavids revived Iran's fortunes as a regional power after a prolonged period of political and economic instability. It was also the Safavids, primarily thanks to the initial efforts of Shah Ismail, who were responsible for the conversion of most of the Iranian population to Shi'ism, a form of Islam that by extension profoundly influenced Iran's form of governance and foreign policy, shaping its relations with its overwhelmingly Sunni Muslim neighbours within the region and beyond.

With regard to unification with Northern Azerbaijan, despite a close bond resulting from their shared history, religion, culture and language, it is by no means a given that, even if international politics would allow, Northern and Southern Azeris would share a common vision that could readily underpin a unified Azerbaijan. An independent political Azeri union has no precedence: prior to the Russian-Iranian war the northern region was never a unified Azeri state but a collection of khanates that enjoyed varying degrees of autonomy, granted for the most part by the Persian Empire. Furthermore, the secularist outlook of Northern Azeris, brought about by prolonged exposure to Western influences as a result of Russian and Soviet rule, has become well established and marks a difference in outlook that can challenge relations with their cousins to the south. Added to this are the realities of global politics, which alone make it reasonable to assume that the two Azerbaijans are more than likely to continue as separate political entities.

*

# From Ancient Times to the Safavid Era: A Regional History of Azerbaijan

Nicholas Awde & Fred James Hill

HUMANS ARE known to have a long-established presence in the region of Azerbaijan. The jawbone of the so-called 'Azikh woman', discovered near Fuzuli in the Lesser Caucasus Mountains of southeast Azerbaijan in 1968, is thought to be between 350,000 to 400,000 years old. In the region of Baku there is also abundant evidence to show that Paleolithic humans roamed the land. Early hunters left behind them tantalising glimpses of their world with the famous drawings carved into the rock of caves at Gobustan, located on the Caspian coast some thirty miles southwest of Baku, the oldest of which may have been created some 10,000 years ago. Along with engravings of animals, including bulls, horses, wild boar and dogs, Gobustan also boasts some of the earliest known representations of humans, both men and women—the former shown dressed in loin-cloths and wielding bows and arrows. Also depicted are lively hunting and battle scenes, including bulls being shot by hunters with arrows.

Archeologists have uncovered numerous sites showing the existence of a thriving farming culture across the South Caucasus dating from around the sixth and fifth millennia BC. Round or oval multi-level houses of mud brick with stone foundations were typical dwellings constructed in the region. Discoveries of painted pottery indicate that inhabitants living in the region of Karabakh and the Mil and Mughan Steppes may have been influenced by the Dalma culture, which flourished in the Urumia region of present-day Iranian Azerbaijan during the fifth millennium BC.

Azerbaijan also functioned as a vital Eurasian gateway. The western coastline of the Caspian coast provided an accessible alternative to the Central Asian routes by which proto-Indo-Europeans filtered from eastern-central Europe into the Iranian highlands (spreading their Indo-European dialects in the process). While other north-south routes through the Caucasus existed, they were unsuitable for mass movements of people with families. For example, in ancient times, the route via the Black Sea coast in the western Caucasus was densely overgrown with sub-tropical forest, while the narrow strip of coastline was strewn with large boulders.[1] Meanwhile, the mountain passes of the Great Caucasus would have proved highly dangerous, making the slow-moving groups easy prey for hostile mountain dwellers.

Between the third and first millennia BC, considerable numbers of people living in the region bred cattle and practised subsistence farming. By the first millennium BC, a more complex social structure had begun to develop as Azerbaijan embarked on its long and stormy relationship with the many regional powers based in the Middle East. The overall extent of the influence of early kingdoms on the people of region remains uncertain. With continuous fighting between feudal clans over land, the territory was in a state of perpetual upheaval. Furthermore, attempting to rein in the northernmost region of Azerbaijan was a daunting task for would-be conquerors. For most of Azeri history these lands were frequently invaded by warlike tribes based on the northern side of the Caucasus, making it a wild and dangerous frontier that future empires would go to considerable lengths to pacify.

Amongst the earliest of the known political units to include part of Azerbaijan were the primitive city-states of Zamia, subsequently known as Mannae, which were the target of military campaigns by the mighty empire of the Assyrians in the tenth and ninth centuries BC. The city-states were centred around Lake Urumia, yet touched upon the southeast region of Northern Azerbaijan. Their inhabitants, who had links to the wider regional trade routes that reached the Mediterranean, practised agriculture (including the cultivation of wheat, barley and grapes) and the rearing of livestock (including sheep, cattle, donkeys and even Bactrian camels).[2] Handicrafts were also highly developed and examples have been found of metal artwork fashioned by Mannaean craftsmen. At the end of the ninth century BC, Mannae came under the domination of the recently founded kingdom of Urartu, a political entity formed by a coalition of various regional tribes. With territory that included present-day Armenia and Nakhchivan, Urartu launched effective military campaigns against the Assyrians.

Urartu itself was conquered by the highly influential state of the Medes, which emerged around 700 BC. The Medes were an Indo-European people who had arrived in the region of northern Iran around

1000 BC. While their capital was at Ecbatana (now Hamadan, northwest Iran), they were also well established in Southern Azerbaijan—their state frontiers extended as far north as the Kura River. It was from the Medes that the hereditary class of priests known as the Magi(ans) came. They were later to play a hugely influential role in the spread of Zoroastrianism, a religion that became intricately linked with Azerbaijan.

The Medes were also responsible for the overthrow of the Assyrians in 612 BC. Like the other powers of the day, they had the additional challenge of tackling the formidable Scythian tribes—nomads of Indo-European stock who hailed from lands north of the Black Sea, in the region of present-day Ukraine. The Scythians appear to have first entered the South Caucasus around 700BC, most likely via the Mamison and Daryal passes of the Great Caucasus as well as the Caspian littoral. Their considerable equestrian and archery skills made them formidable fighters[3] who, though failing to create their own state, plundered and levied contributions from the Medes.[4] The inhabitants of Media are said to have 'sent their boys to the Scythians to learn from them the technique of archery and even their language'.[5] Eschewing permanent homes, the Scythians (men, women and children) lived in mobile wagons, and so left tombs across the entire South Caucasus, containing weapons and other artefacts typical to their culture. Herodotus tells how the great Median king Cyaxares dealt with the troublesome people by wiping out their drunken chieftains at a feast in the seventh century BC—an event that led to the Scythians' abandonment of the Caucasus.

A major turning came with the rise of the Achaemenids, a dynasty that toppled the Medes in 550 BC. It was the Achaemenid Empire that was to bring Azerbaijan, and the South Caucasus in general, into the Perso-Iranian cultural and political sphere—a state of affairs that, despite lapses, would endure until the 19th century. The Achaemenid Empire was vast, bringing into its political and economic orbit territories stretching from the Mediterranean Sea eastwards to what is now Pakistan and from the Gulf of Oman northwards to the Caucasus Mountains and Central Asia.

The founder of the Achaemenids was Cyrus the Great, who named his new kingdom Persia and distinguished himself by becoming the first of the Persian rulers to be referred to as 'shah'. Under his successors, the empire was divided into some 20 satrapies (provinces). Much of present-day Azerbaijan corresponded to the 11th satrapy, although western areas including Nakhchivan came under the 18th along with territory corresponding to present-day Armenia. The Achaemenids did not rigorously impose central uniformity on the empire. Local dynasties provided regional satraps (or governors), and their armies played key roles in maintaining imperial order. In fact, satraps often ruled like kings, blatantly ignoring or even defying the authorities in the far-off Persian capital.[6]

Ancient stone horses.

Darius I, one of the greatest Achaemenid kings, turned Zoroastrianism into the state religion (although the dynasty's reputation for tolerance ensured the survival of local age-old pagan religious practices). The faith, with its strong tendency to monotheism, had gained ground under the Median kings, themselves close followers of the religion who did much to facilitate its spread. The influence of Zoroastrianism on the Persians was profound. By fusing key Aryan deities into the single powerful god Ahura-Mazda, 'the wise lord', the religion changed the Persians from polytheism to near monotheism, thereby helping them shed their nomadic hunter-gathering past and providing them with a unifying religion that cemented their new civilization with its base in agriculture.[7]

With the help of the Magi priestly caste, both Northern and Southern Azerbaijan came to be especially closely identified with Zoroastrianism, a religion whose key ritual centred on the veneration of fire as a symbol of immortality and the purity of Ahura-Mazda. Baku and the Apsheron Peninsula, with its abundance of oil and eerie natural gas flares rising from the ground, was a perfect site for fire temples and their presence in the region is known to stretch back 2,500 years at the very least. This has given rise to a commonly held belief that the name Azerbaijan is derived from the Persian word for fire, *azar*—literally making it the 'Land of Fire'. Priests and pilgrims braved long and hazardous journeys to get the chance to worship at such a holy place. Zoroaster himself was even said to have taught in the region and popular legend places his birthplace not so far away in the region of

Ancient rock carvings at Gobustan and detail (inset) of various designs found in the area.

Urumia. (In fact, he most likely hailed from northeastern Iran or southern Afghanistan.)

## Rise of Albania, Atropatena and Armenia

The Achaemenids continued to hold sway over the region until a formidable new challenger came from the west in the fourth century BC, in the form of Alexander the Great. The young Macedonian commander dealt the Achaemenids a mortal blow in 331 BC, destroying the palace of Persepolis and killing the all-powerful royal priests.

The extent of Alexander's new empire was enormous, at its peak stretching all the way from his native Greece to India. Yet it was short-lived and Alexander himself never set foot in the Caucasus. His early death in 323 BC at the age of 32 saw his empire carved up amongst his generals. Persia went to one named Seleucus, founder of the Seleucid Empire, which extended from Turkey (Anatolia) to Central Asia and which also included Syria and Babylonia. While Greek influences certainly began to filter into the new empire, the Seleucids left the existing Achaemenid decentralized political and administrative system more or less in place. Meanwhile, they faced an uphill struggle attempting to prevent regional dynasties from eroding their authority. The principal challenge came from the Parths, a people whose exact origins are uncertain but whose territory lay to the east of the Caspian. A Parthian dynasty was founded in around 245 BC by Arsaces I, who overthrew the local Seleucid satrap. In time, the Parths would extend their rule across Persia, proving an enduring empire that spanned five centuries. As with their Achaemenid predecessors, the Parths had a reputation for religious tolerance.

Alexander's victory also gave rise to the creation of a state that was to figure large in Azeri history, that of Atropatena, formerly the Achaemenid satrapy of Media, governed under Darius III by the satrap Atropates. Possibly a Mede himself, Atropates had allied himself with Alexander and was rewarded by being declared sovereign of the former-province. The kingdom of Atropatena (another of the possible orgins of the name Azerbaijan) incorporated Southern Azerbaijan, its northern frontier reaching up to the River Aras and taking in part of the southeast of the present-day Republic of Azerbaijan. Following the Macedonian destruction of the holy city of Raga (now Rayy, near present-day Tehran), the Atropatenian city of Ganzak near Lake Urumia (at the site of Takht-e-Soleiman in modern-day Iranian Azerbaijan) became the new home of the immensely important and holy fire of Adur Gushnasp—ensuring that Atropatena became a major bastion of Zoroastrianism.[8]

Meanwhile, to the north of Atropatena, another political entity that was to prove enormously influential in Azeri history was beginning to blossom—the Kingdom of Albania. Although its boundaries fluctuated over time, Classical Albania (not to be confused with today's Albania of the Balkans) covered a significant area of Northern Azerbaijan, lying within the great triangle of land formed by the junction of the Rivers Kura and Aras.[9] Very little is actually known of the culture of the kingdom, since no documented Albanian history survives[10]—historians have been left with little more than second-hand accounts penned by Classical scholars. Nevertheless, it proved an enduring kingdom, which for centuries steadfastly maintained its autonomy, if not quite its independence. This it did by paying tribute to the greater regional powers and, when all else failed, by engaging in fierce armed resistance.

From what is known, the inhabitants of the kingdom belonged to a number of indigenous Caucasian tribes whose eventual union evolved into a feudal society with its own language, most likely belonging to the Northeastern Caucasian linguistic family. The distinctive language was still reportedly spoken in areas such as Barda well into the tenth century AD, long after Albania had been incorporated into the Islamic Empire. (Their descendants, the Udins, still live in Azerbaijan and speak a modern form of the language.) The Albanians established their capital at Qabala, and by all accounts their kingdom developed into 'a rich country with diverse economic activity', with 'gardens, orchards, viticulture, arable land, pastures, large herds of cattle and horses, fishing, and hunting' and numerous trading and cultural centres.[11] The existence of such a sizeable and long-lived kingdom located within the borders of the Republic of Azerbaijan has often been used to suggest the existence of an embryonic Azeri nation.

Following the fall of the Achaemenids, the Armenians had also managed to forge an independent state centred between Lake Van (now in eastern Turkey) and Lake Sevan (in present-day Armenia). Although the state fell under the direct rule of the Seleucids, it would later break free to become a key power in the South Caucasus during the following centuries.

Rome's ongoing policies in the region and its victory over the Seleucids in 188 BC in Asia Minor gave Armenia a massive boost. That same year saw the formation of the extensive Greater Kingdom of Armenia under King Artashes I, which, having been recognized by the Roman Empire, now became a major political player in the region. It came to occupy the lion's share of the South Caucasus, extending from the Caspian (where it carved a corridor between Albania and Atropatena) across Karabakh and Nakhchivan and stretching a further hundred kilometres west of Lake Van.

For a while it seemed that the Armenians were unstoppable. Under the lengthy rule of the Tigran the Great (*r.*95-55 BC), successful campaigns were waged against the Parthians,[12] who had by now supplanted the Seleucids in Persia. This enabled Tigran to dramatically increase his kingdom's standing, gaining control of Syria (as far as Egypt), Atropatena and considerable territorial gains to the west.[13] While there is no record of Albania actually being subjugated by Tigran,[14] there was little choice for the state, along with Iberia (Georgia), but to accept Armenian suzerainty.

When the Romans besieged the Armenian capital in 69 BC, Albania was amongst a wide array of willing allies to lend Tigran their support.[15] Nevertheless, it was not long before the Roman legions were on the offensive again. With the eastern frontiers of its empire in a state of disarray, Rome charged the great general Pompey with the task of bringing about a semblance of order and in 66 BC, after marching into Syria and finishing off the last remnants of the Seleucid dynasty, he turned his attention to Armenia.

This time the situation was somewhat different. The ageing Tigran had little desire for a head-on confrontation with Pompey's forces. Instead, he opted to make peace, which he did by agreeing to pay Rome huge sums of money and treasure.[16] The deal secured the loyalty and obedience not only of Armenia but also, at least theoretically, of its vassals. However, the Albanians appeared to have jealously clung on to their autonomy, cementing their reputation for fierce resistance to the meddling hands of outside powers, especially Rome. When the territories of the Armenian Empire were parcelled out by the Romans, the Albanians ensured that they were not left out and they even gained Caspiane, the territory just below Albania and above Atropatena.[17] (Interestingly, Roman military activity in the region of Northern Azerbaijan during the first century AD is attested to by a soldier of the 12th Roman legion who saw fit to leave an inscription on a rock in Gobustan.)

Pompey's political reorganization of the East had the effect of turning the region of Northern Azerbaijan into part of a larger Caucasian buffer zone between Rome and its eastern Parthian rivals. Overall, Rome's influence in the South Caucasus proved to be highly limited and it never succeeded in dislodging the predominance of Persian and indigenous cultures in the region. Furthermore, in the complex regional politics aimed at maintaining the balance of power, in time Rome saw fit to sanction the installation, as representatives of its authority, of ruling branches of the Parthian Arsacid royal family in both Albania and Armenia.[18]

## The South Caucasus under the Sassanians

A major development in South Caucasian history was the early arrival of Christianity. Shortly after Armenia officially adopted the religion at the beginning of the fourth century—making it the first state in the world to do so—Albania, along with Iberia, followed suit. The fact that Albania became Christian has had a significant impact on the national identity of the modern Republic of Azerbaijan. The existence of an independent-minded people with its own state and Caucasian language, who adopted

Christianity in defiance of the Zoroastrian rulers of Persia, has served to strengthen the bond felt by modern Azeris towards the territory they now inhabit, as well as to counter claims that the history of the Republic of Azerbaijan is merely a detail within the wider history of Iran. However, differing views of the history of Christianity in the region have given rise to a great deal of controversy. In particular, the extent to which the Albanian Church was separate from the Armenian Church, and therefore the degree to which Albanians and Armenians have a shared common past, has remained a subject of intense debate with important implications for the ongoing territorial dispute between Azerbaijan and Armenia.

Religion also figured large in the workings of the new native Persian Sassanian dynasty, which toppled the Parthians in 224 AD and seized power for itself. The legitimacy of Sassanian power was deeply rooted in their defence of a more intense brand of Zoroastrianism, making for a powerful combination of religion and politics that, while proving highly effective in uniting much of Persia, would prove to be highly divisive in the South Caucasus. The Sassanian authorities eventually embarked on a mission to impose religious uniformity in the empire, leaving the Christians of the Caucasus in a precarious position.

Three decades into Sassanian rule, under Shapur I, the Persians flexed their military muscle in the Caucasus with successful campaigns in Albania, Armenia and Iberia setting off a new round of alternating political alliances between the local Caucasian rulers and the empires of Rome and Persia. In the fourth century, under the lengthy rule of Shapur II (*r*:309-379 AD), all three South Caucasian states were listed as vassals of the Sassanian Empire[19] (Atropatena had already ceased to function as an independent state, having been annexed by Persia in the previous century).

The archrivals of the Sassanians were the Byzantines, whose state had emerged after the fracture of the Roman Empire. (The western half of the Roman Empire maintained Rome as its spiritual centre but rapidly split up into smaller kingdoms, while the eastern half, with its capital in Constantinople [today's Istanbul] became known as the Byzantine Empire and adopted Christianity as the state religion with the Holy Roman Emperor at its head.)

Fierce battles between the Byzantines and the Sassanians resulted in a redrawing of imperial boundaries during the fourth century. Caught in the middle, Armenia did not fare so well and was partitioned by the two empires in 387. In 428, the Armenian monarchy was dissolved by the Sassanians and the territory patched onto the Persian empire proper as a marzpanate (province). In place of kings, for the next two centuries a series of governors took over the administration of the land. Albania, on the other hand, maintained its fragile autonomy, lending its support to the Sassanians against the Romans, an act for which it was rewarded with a portion of eastern Armenia, including the province of Utik.[20] While the kingdom subsequently came to be part of a single administrative unit combined with Persian Armenia, Atropatena and Iberia,[21] it nevertheless continued to thrive and, as was the case with Iberia, retained its own monarchy.

In an attempt to strengthen its control over the South Caucasus and prevent territorial losses to the Byzantine Empire, the Sassanians launched a vigorous campaign to impose Zoroastrianism. Summoned to the court of the Persian ruler:

> ... the magnates and senior members of the lesser nobility in Armenia, Iberia and Albania ... feigned apostasy and returned home with Zoroastrian teachers. There the sad and scornful reaction of their compatriots caused the princes to swear an oath, form a covenant and, taking advantage of Persia's military engagement in the east, to rebel.[22]

Albania's Arsacid ruler Vache II (*r.c.*451-*c.*463) sent his cavalry to aid the Armenians, who were leading the resistance. A showdown against the Sassanians took place at the Battle of Avarayr in 451 in the region of Nakhchivan. Although the rebellion was quashed by the Sassanian king Yazdgard II, in the ensuing peace deal the Armenians secured the right to remain Christian. In 457, Vache II renounced fire worship and proclaimed Christianity the official religion of the Albanian kingdom.

Following Yazdgard's death in the same year, a power struggle between his two sons gave Albania the opportunity to declare independence from Persia—it proved short-lived with the Sassanians retaking control once the crisis was resolved.[23] Vache II for his part was forced to surrender his crown[24] but Albania was able to cling on to its fragile autonomy and Christian faith by declaring its clear recognition of Sassanian suzerainty and paying tribute.

Towards the end of the sixth century a dynasty of Persian (Sassanian) royal descent known as the Mihranids was installed in Albania.[25] Converts to Christianity,[26] these rulers struggled hard to fend off a series of punishing attacks from the north by the Gok ('Blue') Turk empire and the Khazars. The perennial invasions of such nomadic tribes from the north was a major preoccupation for the regional powers and resulted in treaties in which the Byzantines, concerned about intrusions into their Anatolian provinces, made funds available to the Persians to contribute to the costs of defending the Derbend Pass. One agreement in 533 provided for a Byzantine payment of 11,000 pounds of gold to help for the upkeep of Caucasian defences.[27]

Towards the latter part of the sixth century the Sassanian grip on the Caucasus had severely weakened and much of its Armenian territory had already been lost to Byzantium. In 623, the Byzantine emperor Heraclius invaded the remnants of Persian Armenia, and, building up his army in the Caucasus region, launched attacks on Azerbaijan, plundering and destroying one of Persia's three great fire temples—that of Gushnasp at Ganzak, the former capital of Atropatena.[28] Heraclius similarly turned his attention to Albania and, in 628, installed a ruler sympathetic to Byzantium.[29]

Little prepared the Persians for the cataclysm that was to come. Within the space of a few years, the Sassanian-Byzantine balance of power that had defined the politics of the entire region fell apart thanks to the highly efficient military skills of a new force in the region: the Arabs. After increasingly frequent raids on Persian territory for booty, the Arabs launched a major attack on the Sassanians and, defeating them in 642, they began to incorporate Sassanian territories wholesale into their own rapidly expanding empire. Having established their capital in Damascus in 661, Syria would provide the first great Muslim Arab dynasty, the Umayyads, with a base from which to launch further campaigns into the South Caucasus, thereby bringing the region into the realm of their new Islamic empire.

By the end of a few decades, the Arabs had forced the Sassanian marzpans (governors) of Armenia and Atropatena and the rulers of Sheki and Shirvan (later to become key components in the tapestry of khanates in Northern Azerbaijan) to accept Arab suzerainty and pay tribute. Yet Albania put up a spirited resistance, especially under its Mihranid ruler, Javanshir (638-70). The Arabs would have to wait until 705 AD to finally get the Albanians to bow to the authority of the caliph (the name given to the all-powerful Muslim rulers who were the ultimate authority in the Islamic Empire), although the latter would continue to display their characteristically independent streak.

In exchange for helping to counter the marauding Khazars, the Arabs pragmatically offered the Albanians a free hand in running their own affairs. The Khazars, who had been seriously disrupting trade patterns throughout the region, had earlier profoundly traumatized the Albanians in 629 with the seizure of their capital. The Albanian nobility and clergy were forced to flee to safety and it was a long year before the invaders were finally removed and a degree of normality returned.

The curtain would finally fall on Albania in the early ninth century with the assassination of the Mihranid ruler Varaz-Trdat II in *c.*822. The region of Albania was incorporated into the Muslim empire as part of the province the Arabs referred to as Arran (Ar-Ran), with its administrative capital at Barda.

## The Arabs and the Islamic Caliphate

Azerbaijan and the South Caucasus constituted an exposed frontier zone, one that the caliphate would always go to great lengths to secure. The region presented the Arabs with an immensely complex administrative challenge, one in which there could be no dramatic dismantling of local regimes:

> The variety of the population as well as the mountainous fragmentation of the region, favoured the survival of numerous petty principalities, some of which had been established by the Sassanians with the aim of strengthening the border defence. These local dynasties became tributaries of the Arab conquerors and generally survived intact at least until the late Umayyad Age [ended 750], though little is known about their history. Later some of them disappeared, while in other principalities the rule was taken over by members of the new nobility of the conquerers.[30]

The Arabs were keen to ensure trade routes were kept open and that taxes and tribute were paid.[31] Governors for each region, appointed by the caliph, oversaw their collection and also made sure the army received its due. The payment of tribute was normally sufficient to ensure that local rulers were left to their own devices.

The population at the time of the conquest in Southern Azerbaijan had become predominantly Iranian and spoke numerous Iranian dialects while 'groups of Kurds had already penetrated into some parts of the province'.[32] In Northern Azerbaijan, in addition to the Albanian people, there were also substantial numbers of Iranian immigrants who had settled permanently whose 'local names like Laizan, Sharvan, Bailaqan suggest that they came from Dailaman and other areas south of the Caspian Sea'.[33]

Furthermore, there were also numbers of settlements established by the various tribes that had invaded from the north—most important at the time were the Khazars 'who had occupied the town of Qabala to the west of Shirvan'.[34] The Khazars, along with other invaders, continued to blight Arab ambitions in the region until the mid-eighth century, when, under the governor Marwan ibn Muhammad, they were finally subdued.[35] (An

Chiraq Qala, an imposing fortress built 1,600 years ago in the mountainous stronghold of northern Azerbaijan (picture by Jason Thomson).

interesting legacy of the Khazars is the lending of their name to the Caspian Sea—in Azeri it is known as Khazar Deniz, literally 'Khazar Sea'.)

Barda, in Northern Azerbaijan, conquered by the Arabs in 645, would remain the key regional city of Arran during Arab rule. In addition to stationing garrisons there, important garrisons were also established in Nakhchivan (also in the present-day Republic of Azerbaijan) and Ardabil and Maragha in Southern Azerbaijan (present-day northwestern Iran). The Arabs followed in the well-trodden footsteps of previous rulers and carefully attended to the most northerly point of the empire, Derbend, or as it was known in Arabic, Al-Bab ('The Gate'). The important stategic trading city, now in modern Daghestan and known as Derbent, became a major Arab bastion. In 731 the its fortifications were greatly strengthened and 24,000 Syrian soldiers settled there.[36]

Although Islam did begin slowly to take root in the Caucasus, it was a relatively slow process, and the Arabs, during their early rule at least, were noted for their religious tolerance. There was, in fact, usually little incentive and thus little attempt by the Arabs to gain Muslim converts. These would have merely competed with Arabs for privileges and affected revenues gained from taxing non-Muslims. Under the Arabs, as in the rest of the Islamic Empire, Christians and Jews were considered 'Peoples of the Book' on account of their belief, shared with the Muslims, in the Old Testament and its prophet) and accorded the status of 'protected people', known by the Arabic term *dhimmi*. Accordingly they were permitted to continue to worship freely on payment of the religious *jizya* tax. The Zoroastrians—who have their own religious scripture, the Avesta, and thus also came to be considered as a People of the Book—were also able to buy themselves protection with the tax, but their status was far more precarious and they would later face mounting persecution, leading in turn to the massive decline of the ancient religion.

In the early eighth century, the Albanian Church was officially absorbed into the Armenian Church with the approval of the caliph.[37] However, descendants of the Mihranid family restored the Albanian kingdom in Karabakh in the ninth century and an Albanian catholicos managed to survive into the 11th century at Ganja until the city was seized by the Seljuk Turks under their leader, Togrul, in 1054. The Albanian Church subsequently lived on in the Khachen Principality, which lay in the mountainous region of Karabakh. An autonomous patriarch-catholicate managed to survive until 1836, when Russia had it merged with the Armenian Church. The last surviving descendants of the Albanian Christians are the Udin people who still live in Azerbaijan and Georgia.

Political upheavals in the Arab world brought a change of capitals and dynasties. The Muslim Umayyad dynasty, based in Damascus, which had overseen the phenomenal expanse of the Arab Empire and which stretched from Spain and Morocco in the west to the borders of China in the east, was overthrown in 750 by a rival Arab dynasty, the Abbasids. The caliphs of the latter ran their empire from Baghdad, but eventually faced insurmountable problems asserting their authority over their far-flung territories. Azerbaijan turned out to be a particularly challenging region.

The Abbasids' Persian territories had seen the emergence of various groups and movements opposed to their authority—ones that were prepared to reassert their own identity and culture by armed struggle. Some of these, known collectively as the Khurramites, subscribed to traditional Persian religious beliefs tinged with certain Islamic characteristics. By siding with a peasantry embittered by the excesses of the large landowners who had been assimilated into the caliphal system, the Khurramites took on the character of populist movements. Linked with these groups were the neo-Mazdakites, whose highly obscure beliefs had their roots in Mazdakism, a heretical Zoroastrian movement from the Sassanian times. The Mazdakist faith upheld the idea of universal equality and has since been likened to a kind of religious communism. The most famous Khurramite–neo-Mazdakite rebellion was led by one of Azerbaijan's most enduring folk legends, Babek, a figure whose battle against the Arab caliphate became synonymous with the struggle against oppression.

Until modern times, Babek has remained a potent symbol of the defiant spirit of the Azeri people in the face of occupation by foreign powers. While the mists of time have seen Babek's life embellished with layers of wildly rich and colourful myths, he was a very real leader who temporarily disabled the Abbasids' rule over the region of Azerbaijan. According to some sources, Babek was the son of an itinerant oil vendor and a blind woman and spent his early life working as a shepherd.[38] His rebellion, which began around 816, was centred in Badhdh just to the south of the River Aras, where, aided by local warlords he managed to seize control over a substantial part of the region and succeeded in holding the armies of the Caliphate at bay for two decades. In 835, the caliph Al-Mutasim instructed his governor of Azerbaijan to put an end to Babek's rebellion, which he did in 837. Babek was caught after being betrayed by his allies and taken to Samarra (in modern-day Iraq) where he was tortured to death in 838 on the orders of the caliph.

## The Sajid, Sallarid and Rawwadid dynasties

Although Babek's venture ultimately failed, it was a clear illustration of how precarious the hold of the Abbasid caliphate over the region was. In the late ninth century, in an attempt to impose its authority over the troublesome and powerful Arab chieftains that had established themselves in the region and to check the ascendancy of the Bagratid kings of Armenia, the Abbasid Caliphate unintentionally helped to establish a succession of Muslim dynasties in Northern and Southern Azerbaijan that would prove highly influential and gain an enormous degree of independence.

The Sajids, a family which originated in Ushrusana, Central Asia, were handed Azerbaijan around 889 after the caliph Al-Mu'tamid appointed one of his top commanders, Muhammad bin Abi 'l-Saj, governor of Azerbaijan and Armenia. Muhammad made Maragha his capital but later usually resided in Barda.[39]

Loyalty to Baghdad was not foremost in Muhammad's mind and he embarked on a career that served his own ambitions. In Barda, in 898, he began to have coins minted in his name, along with the titular surname Al-Afshin—the traditional title of the kings of Ushrusana.[40] After

Muhammad, the throne went to his quarrelsome descendants and the capital was subsequently transferred to Ardabil. Relations between the Sajids and the Caliphate remained volatile, oscillating opportunistically between compliance and defiance. The family engaged in a lengthy and bloody campaign to subdue the Armenian Bagratid king Smbat I (*r.* from 890) during the course of which they took Dvin and Kars (now in Eastern Turkey), as well as bringing Nakhchivan under their suzerainty. The Sajid family's hold over Azerbaijan came to an end in 929 when their leader was poisoned by a slave in Ardabil.[41]

Following the Sajid period, Azerbaijan did not revert to the rule of governors appointed by the caliph. After a brief interlude that saw several warlords jostle for control, Azerbaijan was seized by the Sallarid ruler Al-Marzuban, who invaded in 941-2. The Sallarids (named after their founder Salar, a derivative of *sardar* meaning 'prince-leader') were members of a family that had established itself in Tarum (today in west-central Afghanistan). Al-Marzuban's rule was undisturbed until his death in 957. Furthermore, judging from a list of his tributaries in 955-6 (quoted by Ibn Hauqal), his suzerainty was recognized by most of the petty princes in the Caucasus region. [42]

It was under Al-Marzuban's rule that a celebrated 'Viking' invasion of Barda took place in 943. The invaders were known by the Arab chroniclers as the 'Rus', a term taken by most Western scholars to mean Scandinavian settlers in Russia.[43] The Rus made a number of expeditions around the northern and western coasts of the Caspian in the ninth and tenth centuries but their foray into the heartland of Northern Azerbaijan was by far the most audacious, and one that illustrated the vulnerability of the Muslim rulers in the region.

Having made their way into the Caspian (exactly how is not known for sure):

> [The Rus] arrived at the mouth of the River Kura in Azerbaijan and sailed some 200 miles upstream to Barda on the Terter. This town, the ancient capital of the Arran province, they took, after defeating a levy of 5,000 Mohammedans, and subsequently put most of the wretched inhabitants to the sword. After this the Muslim governor, El-Marzoban, collected an army of 30,000 men from out of his province and threatened the Russians [Rus]. His attacks were beaten off, but by this time the Russian ranks were being thinned to an alarming degree by an epidemic of dysentery.[44]

Eventually Al-Marzuban laid an ambush, during which it is said that 'the Rus commander and 700 of his men were killed, while the rest retreated to a fortress inside the town and there were besieged'.[45] Meanwhile, the epidemic, which may have been caused by the women of town tampering with food and water supplies,[46] intensified. Having buried as many of their dead as possible, the Rus 'slipped away by night, taking with them what booty they could carry and the most valuable captives; they made for the river Kura and rowed away'.[47] The Arab chronicler Ibn Al-Athir stressed that 'the Rus behaved well in Barda until provocation from the inhabitants made it impossible to come to terms with them' and added that Marzuban's forces 'dared not pursue the Rus after they left the town, because they had such respect for the fighting power of their opponents'.[48]

The Sallarid family fell into bitter dispute over the throne. Their control over the region came to an end with the death of Al-Marzuban's son and successor, Ibrahim, in 983. Azerbaijan was subsequently taken over by the Rawwadids, a family that had already, in 961, made Tabriz their capital after seizing it from the Sallarids. The Rawwadids were descendants of the Azdi Arab family of Al-Rawwad bin Al-Muthanna, a highly influential clan that had dominated Tabriz in the eighth and ninth centuries. They had come to be closely identified with the increasingly powerful Kurds of Azerbaijan, to the extent that in the tenth century 'they were themselves generally considered as Kurds'.[49] In the 990s, the Rawwadid ruler Mamlan (*d.c.*1001) took it upon himself to act as 'defender of the Muslim cause' against the Georgians and Armenians but with unsuccessful results.[50]

## The Yazidids of Shirvan

Amongst the various smaller feudal Islamic principalities that had emerged in the eastern region of the Caucasus during the Abbasid period were the fractious and feuding Yazidids of Shirvan and the Hashimids of Derbend.

The Yazidids established their hereditary rule in the province of Shirvan (Sharvan) in the middle of the ninth century. Until the late Sallarid period they remained generally under the overlordship of the governors and rulers of Azerbaijan and Arran but were mostly left to their own devices.[51] Amidst constant feuding among themselves, they frequently raided non-Muslim petty principalities in the region and likewise repelled their attacks.

The Yazidids were descended from Yazid bin Mazyad, a chief of the Arab tribe of Shaiban and a prominent commander under the legendary caliph Harun Al-Rashid. Yazid had twice been appointed governor of Azerbaijan and Armenia (787-9 and 799-80) and had earned himself a reputation fighting the Khazars.[52] His sons were also sent as governors of Azerbaijan, Armenia and Arran. As a reward for restoring Ganja in 859-60, his grandson Muhammad bin Khalid was granted the town 'together with some estates as a hereditary fief'.[53] Meanwhile, Muhammad's brother Al-Haitham became governor of Shirvan. Taking advantange of upheavals in the Caliphate following the murder of the caliph Al-Mutawakkil in 861, Al-Haitham was able to bequeath his domain to his son. Both Al-Haitham and another brother, Yazid, who had established himself as governor of Laizan (a small region in northern Shirvan), adopted the traditional titles of 'Shirvan Shah' and 'Laizan Shah' respectively and the dynasty soon became Persianized.[54]

Around 913, during the rule of the Shirvanshah Ali bin Al-Haitham, the Rus raided Baku. When they retreated to some islands off the coast 'the Shirvanians attacked them in boats, but were badly mauled and several thousand Muslims were killed'.[55] In 917-18, Ali, was killed by Abu Tahir Yazid, of the Laizan branch of the Yazid family, who then took control of Shirvan. He immediately constructed a new capital, Al-Yazidiyya, near Shemakha and gave Laizan as fief to his son Muhammad, who later seems to have become his co-regent.[56] Yazid also annexed territory to the north at the expense of the fractious Hashimid rulers of Derbend.[57]

In the 940s and 960s, Shirvan suffered the setback of invasion by the Sallarid rulers Al-Marzuban and his son Ibrahim, who were eager to assert their authority in the region, and was forced to pay tribute. Nevertheless, in the 980s the Shirvanshah Muhammad bin Ahmad pursued a policy of expansion taking the town of Qabala (981) and Barda (982). Under the subsequent dynasty of the Kesranids, Shirvan, which grew rich on the trade in oil and salt, would go on to eclipse the other principalities of the region and remained an important political entity until the 15th century.

## The Hashimids of Derbend

The Hashimids rose to prominence after entering into the service of an Arab clan that was powerful in Derbend (Al-Bab). One of their members, Al-Najm bin Hashim, is mentioned as 'the lord of Al-Bab representing the local interests' in the mid-790s.[58] The family continued to maintain its influence and eventually established its rule along hereditary lines in around 870. The Hashimids led raids to the north and fended off new Khazar attacks.

Derbend remained especially volatile and was plagued by frequent popular unrest and rebellion. A succession crisis in 938 led disgruntled chiefs of Al-Bab to install a member of the Yazidid dynasty of Shirvan as ruler. It turned out to be an unsatisfactory measure, and the leadership of the city subsequently oscillated between the Hashimids and Yazidids. While the latter were once again invited to rule over Derbend in the 980s, the Hashimids persevered and were able to re-establish control. Relations between the Shirvanshahs and the Hashimids failed to improve and the next decades were characterised by endless feuding and warfare.

## The Shaddadids of Arran

Another minor dynasty of Northern Azerbaijan was that of the Shaddadids of Arran, descendants of a Kurdish clan that 'roamed the pasture grounds of Armenia'.[59] The family, under Muhammad bin Shadda bin Qurtaq (*d.*955-6), had opportunistically managed to take the Armenian city of Dvin around 951-2 at the time that the Sallarid Al-Marzuban was temporarily imprisoned by a rival. Three years later he was driven out after Al-Marzuban regained control of Azerbaijan. Nevertheless, in 971, Muhammad's two sons, Al-Lashkari and Al-Fadl took control of Ganja from the Sallarids with the support of the local population. The Sallarid ruler, Ibrahim, laid siege to Ganja in 972 but, failing to take it, 'withdrew after concluding a peace which must have practically recognized the independence of the Shaddadid'.[60] Al-Lashkari subsequently established himself as ruler of the region.

By the time of his death in 978-9, Al-Lashkari had managed to extend Shaddadid territory as far as 'Shamkur to the northwest and Barda'a to the East'. Under the long reign of Al-Fadl (*r.*985-1031) the dynasty's realm was expanded down to Bailaqan. Al-Fadl also extended his control into Shothkh (territory lying between Lake Sevan and Barda), and around 1022 brought Dvin under his rule imposing a heavy tribute on the Armenians and appointed his son Abu'l-Asvar governor.[61] Perhaps with an eye to expanding his domains into Azerbaijan, in 1027 the veteran Shaddadid ruler ordered a bridge to be built over the Aras (probably at Khudafarin).[62]

Al-Fadl also waged unsuccessful wars against Christian Georgia, as well as against the Armenian Bagratid king Gurgen and his successor Davit of Tahsir. In an act that was characteristic of the fractious South Caucasian dynasties, Al-Fadl's son and successor Abul-Fadl Musa was subsequenly murdered by his own son Al-Lashkari Ali. Once in power, the latter continued to wage war against the kings of Georgia and Armenia. He also forged links with the Rawwadid leader Vahsudan and the Muslim ruler of Tiflis (Tbilisi), Jafar bin Ali, helping the latter to resist Georgian attacks. After Jafar's death in 1046, Al-Lashkari married his widow. When Ganja suffered a lengthy siege by the Turkic Oghuz tribes in 1045-6, liberation came in the unlikely form of an approaching Byzantine army, supported by the Georgian King Bagrat IV, with the result that Al-Lashkari Ali had little option but to recognize Byzantine suzerainty and offer his son Ardashir as a hostage.

The final years of the Shaddadid ruler were far from secure and he spent the remainder of his life moving from castle to castle until he died in around 1050.[63] The Shaddadids were subsequently paralysed by a succession crisis, yet under the ruler Abul-Asvar, the dynasty was able to claw back some of its former glory.[64]

## The Turkification of Azerbaijan

A major turning point in Azeri history, and indeed in the entire history of the Middle East and beyond, came in the 11th century, after a group of Turks known as the Seljuks invaded Persia. The Seljuks were the ruling family of the wider Oghuz Turk confederation whose origins lay in Central Asia. After entering Baghdad in 1055, the Seljuk warlord Togrul Beg (990-1063) was proclaimed sultan. The once powerful Abbasid caliphs were reduced to mere religious figureheads, losing for good their central role in the politics of the Islamic world.

The Eastern Caucasus region was no newcomer to Turks—for centuries the western shore of the Caspian had been a major migratory route for Turkic tribes hailing from Central Asia. Yet it was the Seljuks who would exert an especially important influence. As they flooded into the area, their Oghuz Turkish language supplanted Persian and eventually became the dominant language of the region, in turn giving rise to the modern-day Azeri tongue. Southern Azerbaijan now served the Turks as a convenient base from which to pursue their expansion:

> This area lay at one end of the route through Rayy and northern Iran along which Turkmen passed from Khurasan and beyond, and its fertile valleys—Azerbaijan is one of the few regions of Iran where dry farming can be practised to any considerable extent—provided pasture for the nomads' herds. Political authority in the region was fragmented, which gave numerous opportunities for employment in the service of local rulers. Moreover, as a frontier province sharing a border with Christian powers, Azerbaijan had long-established traditions of *ghazi* [raiding] warfare, in which families like the Shaddadids were prominent... All these factors combined to make Azerbaijan a concentration point for the Turkmen, and at this period it began to acquire the Turkish ethnic and linguistic colouring which it still has today.[65]

The initial waves of Oghuz Turks reached Azerbaijan under the rule of the Rawwadid leader Vahsudan (*r.* from 1025) and belonged to tribes that had been expelled from Khurasan by the Gahznavids (their leader Arslan Israi'il bin Saljuk was cast into prison where he died around 1034). The first contingent of nomadic Oghuz arrived in 1029 and consisted of 'about 2,000 tents'. Vahsudan welcomed them and, on account of their impressive archery skills employed them effectively against his enemies.[66]

However, in 1037-8, another wave of Oghuz, far stronger than the first, arrived. Despite Vahsudan's efforts to co-opt them, they began to pillage and sack the countryside. In this and a subsequent wave of Ohguz (1044), Vahsudan managed to defeat them and drove them back, yet the newcomers' presence in the region had begun to take root. In 1045-6, with the Oghuz now laying siege to Ganja, the Shirvanshah Qubad took the desperate measure of constructing a defensive wall around the capital Al-Yazidiyya.

In 1054, Togrul finally arrived in Southern and Northern Azerbaijan to receive homage from the local ruling dynasties. In Tabriz, Vahsudan submitted to Togrul, introduced his name in the Friday prayer in the mosque (thus acknowledging in the traditional way the Seljuk's supreme authority) and surrendered his son to him as hostage.[67] From there Togrul went on to Ganja to receive the submission of the Shaddadids of Arran, ruled by Abul-Asvar. Whether or not the rulers of Shirvan and Derbend were among those who formally submitted to Togrul at this particular time is not known, but given that a decade later the region came under mass occupation, their recognition of the Seljuk suzerainty cannot have been long in coming.[68] Under Togrul's successor, Sultan Alp Arslan (1029-72), the Seljuks consolidated their power in Persia and strengthened their hold over the South Caucasus region. Nevertheless, local rulers and tribes would continue to retain a fair degree of power and autonomy. Abul-Asvar for one took an active role in the Seljuk conquest of Armenia and his Shaddadid dynasty survived as Seljuk vassals ruling Ani (now in eastern Turkey) until the end of the 12th century.[69]

Converts to Islam, the Seljuks took it on themselves to champion the Sunni cause, rallying Muslims under the banner of the Caliphate at Baghdad.[70] The security they brought to trade routes in the Caucasus region did much to facilitate the spread of Islam, which now became more deeply rooted. The Seljuks also adopted Persian as their literary language, helping to spread its use throughout their empire, while Arabic was retained principally for the study of the Quran. Older scripts in the Caucasus such as Albanian, Pahlavi and Aramaic disappeared and were replaced by a modified Arabic script that could also be used for Turkish.

During the 12th century, as the Seljuk state fell into chaos, power in the region of Northern and Southern Azerbaijan was divided between two rival dynasties that ran their territories as autonomous states. The Ahmadilis, who were based in Maragha, Southern Azerbaijan, took their name from the Rawwadid Ahmadi bin Ibrahim of Tabriz. Meanwhile to the north in Arran, Shamsaddin Eldiguz (*d.c.*1175), an ex-slave who had been appointed governor by the Seljuks, started his own dynasty. For several decades the Eldiguzids, whose capital was at Ganja, ruled supreme over the region and came to earn themselves a place in history for their role as 'Champions of Muslim Arms' on the northeast frontier, where they faced the resurgent power of the Christian Georgian kings.[71]

The well-fortified city of Ganja was an important centre of silk-production and general trade. It had replaced Barda as the chief town of Arran after the decline of the Abbasid Caliphate, becoming the capital of the Shaddadids during the tenth century. And now, under the Eldiguzids, the city experienced a cultural and literary explosion, producing a number of great poets, including the greatest literary figure in Azerbaijan, the poet Nizami Ganjavi (1141-1209).

Nizami, whose mother is taken to be of Persian origin (in fact described as Kurdish by the poet himself),[72] lived and worked all of his life in Ganja. He was well-versed in Arabic and Persian literature as well as local oral and written traditions. Although he spoke Turkish, it was in fact the Persian language that was the medium for his verse, allowing his genius to radiate outwards from the Caucasus across the Persian-speaking world. His poem *Makhzan al-Asrar* (*The Treasury of Mysteries*) so greatly impressed the ruler of Derbend that he made Nizami a gift of a Qipchaq slave girl, named Afaq, whom he married and with whom he had a son. His intensely moving epic love poems *Khosrow and Shirin* and *Layla and Majnun* are regarded as being amongst the greatest pieces of Persian literature.

The rule of both the Eldiguzids and Ahmadis was eventually brought to an end in the 13th century by the Khwarezmid Empire. Founded by Oghuz Turks in the 12th century, the state of Khwarezm (lying to the east of the Caspian) temporarily became a Seljuk province. With the decline of the Seljuks, the Khwarezm-Shahs managed, prior to their defeat by the Mongols in 1220, to extend their power across Persia, also bringing Southern Azerbaijan and Arran under their suzerainty.

## The Mongols

Azerbaijan's Golden Age was shattered by the ubiquitous and terrifying Mongols. Having wrought devastation in the Russian Steppes to the north and the heart of Persia to the south, they launched a sustained wave of attacks in the Caucasus during the first half of the 13th century, devastating towns and villages and unleashing massacres along the way.

In his *History of the World-Conqueror Jengis Khan*, the contemporary historian Ata-Malik Juvaini describes how the Caucasus became the setting of the climax of a great expedition by one of Jengis Khan's most trusted generals, Jebe, who was ordered to hunt down the shah of Khwarezm, Muhammad II (who ultimately killed himself rather than surrender). The venture began in 1210 and took the general on a journey from Balkh across Khorasan, Iran, Iraq and into Azerbaijan, before finally rounding the Caspian to rejoin the forces of Jengis Khan.

When Jebe's men arrived in Ardabil, Southern Azerbaijan, they unleashed a customary campaign of pillage and massacres. As they headed further north they found their way blocked by snow and opted to winter in the Mughan Steppe, which lies to the west of the Caspian and south of the Aras river (mostly in the present Republic of Azerbaijan).[73] It was from this base that the Mongols most likely launched their initial attack on the neighbouring kingdom of Georgia, on which they inflicted a crushing defeat near Tbilisi in February 1221.[74]

The following spring, Jebe's attention was taken up with quelling a rebellion in Iraq, after which he headed back to the South Caucasus, having subjugated Tabriz, Maragha and Nakhchivan.[75] From Nakhchivan he entered Arran and took the town Bailaqan, before continuing northwards to the province of Shirvan. Another chronicler, Rashid ad-Din,[76] picks up the story in Shemakha (Shemakhi), the chief town of the province, relating how the Mongols 'carried out a general massacre and bore a great numbers of prisoners en route to Derbend'. According to Rashid ad-Din, faced with the formidable task of getting past Derbend, the Mongols hatched a plan to invite the Shirvan Shah (the ruler of Shirvan) to send a delegation to make peace.

The Shirvan Shah took the bait. One of the ten emissaries he dispatched for the peace terms was put to death and the rest threatened with the same fate unless they guided the Mongols through the pass. Rashid ad-Din noted that the people of Derbend made offerings of food and cloth to the Mongols 'and tendered their submission'.[77] From there they made their way back east over the top of the Caspian.

Their epic undertaking was summed up by the 18th-century historian Edward Gibbon:

> They had trampled on the nations which had opposed their passage, penetrated through the gates of Derbend, traversed the Volga and the desert and accomplished the circuit of the Caspian Sea, by an expedition which had never been attempted and has never been repeated.[78]

Before his death in 1227, Jengis Khan divided his empire between his four sons, resulting in the creation of new Mongol states. One to emerge in the region of Persia was the handiwork of Jengis Khan's grandson, Hulegu (1217-1265), who had been sent by his brother, the Great Khan Mongke, to topple the Abbasid Caliphate. In the mid-1250s, after invading Persia, Hulegu made Maragha his capital. The city, today in the eastern Azerbaijani province of Iran, provided him with a base from which to build his own empire, which would stretch from Syria in the west to the River Oxus in the east.

The new state became known as the Il-Khanate and was subordinate to the greater Mongol Empire. Hulegu, a shamanist with Buddhist sympathies, encouraged the settlement of large numbers of foreigners in the region including Buddhists and Nestorian Christians. Hulegu's own wife was a Christian (belonging to the Turkish Keray [Kerei] tribe who lived in northern Mongolia and who had adopted Christianity in about 1009),[79] while Mongke Khan himself had a Christian mother.[80]

The real focus of Hulegu's imperial pretensions lay southwards, and, in 1258, according to plan, he infamously captured the great city of Baghdad—seat of the Caliphate and popularly believed to be impregnable. The gratuitous brutality and destruction with which the occupation was carried out left the Islamic world profoundly traumatised. Hulegu's forces butchered thousands upon thousands of the city's Sunni Muslim inhabitants (Shi'ites, Jews and Christians were fortunate to be spared the same fate). After forcing the caliph to reveal where he had hidden his treasure, the Mongols had him stitched into a carpet and trampled to death under the hooves of their horses. They left the bloodstained capital in ruins—its world-famous palaces, mosques, centres of learning and other institutions utterly destroyed.

Hulegu's ambitions were curtailed after he unsuccessfully tried to seize Syria. After his army was defeated by the Egyptian Mamluks, he fell back to Azerbaijan. Nevertheless, by the end of his rule, the Mongol had wrought enough havoc on medieval Islamic culture to ensure it would never recover. After five centuries as the seat of the Abassid Caliphate, Baghdad's history as a great political and cultural centre was over. The new centre of Islam was subsequently transferred to Cairo, under the aegis of the Mamluks (many of whom, interestingly, were of Caucasian origin).

Although Hulegu had declared the Caucasus to be part of his domain—with the states in the region of Northern Azerbaijan becoming vassals of the Il-Khanate—in reality the region remained a peripheral concern over which only a modicum of control was exerted. In 1295, the Il-Khan Ghazan (*r.*1295-1304) declared himself a Sunni Muslim—an example that was followed by a great many of his Turkish and Mongol subjects.[81] Tabriz, the chief town of the province now became the capital of Persia under the Mongols and a flourishing entrepôt for trade between Europe and Baghdad, the Persian Gulf and India.[82] However, after the Il-Khanid Empire disintegrated, trade almost ceased owing to the instability of the region.

Ferocious Mongol interfactional fighting during the 14th century brought little but death, destruction and uncertainty to the Caucasus. Some respite came with the Jalayrids (*r.* from 1336) another Mongol branch, ruling in Baghdad, Tabriz and Samarkand, that had taken advantage of a succession crisis in Hulegu's family line and thereby extended its rule into the region of the South Caucasus. The Jalayrids proved to be somewhat sensitive to local affairs and secured themselves a degree of loyalty from the Azeraijani nobility by marrying into the feudal families.

Yet they soon fell victim to the ferocious leader Timur Leng (known to the West as Tamerlane, *r.* 1369-1405), a zealous Muslim of Turkic-Mongol origins who had worked in the service of Mongol pagan warriors. Timur marched into Samarkand, which subsequently became his own capital, and there massacred the ruling family before launching a wider campaign to eradicate the surviving Jalayrids. In 1380-1, he invaded Persia and, following campaigns into Northern Azerbaijan, Armenia, Georgia and Daghestan during the 1380s and 1390s, he managed to extend his influence into the Caucasus. Accepting him as suzerain, the Shirvanshahs duly put Timur's head on their coins, included his name in their Friday prayer, and agreed to side with him against his enemies, including the powerful Mongol empire of the Golden Horde,[83] which held sway to the north of the Caucasus.

## The 'Black' and 'White Sheep'

After Timur's death in 1405, his son and successor, Shahrukh, opted to shed the western territories of his father's overstretched empire in favour of a more manageable realm to the east. Azerbaijan was subsequently left in the hands of feuding local lords as Turkic tribes continued to drift in and out of the region. It was not long before some of the latter took advantage of the power vacuum that had opened up. The first of these groups was the Qara-Qoyunlu (the 'Black Sheep', so named because of its tribal emblem), of Oghuz descent, which managed to establish its power base in Tabriz and ruled over Azerbaijan, Iraq and parts of Iran.

The Qara-Qoyunlu were soon challenged by the Aq-Qoyunlu (the 'White Sheep'), also of Oghuz descent. From the 1430s to 1450s, the two groups waged near-continuous war against each other, with further devastating effects on the stability of the region. The following decade, after the dust had settled, the Aq-Qoyunlu emerged as the clear winners, holding sway over territories that included Azerbaijan south of the Kura, eastern Anatolia, Mesopotamia and northern Syria.

Despite all the upheavals, to the north of the Kura the Shirvanshahs were thriving. Following Timur's death in 1405, Shirvan had gained its independence under the leadership of Shaykh Ibrahim of Derbend. The Shirvanshah quickly reached an understanding with the Qara-Qoyunlu, and in 1410 he struck a deal accepting the Turks' suzerainty in exchange for territorial concessions.[84] During the course of the 15th century, Shirvan was fortunate enough to enjoy a period of peace and prosperity under Ibrahim's successors Khalil Allah (1417-62) and Farrukh Yasar (1462-1501), who patronised the arts and saw to it that Shemakha (Shemakhi) became renowned for its beautiful and distinctive illuminated manuscripts. The city attracted artists from afar, including from Herat (now in modern-day Afghanistan), which Shahrukh had made his capital and endowed with a magnificent library. Enjoying their continuing prosperity, they moved their capital from Shemakha to Baku, where they built themselves an impressive palace complex that still stands today.

During their short rule, the Aq-Qoyunlu made little mark on the region of Azerbaijan. Leaving the existing feudal system intact, they merely appointed governors and let day-to-day life continue as it had done. Failing to impose any real order, by the end of the 15th century what was left of their venture was little more than a chaotic jumble of petty native principalities. In the absence of a heavyweight regional power, and with little incentive to renew pacts of old, these principalities soon became embroiled in bitter disputes as the various contenders put forward their claims on the region. One such prince was Ismail, the heir of a powerful family based in Ardabil, Southern Azerbaijan. Within the space of a few years, as head of the ruling Safavids, Ismail (*r.*1501-1524) would profoundly alter the course of Persian history.

## Azerbaijan and the Safavid dynasty

The Persian Safavid Empire (1501-1736) was of immense significance in the history of Azerbaijan. For more than two hundred years it would remain under Safavid rule, a time that would see a revival of Persian culture as well as the promotion of the minority Islamic rite of Shi'ism at the expense of its rival, Sunnism. The state created by the Safavid dynasty reflected its Azeri roots: it was ruled from Tabriz by the Azeri nobility, the court language was Azeri Turkish and its army depended on key Azeri tribes. It was only later in the 16th century, when the capital was

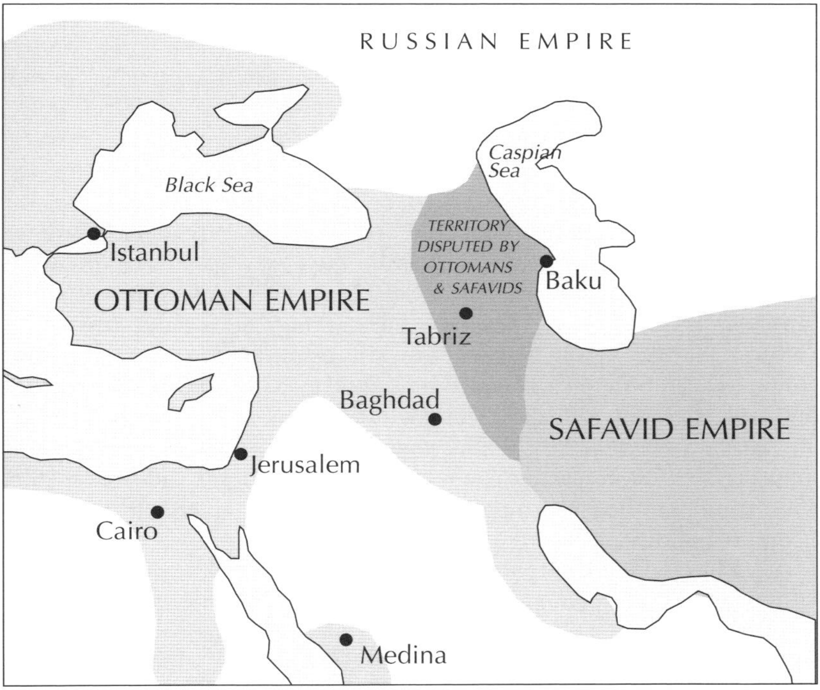


The khanates of Azerbaijan at the heart of territory disputed by the Safavid and Ottoman empires.

moved southwards to Esfahan, that Persian influences became more predominant.

Reflecting the continuous mix of peoples in the region, the Safavids were probably of Kurdish origin. Ismail was a direct descendant of Safi ad-Din Ardabili ('of Ardabil', 1252-1334) from whom the dynasty took its name. A devout Sufi with a Kurdish background, Safi ad-Din was an immensely popular figure with the people and the rulers of his day. In 1301, he established the Sufi Safaviye order and both family and order went from strength to strength, even gaining the support of the Mongol Empire and possibly from Timur.[85]

At some point during the mid-15th century the order underwent a dramatic change, becoming a highly militarized and powerful force in western Persia and eastern Turkey. Previously Sunni, it now openly embraced Shi'ism, which rejected the orthodox Sunni rite and its line of caliphs. Shi'ites instead pledged allegiance to their own rival lineage of religious leaders (imams) based on the descendants of Ali, the Prophet

Muhammad's son-in-law. The order became a channel for the popular following Ali enjoyed, not just amongst Shi'is, but Sunnis too. It also counted on a great deal of support from the various Turkic tribes in the region.

Safavid leaders, like Safi ad-Din were treated with enormous respect by their supporters and were considered to have special religious powers—Ismail's father, Haydar, had been widely held to be semi-divine.[86] He had led his army on a number of successful religious campaigns, or *jihads*, against Christians in the Caucasus. His troops were known as the Qizilbash (literally 'Red Heads') on account of their red caps that featured twelve scallops representing the Twelve Imams of Shi'ism.[87] In the 1480s, Haydar unwisely made enemies with the Aq-Qoyunlu leader Ya'qub, who also happened to be his brother-in-law. In 1488, Haydar was killed in Shirvan by the forces of Yaqub and the Shirvanshah Farrukh Yasar. The young Ismail himself was held by his supporters to be preparing the way for the coming of the Mahdi (the Twelfth Imam who, according to Shi'ite beliefs, will emerge from hiding at the end of time, ushering in a new age of peace).

After Haydar's death, Ismail spent the next few years imprisoned by his father's enemies. On gaining his freedom he was forced to lie low and bide his time until he was old enough lead a campaign to avenge the wrongdoings suffered by his family. He proved to be a more than able leader: in 1500, he defeated Farrukh Yasar and took Shirvan, while the following year he gained a victory over the Aq-Qoyunlyu at the Battle of Shurur. After securing Tabriz, he proclaimed himself Shah of Persia, thereby installing the Safavid dynasty. Further Safavid campaigns put a decisive end to the Aq-Qoyunlu and confirmed his new status as the new ruler of the region.

From Tabriz, and their subsequent capitals of Qazvin and Esfahan, the Safavids oversaw a period of great empire building across Persia and surrounding regions. Their realm extended from the Euphrates to the Amu-Darya and the Persian Gulf to Derbend (where they took the precaution of strengthening the northern walls that had for centuries served as a defence from invasion).[88] Under the Safavids, the South Caucasus found itself divided along the following lines:

> In the northwest of the country, in the angle formed by the Caucasus range and the Turkish frontier, was the Persian part of Georgia, consisting of the kingdom of Kartli in the northwest and that of Kakheti in the southeast. In view of its situation and importance, Persian Georgia was governed by one of the four Valis or Viceroys of Persia; this post having

Views of the Shirvanshah Palace complex in Baku (above and below), built in the 12th-15th centuries.

> for long been hereditary in the Bagratid royal line. The capital of Persian Georgia and also of Kartli was Tbilisi.
>
> To the south and southeast of Georgia was the vast province of Adharbaijan. In those days it was very much larger than it is now because it contained a number of smaller provinces and districts [including] Chukhur-i-Sa'd, [...] Nakhchivan and Qarabagh. Tabriz was, as it is today, the capital of Adharbaijan, and the residence of the Beglarbegi or Governor-General of the province.
>
> Other important centres of population in Adharbaijan were Erivan, Ganja and Ardabil. Erivan, the capital of Chukhur-i-Sa'd, was the seat of government of a Beglarbegi and the chief town of Persian Armenia. Ganja was likewise the seat of government of a Beglarbegi who exercised jurisdiction also over the adjoining district of Qarabagh.[89]
>
> Separated from the northern limits of Gilan by the district of Talysh and the Mughan steppe, both of which formed part of Adharbaijan, was the province of Shirvan. It was under a Beglarbegi whose seat of government was at Shemakha. This province then included the comparatively small part of Daghistan that lay within the borders of Persia proper; in this area was the strongly fortified fortress town of Darband, which was under a governor. To the north of Darband, along the coastal strip, the authority of Persia grew progressively more shadowy as one proceeded northwards. Lezgins and other mountain tribes acknowledged no jurisdiction by Persia.[90]

Ismail wasted no time imposing Shi'ism as the state religion. He subsequently launched a massive and highly effective campaign to convert the predominantly Sunni population of his new empire, helping to forge a strong Shi'ite Persian identity that continues to be a key national trait in present-day Iran. The other countries that now have a Shi'ite majority are Iraq, Bahrain and the Republic of Azerbaijan itself. In fact, Northern Azerbaijan was slower to adopt Shi'ism than other parts of the Safavid Empire—it was not until much later, as a result of Russia imperial policies during the 19th century, that Shi'ites would become a majority.

The Safavids energetically promoted the arts and literature and transformed the Iranian city of Esfahan into a major cultural centre whose influence radiated outwards across the Persian Empire and beyond. Shah Ismail himself was an accomplished poet and a key figure in Azeri literature, who wrote in the Azeri language under the pen-name of 'Khatai' and who also encouraged Muhammad Fizuli (1498-1556), another of Azerbaijan's great literary figures, to write in Azeri.

## The decline of the Safavids

For more than two centuries, Azerbaijan would find itself caught up in the stormy rivalry of two of the Islamic world's greatest empires. While the Safavid star was rising sharply, the Ottomans had been consolidating their position to the west as the masters of the eastern half of the Mediterranean. Descended from the same Turkic tribes as the Seljuks, the Ottomans put a decisive end to the Christian Byzantine Empire, transforming Constantinople into the capital of their own empire in 1453 and renaming it Istanbul. The Ottomans and Safavids spent the better part of the 16th and 17th centuries pitting their wits against each other in a near continuous state of war. As a result, territories within Azerbaijan would frequently change hands in the exhausting cycle of battles and treaties. Their rivalry found its clearest expression in their antagonistic stances on Islam—while the Persians rallied behind the banner of Shi'ism, the Ottomans did so behind Sunnism and the spiritual authority of their sultan.

The Safavids had more than just the Ottomans to contend with. Uzbek attacks in Khorasan (to the northeast of Persia) became so acute that the Safavid ruler Shah Abbas I was obliged to sue for peace with the Ottomans in order to turn his attention to the crisis. Accordingly, in 1590, he agreed to relinquish Georgia, Azerbaijan, Tabriz, Luristan and Shirvan, thereby extending Ottoman control across the South Caucasus to the Caspian Sea. The gambit paid off and Abbas I was free to subdue the Uzbeks. Peace with the Ottomans was short-lived—by the early 17th century war had resumed once more and Abbas was able to snatch back much of territory he had lost.

The costs of war, combined with the lack of leadership under a succession of puppet shahs, took its toll on the Safavid dynasty. Persia's pivotal role in east-west trade also went into serious decline. Not only had the sea-route from Europe to Asia via the Cape of Good Hope, pioneered by the Portuguese, gradually undermined Persia's position as a vital link between Europe and Asia, access was also blocked by the Ottomans. Instead, Persian trade now had to find its way to Europe by ship across the Caspian Sea from Gilan to Baku and then overland through tsarist Russia—which itself threatened to become a serious rival in the region.

The curtain finally came down on the Safavids in the 18th century, after an invasion of the Afghans in 1722 threw the foundering empire into chaos. Persia's salvation appeared to come in the form of the outstanding Afshar general, Nadir Shah, who repelled the Afghans and reinstalled the Safavids. Yet in 1736 Nadir Shah took the throne himself and subsequently terminated the Safavid line by killing the last of its shahs.

Despite considerable military successes, however, Nadir Shah failed to restore Persia to its former glory. With the disintegration of the once centralized Persian state, the South Caucasus splintered into numerous rival independent or semi-independent feudal khanates, amongst them Karabakh, Baku, Sheki, Quba, Ganja, Shirvan, Derbend, Erivan (Yerevan) and Nakhchivan. With the region effectively divided and the Persian Empire bereft of a strong leadership capable of restoring a degree of unity, the South Caucasus became easy prey for the ambitious Ottoman and Russian powers. Yet it was opportunistic Russia, with its modernized army and brilliant military and political strategists, that would, in the 19th century, win the prize of the Caucasus—thereby absorbing into its imperial collection the territory that is now home to the modern states of Georgia, Armenia and, of course, Azerbaijan.

* *
*

# Further Reading

Azeri carpet dealers in Tbilisi at the turn of the 20th century.

# Azeri proverbs

**Qonaqsız ev susuz dəyirman kimidir.**
A house without a guest is like a mill without water.

**Qonaq evin nurudur.**
A guest is a light in the house.

**Qonağin ruzisi özündən qabaq gələr.**
A guest's meal should arrive before he comes.

**Qonşunu iki inəkli istə ki, özün bir inəkli olasan.**
Wish your neighbour two cows so that you may have one for yourself.

**Vəfalı dost yad olmaz, görməsə yüz il səni.**
A faithful friend never becomes a stranger, never mind if he hasn't seen you for a hundred years.

**Yaxşı qonşu pis qohumdan yaxşıdır.**
Better a good neighbour than a bad relative.

**Bir əldə iki qarpız tutmaq olmaz.**
It's impossible to hold two watermelons in one hand.

**Çox bilirsən, az danış.**
The more you know, the less you should talk.

**Gözəllik ondur, doqquzu dondur.**
Beauty is ten, nine of which is knowing how to dress.

**Allah sol əli də sağ ələ möhtac eləməsin.**
I wish God had not made the left hand to need the right hand.

**Palaza bürün, el ilə sürün.**
Wrap yourself in a carpet and roll together with your kinsmen.

**Ev alma, qonşu al.**
Don't buy a house, buy a neighbour.

**Yaxşılığa yaxşılıq hər kişinin işidir, yamanlığa yaxşılıq ər kişinin işidir.**
Doing good in return for good is the deed of every man. Doing good for bad is the hallmark of an honourable man.

**Ağ pulu qara gün üçün yığarlar.**
White money should be collected for a black day.

**Pul əl çirkidir, yuyarsan gedər.**
Money is dirt on the hands. It washes off very quickly.

**Yüz ölç, bir biç.**
Take one hundred measurements, make one cut.

**Allaha da özünü plov yeyən tanıt.**
Let even God think that you eat pilaf rice every day.

**Qohum sənin ətini yesə də, sümüyünü atmaz.**
Even if your relative eats your meat, he shall never discard your bones.

**Dost yolunda boran olar, qar olar.**
Never mind storms and snows for the sake of a friend.

**Yaxşılığı, at dəryaya, baliq bilməsə də, xalıq bilər.**
Do a good deed, and throw it into the sea. If the fish don't appreciate it, the Creator will.

**Adım anılsın bir çürük qozla.**
Give a gift, even if it's a rotten nut.

**Yeməkdənsə ümid yaxşıdır.**
Hope is better than eating.

**Ucuz ətin şorbası olmaz.**
Cheap meat never makes a good soup.

**Halva-halva deməklə ağiz şirin olmaz.**
Saying 'halva-halva' won't make a sweet mouth.

**Adamın öz yavan çörəyi özgənin plovundan yaxşıdır.**
One's own simple bread is much better than someone else's pilaf.

**Yaxşı at özünə qəmçı vurdurmaz.**
A good horse never needs a whip.

**Gülüş min bir dərdin dərmanıdır.**
Laughter is the remedy for 1,001 illnesses.

**Ağrımaz başına sarımsağ bağlama.**
Don't tie garlic on your head if you don't have a headache.

**Qocalığında öyrənən gorunda çalar.**
He who who learns (music) late in life will play in his grave.

**Utananın oğlu olmaz.**
A shy person will never have a child.

**Qaş düzəltdiyim yerdə göz çıxartdım.**
I wanted to draw an eyebrow, but instead I poked an eye.

**İt hürər, karvan keçər.**
The dog barks, a caravan passes.

**Bilməmək ayıb deyil, soruşmamaq ayıbdır.**
Not knowing is not a shame, but not asking is.

*

# Chronology of Azerbaijan and Neighbouring Regions

## BC

| | |
|---|---|
| c.800 BC | Founding of kingdom of Mannae in region of Urumia, Southern Azerbaijan. |
| c700 BC | Emergence of the state of the Medes in northwestern Iran, extends influence into Southern Azerbaijan up to Kura and plays important role in early spread of Zoroastrian religion. |
| c.550 BC | First Persian rule over the region of Azerbaijan and South Caucasus under the Achaemenid Empire. |
| c.400 BC | Emergence of Kingdom of Albania. |
| 331 BC | Conquest of Achaemenid Empire by Alexander the Great and rise of the Seleucids; founding of Atropatena. |
| c. 230s B.C. | Parthia begins to emerge as major regional power. |
| 95-55 BC | Rule of Tigran the Great sees major Armenian expansion. Atropatena comes under control of Armenia. Albania and Iberia (Georgia) accept Armenian suzerainty. |
| 66 BC | Roman campaign under Pompey in South Caucasus. |

## AD

| | |
|---|---|
| 226 | Sassanian dynasty topples Parthians and rules Persia. |
| 451 | Resistance of Armenia to oppressive Sassanian policies in region culminates in Battle of Avarayr in region of Nakhchivan. Albania sides with Armenians. |
| c.451-c463 | Reign of Albanian King Vache who officially renounces Zoroastrianism and proclaims Christianity official religion in Albania. |
| 622 | The Prophet Muhammad's flight from Mecca to Medina marks the beginning of the Islamic Era. |
| 623 | Byzantine Emperor Heraclius invades South Caucasus. Destroys major Zoroastrian fire temple of Gushnasp at Ganzak in Southern Azerbaijan. |
| 629 | Khazars invade Albania forcing the Albanian nobility and clergy to flee Barda to the last Albanian stronghold of Mountaineous Karabakh The following year the Khazars withdraw. |
| c.640 | Sassanian Persia falls to the Arabs. |
| 660 | Albanian ruler Javanshir successfully repels the Khazar invasion in Albania. |

## Chronology

| | |
|---|---|
| 661 | Umayyad Caliphate established in Damascus—oversees major era of Arab expansion. |
| 690s | Derbend conquered by Arabs. |
| 705 | Albanians finally brought under control of caliphate in Damascus. |
| 750 | Umayyad dynasty overthrown by Abbasids, who subsequently rule from Baghdad. |
| 816 | Babek's major rebellion against Arab rule begins in Badhdh, Azerbaijan—finally quelled in 837. Babek executed in 838. |
| c.822 | Death of last Mihranid ruler, Varaz-Trdat II, sees Albania finally incorporated into province of Muslim empire and referred to by Arabs as Arran (Ar-ran) with capital at Barda. |
| c.850s | Yazidids establish minor dynasty in Shirvan. |
| c.870 | Hashimids establish minor dynasty in Derbend. |
| c.889-929 | Sajid state in Southern and Northern Azerbaijan. |
| 941-2 | Sallarid dynasty, established by Al-Marzuban, supplants Sajid dynasty and subsequently gains recognition as suzerain of most of petty principalities in South Caucasus. |
| 943 | Celebrated Rus ('Viking') invasion of Azerbaijan. Rus take temporary control of Barda but soon expelled. |
| 970s | Shaddadids establish minor dynasty in Arran. |
| 980s | Rawwadids seize power from Sallarids in Tabriz. |
| 1020s-30s | Major waves of Oghuz Turks arrive in region of Azerbaijan. |
| 1054 | Leader of the Seljuk Turks, Togrul, arrives in Southern and Northern Azerbaijan and is recognized as suzerain. |
| 1141 | Birth of Nizami Ganjavi, major figure in Azeri literature. |
| 1150s | Rise of Shamsaddin Eldiguz and start of Eldiguzid dynasty in Azerbaijan following weakening of the Seljuk state. Eldiguzid capital located at Ganja. |
| 1220s | Mongol campaigns in South Caucasus. |
| 1250s | Azerbaijan becomes a part of the Il-Khanid Empire founded by the Mongol Hulegu, with its capital at Maragha and later Tabriz. |
| 1258 | Hulegu destroys Baghdad. |
| 1380 | Invasion of Persia by Timur Leng ('Tamerlane') followed by campaigns in Northern Azerbaijan, Armenia, Georgia and Daghestan. |
| 1405 | Death of Timur Leng. Power passes to his son Miranshah. |
| 1410 | Southern Azerbaijan becomes part of Qara-Qoyunlu state with capital in Tabriz. Meanwhile, the Shirvanshahs control Northern Azerbaijan. |
| 1453 | Ottoman Turks take Constantinople and rename it Istanbul. |
| 1460s | Collapse of Qara-Qoyunlu state under Jahanshah. Formation of Aq-Qoyunlu state with capital in Tabriz. |
| 1501 | Creation of Safavid Empire under Shah Ismail I, with capital in Tabriz. Ismail imposes Shi'ite Islam as official religion of the empire. |
| 1550s | Sheki feudal state collapses under Safavid pressure. Azerbaijan is |

| | |
|---|---|
| | divided into following principalities (beglerbeydoms): Shirvan, Karabakh (Ganja beglerbeydom), Chukhur-Saad (Yerevan beglerbeydom), and Tabriz. |
| 1590s | Significant parts of Northern and Southern Azerbaijan temporarily fall under the control of Ottoman Empire. |
| 1722 | Mahmud of Kandahar invades Persia forcing the Safavid Shah Husain to abdicate. |
| 1722 | Russian troops march into South Caucasus under pretext of aiding beleaguered Safavid rulers. |
| 1724 (June) | Russians sign Treaty of Constantinople and agree to share territory in Persia. |
| 1725 | Mahmud unleashes massacre of Safavid royal family. |
| 1729 | Nadir Shah (Tahmasp Quli Khan) successfully challenges Afghans in Persia. |
| 1732-1735 | Nadir Shah successfully combats Russians and Ottomans. Russia signs peace treaty with Persia in February 1732 agreeing to restore territories south of the Kura river. Derbend and Baku are returned in a separate treaty signed in Ganja in 1735. |
| 1736 | Reign of Nadir Shah marks the end of the Safavid dynasty. Last Safavid rulers assassinated by Nadir Shah in 1740 |
| 1747 | Assassination of Nadir-Shah. |
| c.1750-1813 | Khanate period in Azerbaijan. South Caucasus divided numerous khanates including: Karabakh, Baku, Sheki, Quba, Ganja, Shirvan, Derbend, Erivan [Yerevan] and Nakhchivan. |
| 1795 | Qajar Agha Muhammad Khan's army launches campaign in South Caucasus and faces resistance from Ibrahim Khan at Shusha. Sacks Tbilisi and unleashes massacre. |
| 1796 | Russian army invades Azerbaijan, Agha Khan withdraws to Iran. In the same year Russian army leaves Azerbaijan as Catherine II dies. |
| 1797 | Second invasion of Agha Muhammed Khan and his successor Babakhan, fall of Shusha. |
| 1801 | Russia annexes Eastern Georgia, provides base from which to launch military campaign to dominate the South Caucasus. |
| 1802-1806 | Russia begins to occupy Azeri khanates. |
| 1804-1813 | First Russo-Persian war. Ends with the Treaty of Gulistan (1813)—establishes the border between the two powers along the Aras (Arax) River and formalizes Russia's dominion over Baku, Karabakh, Ganja, Sheki, Shirvan, Derbend, and Quba, together with part of Talysh and the fortress of Lenkoran. Persia also relinquishes claims to Georgia, and Daghestan. |
| 1826-1828 | Second Russo-Persian war. Ends with the Treaty of Turkmanchai (1828), which allows for the Russian annexation of the Khanates of Erivan and Nakhchivan and ends Persia's domination of the Caucasus. Northern and Southern Azerbaijan decisively separated by border. |
| 1867 | South Caucasus divided into five provinces: Kutayis (Kutaisi), |

| | |
|---|---|
| | Tiflis (Tbilisi), Erivan (Yerevan), Elizavetpol (Ganja) and Baku. The last two provinces form the core territory that today makes up the Republic of Azerbaijan. |
| 1870s | Foreign investment flows into Baku launching oil boom. |
| 1905 | Russian Revolution leads to outbreak of ethnic violence between Azerbaijanis and Armenians. |
| 1906-1911 | Constitutional Revolution in Iran. Tabriz headed by Sattar Khan plays leading role in challenging the Iranian monarchy. |
| 1917 | Russian Revolution and seizure of power in Russia by Bolsheviks. |
| 1918 (March) | Notorious 'March Days' massacre in which Dashnaks (Armenian revolutionary nationalists) go on rampage in Baku with great loss of Azeri lives. |
| 1918 (May) | Republic of Azerbaijan founded after Transcaucasian Federation disbanded—government based in Ganja. Baku remains under control of Bolshevik Council of Commissars. Republics of Georgia and Azerbaijan also proclaimed. |
| 1918 (Sep) | Downfall of the Baku Commune and installation of Republican control over all of Azerbaijan with capital at Baku; outbreak of interethnic war in Nagorno-Karabakh. |
| 1920 | Shaikh Muhammad Khiyabani leads rebellion in Southern Azerbaijan, declares autonomous Republic of Azadistan—quashed six months later. |
| 1920 (April) | Downfall of Republic of Azerbaijan. Russian troops enter Azerbaijan and establish Soviet government under Nariman Narimanov. |
| 1923 | Zangezur becomes Armenian territory and Nakhchivan and Nagorno-Karabakh made autonomous republics within the Azerbaijan SSR. |
| 1938-1940 | Stalin's Great Purge |
| 1942 | Baku oilfields scuttled by Soviet authorities to prevent them falling into enemy hands during World War II—Azeri oil industry left in ruins. |
| 1945 | Iranian Marxist Jafar Pishavari establishes National Government of Iranian Azerbaijan with backing of Soviet Union—quashed in 1946. |
| 1946 | Soviet Union's reluctance to leave Southern Azerbaijan/northern Iran prompts famous Iron Curtain Speech by Winston Churchill, one of the earliest incidences in the Cold War. |
| 1969 | Rise of Heydar Aliyev, First Secretary of the Azerbaijan Communist Party. |
| 1988 (Feb) | Nagorno-Karabakh soviet votes to transfer territory from Azerbaijan to Armenia. |
| 1989 (Dec) | Armenian Supreme Soviet passes resolution to annex Nagorno-Karabakh. |
| 1990 (Jan) | 'Black January'—Nationalist protests in Baku bloodily put down by the Soviet army. |
| 1990 (Aug) | Azerbaijan Supreme Soviet votes to restore independence on |

| | |
|---|---|
| | August 30; Azerbaijan officially becomes independent on October 18. |
| 1991 (Sept) | Ayaz Mutalibov elected president of Azerbaijan. |
| 1992 (Jan) | Armenians in Nagorno-Karabakh declare the territory the Republic of Mountainous Karabakh and begin to consolidate their military hold over the region. |
| 1992 (May) | Mutalibov ousted. |
| 1992 (June) | Abulfaz Elchibey elected president. |
| 1993 (June) | Azeri military campaign in Nagorno-Karabakh founders. Rebellion staged by Azeri colonel, Surat Husseinov. Elchibey forced to flee to Nakhchivan. Heydar Aliyev strikes deal with Husseinov and assumes presidential powers. |
| 1993 (Oct) | Aliyev elected president. |
| 1994 (Jan) | Failed Azeri military offensive. (May) Russian-brokered cease-fire declared. |
| 1995 (Nov) | Azerbaijan adopts new secular constitution, back by popular referendum. |
| 2003 (Oct) | Ilham Aliyev, son of Heydar, elected president. |
| 2003 (Dec) | Heydar Aliyev dies. |
| 2006 (July) | Baku-Tbilisi-Ceyhan pipeline officially opened. |
| 2007 (Jan) | Azerbaijani state oil company stops pumping oil to Russia in dispute over energy prices. |
| 2007 (June) | Russian president Vladimir Putin offers United States use of Russian-leased radar station in Azerbaijan (Qabala) as alternative to US plans to build new missile defence system in Europe. |
| 2008 (Oct) | Ilham Aliyev elected as president for a second term. |

*

# Notes

*For full bibliographical details, see the Select Bibliography on page 241.*

## Chapter 1. Khans, Tsars and Commissars

1. Wixman, p17.
2. Cornell, p32.
3. Quoted in Lockhart, pp 244-245.
4. ibid.
5. Atkin, M., p4.
6. ibid.
7. Solovioff, quoted in Baddeley, p80.
8. Quoted in Henry, p21.
9. Quoted in Lockhar, pp 244-245.
10. J.S. Bromley, p739.
11. Kazemzadeh, F. (1991), p320.
12. Lockhart, L., p266.
13. Roemer, H.R., p328.
14. Altstadt, p8.
15. Atkin, M., p17.
16. Hambly, G.R.V., p146.
17. ibid.
18. ibid.
19. Kazemzadeh, F. (1991), p325.
20. ibid.
21. Hambly, G.R.V., p126.
22. ibid., p131.
23. ibid.
24. Kazemzadeh, F. (1991), p332.
25. Baddeley, p68.
26. ibid., pp 71-72.
27. Kazemzadeh (1991), p332.
28. Baddeley, p67.
29. ibid.
30. ibid., p69.
31. Hambly, G.R.V., p146.
32. ibid.
33. Kazemzadeh (1991).
34. Baddeley, p71.
35. ibid., p74.
36. Gordon (1896), p13.
37. Cornel S, p31.
38. Kazemzadeh (1951), p17.
39. ibid., p23.
40. Henry, p24.
41. Lerche quoted in Henry, p24.
42. Henry, p5.
43. Leeuw, C. van der, *Azerbaijan: A Quest for Identity*, p99 and *Oil and Gas in the Caucasus and Caspian*, p48.
44. Gordon T.E., p7-8.
45. ibid., p13.
46. Kazemzadeh (1951), p14.
47. Gordon, p8.
48. Ulam A.B., p59.
49. ibid., p65.
50 Bobrovskaya, Cecilia, chap. 7 "Work in the Caucasus" in *Twenty Years in Underground Russia: Memoirs of a Rank-and-File Bolshevik*
51. Ulam A.B., p65.
52. Deutscher, I., p109.
53. ibid., p108.
54. Altstadt, A., pp 79-82.
55. ibid., p80.
56. ibid., p90).
57. Buxton, H.
58. Altstadt, p150 (who in fact quotes a possible figure of 120,000 for the years 1937/8).
59. Swietochowski, Tedeusz.
60. Altstadt A., p183.
61. Shaw, W. and Pryce, D.; Leeuw, Charles van der, *Azerbaijan: A Question of Identity*, p156.

62. Fuller, E., p5.
63. Herzig, Edmund.
64. Amirbayov, Elchin.
65. ibid.

## Chapter 2. History Mirrored in Words

1. The research for this article was realised in part with the help of a fellowship the author received from the Leverhulme Trust.
2. This translatation is taken from Altstadt 1992, p189.
3. Transliteration is a problem when dealing with languages where several alphabets are involved and where authors of different nationalities have used different systems of transliteration in their works. Unless there is an established transliteration in Western literature, the letters of the Azeri Latin Alphabet of 1991 will be used.
4. In Iran, Azerbaijani is written in Perso-Arabic script although it does not have an official status.
5. The apostrophe (') occurred in loan words from Arabic and corresponded to a word-medial glottal stop. In Azeri pronunciation the use of this sign results in the lengthening of the vowel. The apostrophe has since been dropped from use.

## Chapter 3. The Birth of the Independent Azeri Media

1. All data by the independent journalists' union Yeni Nasil, with special thanks to Islam Atakishiyev for providing historical material.

## Chapter 4. Heritage of the epics

1 Vahabzade, Bahtiyar, pp 70-71.
2. For details of his life, see Shissler, p103.
3. Shissler, p130.
4. Altstadt, p53.
5. Hitchins, p627.
6. Tyrell, p85.
7. *Azerbaijan International* (12.1), Spring 2004.
8 Vatanabadi 2003.
9. 'Latin Dili' ('The Latin Language'), written in 1967, p53 in *Selected Works of Bahtiyar Vahabzade.*
10. Altstadt.
11. For a full translation of the poem, see *Azerbaijan International* (4.1), Spring 1996.
12. For a translation of the story, see *Azerbaijan International* (4.1), Spring 1996.
13. Vatanabi, p637.

## Chapter 6. Sacred Flames

1. Gnoli, Gherardo, p580, vol 15.
2. Schwartz, M., p697.
3. Yarshater, Eshan, p7.
4. Chaumont, M. L., *Encyclopaedia Iranica*, vol. 3, pp 17-18; Boyce, M., *History of Zoroastrianism*, vol. 3, p69.
5. Quoted from Henry, J.D. p124.
6. Altstadt, p7.
7. Zarrinkub, p31.

8. Gnoli, Gherardo, p165, vol 9.
9. Tapper, R., p41.
10. Lapidus, p234.
11. Altstadt, A., p8, quoting Muriel Atkin.
12. Hannan, Shah Abdul, *Islam in Russia & Central Asia*, p7.
13. Altstadt, A., p58.
14. Henry, J.D., p170.
15. Hannan, Shah Abdul, p15.
16. ibid.
17. ibid.

## Chapter 8. Politics and Revolution in Iranian Azerbaijan

1. Issawi, p600.
2. Scarce, p946.
3. Curzon, quoted in Chaqueri, p61.
4. Scarce, p947.
5. Chaqueri, p60.
6. Chaqueri, p62.
7. Issawi, p600.
8. ibid.
9. ibid.
10. Chaqueri, p62.
11. Issawi, p600.
12. Chaqueri, p58.
13. Gordon, p8.
14. Iranian Constitution 1906, 44. The Supplementary Fundamental Laws of October 7, 1907, 4.2 Rights of the Persian Nation (Articles 9 & 10).
15. Brenda Shaffer, pp 40-41.
16. ibid.
17. Chaqueri, p102.
18. Bayat, p104.
19. ibid., p241.
20. ibid., p103.
21. Quoted in Bayat, p103.
22. Bayat, p103.
23. Chaqueri, p126.
24. Bayat, p241.
25. Kazemazdeh, 1991, p343.
26. Keddie, Nikki, & Amanat, Mehrdad, p207.
27. ibid., p209.
28. Atabaki, p86.
29. Katouzian, Homa, p26.
30. ibid.
31. Abrahamian, p398.
32. Quote from the British consul in Tabriz in Abrahamian, p398.
33. Atabaki, Touraj, p98.
34. Abrahamian, p107.
35. Atabaki, p117.
36. Abrahamian, p400.
37. ibid., p400-1.
38. ibid., p401.
39. Azarsina & Mamedova.
40. ibid.
41. Azarsian, H.

## Chapter 9. From Ancient Times to the Safavid Era

1. Diakonoff, I.M., p50-2.
2. ibid., p72.
3. Sulimirski, T., p153.
4. Diakonoff, I.M., p118.
5. ibid.
6. Chahin, M., p185.
7. Dorraj, Manochehr.
8. Chaumont, *Encyclopaedia Iranica*, vol. 3, pp17-18; Boyce, M, *History of Zoroastrianism*, p69.
9. Juvaini, p148 (editor's footnote no. 30).
10. Garsoïan, N.G., p7.
11. Altstadt, A., p3.
12. Chahin, M. pp 197-8.
13. Redgate, A.E., p69.
14. ibid.
15. Chahin, M., p201.

16. ibid., p205.
17. Redgate, A.E., p71.
18. Chahin, M., pp 214-216; Donabedian, P., pp 54-55.
19. Frye, R.N., p141.
20. Mutafian, C., Ducellier, A., & Lauwe, E. van, p38.
21. Redgate, A.E., p69.
22. ibid., p142.
23. Frye, R.N., p141.
24. Donabedian, P., p56.
25. Golden, P., p51.
26. Donabedian, P. pp 58-9.
27. Langer, W.L. (ed.), p139.
28. Redgate, A.E., p158; and Frye, R.N., p172.
29. Redgate, A.E., p158.
30. Madelung, W., p226.
31. Lambton, A., p43.
32. Madelung, W., p226.
33. ibid.
34. Madelung, W., p226.
35. Bennigsen, A & Bryan F.E., p357.
36. Madelung, W., p227.
37. Altstadt A., p7.
38. Amoretti, B.S., pp 505-7.
39. Madelung, W., p228.
40. ibid.
41. ibid., p331.
42. ibid., p335.
43. Davidson H.R., p57.
44. Kendrick, T. D., p162.
45. Davidson, H.R., p133.
46. ibid.
47. ibid., p134.
48. ibid.
49. Madelung, W., p236.
50. ibid., p237.
51. ibid., p242.
52. ibid., p243.
53. ibid.
54. ibid., pp 243-4.
55. ibid., pp 244-5.
56. ibid., p245.
57. ibid.
58. ibid., p244.
59. ibid., p239.
60. ibid., p240.
61. ibid., p241.
62. ibid.
63. ibid., pp 241-2.
64. ibid., p243.
65. Bosworth, C.E., p43.
66. Madelung, W., pp 237-8.
67. ibid., p239.
68. ibid., p249.
69. ibid., p243.
70. Golden P., p57.
71. Bosworth, C.E., p170.
72. Rypka, J., p578.
73. Juvaini, p147.
74. ibid.
75. ibid., p148.
76. Quoted by editor in Juvaini, p149 (editor's note no. 32).
77. Juvaini, p149 (editor's note no. 33).
78. Quoted from Gibbon, *VII, 10* by Boyce, J.A. in Juvaini, p149 (note 36).
79. Arberry A.J., p293 (Vol 1).
80. ibid.
81. ibid., p294.
82. Lambton, A.
83. Altstadt A., p4.
84. ibid.
85. Tapper, R., p41.
86. Dorraj, M., p83.
87. Tapper, R., p42.
88. Altstadt, A., p9.
89. Lockhart, L. pp 4-5.
90. ibid., p8.

*

# Select Bibliography


Abdullazade, Fatina, & Vagif Bahmenli, *Azerbaijan* (Tisamat Printing Co., Ankara, 1998).

Abrahamian, Ervand, *Iran Between Two Revolutions* (Princeton University Press, 1982).

Acar, Feride, & Ayşe Güneş-Ayata (eds.), *Gender and Identity Construction: Women of Central Asia, the Caucasus and Turkey* (Brill, Leiden, 2000).

*Adabiyyat Gazeti* (November 13, 1992, Baku).

*After the Fall: The Human Impact of Ten Years of Transition* (UNICEF Innocenti Research Centre, Florence, 1999).

Ahmedov, R. J., *Ceramics of Baku in the IX-XVII centuries* (Baku, 1992).

Akhundov, D. A., & M. D. Akhundov, 'The Question of "Disputed Moments" in the History of Culture of Caucasian Albania', in *News of the Academy of Sciences of Azerbaijan No. 2* (Elm, Baku, 1986).

Alijarly, S., 'The Republic of Azerbaijan: Notes on the State Borders in the Past and the Present', in *Transcaucasian Boundaries*, edited by John F. R. Wright, Suzanne Goldenberg & Richard Schofield, (SOAS/GRC Geopolitics Series 4, London, 1995).

Alstadt, Audrey L., *The Azerbaijani Turks: Power and Identity Under Russian Rule* (Hoover Institution Press, Stanford, 1992).

Amirbayov, Elchin, *Shusha's Pivotal Role in a Nagorno-Karabakh Settlement: Caspian Studies Program Policy Brief, No. 6* (Harvard University, John F. Kennedy School of Government, 2001).

Amoretti, B. S., 'Sects and Heresies', in *The Cambridge History of Iran, Vol 4: From the Arab Invasion to the Saljuqs*, edited by R. N. Frye (Cambridge University Press, 1975, pp 481-519).

Aras, Bulent, & George K. Foster, 'Turkey and the Azerbaijan Oil Controversies: Looking for a Light at the End of the Pipeline' (www.biu.ac.il/Besa/meria/books/azerbaijan.htm).

Arberry, A. J. (ed.), *Religion in the Middle East, Volumes 1 & 2*, (Cambridge University Press, 1969).

Ash, Timothy Garton, *The Uses of Adversity: Essays on the Fate of Central Europe* (Granta Books, Cambridge, 1989).

Atabaki, Touraj, *Azerbaijan: Ethnicity and the Struggle for Power in Iran* (I.B.Tauris, 2000).

Atkin, Muriel, *Russia and Iran 1780-1828* (University of Minnesota Press, Minneapolis, 1980).

Avery, Peter Printing, 'The Press and Literature in Modern Iran' in *The Cambridge History of Iran, Vol 7: From Nadir Shah to the Islamic Republic* ed. Laurence Lockhart (Cambrdge University Press, 1991).

Awde, Nicholas, & Famil Ismailov, *Azerbaijani Dictionary and Phrasebook* (Hippocrene Books, New York, 1999).

Ayvasian, Kourken, *The Theater in Soviet Azerbaidzhan* (Research Program on the USSR, New York, 1955).

*Azerbaijan Human Development Report 1998* (UNDP, Baku, 1998).

*Azerbaijan International Magazine*, (Sherman Oaks, 1993–).

*Azerbaijan Soviet Socialist Republic* (Novosti Press, Moscow, 1967).

Azarsina, Habib, 'Azerbaijani Press in Iran', *Azerbaijan International*, no. 8.2, 2000.

Azarsina, Habib, & Naida Mamedova, 'Azerbaijani: Language of a Divided Nation', *Azerbaijan International*, no. 1.3, 1993.

Baddeley, J. F., *The Russian Conquest of the Caucasus* (Caucasus World, Curzon Press, London, 1998).

Baranovsky, P. D., *The Monuments in Qum and Lekit Villages* (Baku, 1947).

Bayat, Mangol, *Iran's First Revolution: Shi'ism and the Constitutional Revolution of 1905-1909* (Oxford University Press, 1991).

Benet, Sula, *How to Live to be 100: The Life-Style of the People of the Caucasus* (Dial, New York, 1976).

Bennigsen, Alexandre, & Fanny E. Bryan, 'Islam in the Caucasus and the Middle Volga', in *The Encyclopedia of Religion, Vol* 7, ed. Mircea Eliade (Macmillan, 1987, pp 357-367).

Bertsch, Gary K., Cassady Craft, Scott A. James, & Michael Beck (eds.), *Crossroads and Conflict: Security and Foreign Policy in the Caucasus and Central Asia* (Routledge, 1999).

Bobrovskaya, Cecilia, *Twenty Years in Underground Russia: Memoirs of a Rank-and-File Bolshevik* (1934; online version: Cecilia Bobrovskaya History Archive, published 2002: http://www.marxists.org/archive/bobrovskaya/twenty-years/index.htm).

Bosworth, C. E., 'The Political and Dynastic History of the Iranian World (A.D. 1000-1217)', in *The Cambridge History of Iran, Vol 5: The Saljuq and Mongol Periods*, ed. J. A. Boyle (Cambridge University Press, 1968).

Boyce, M., *A History of Zoroastrianism, Vol. 3: Zoroastrianism under Macedonian and Roman Rule* (E. J. Brill, Leiden, 1991).

Boyce, M., *Zoroastrians: Their Religious Beliefs and Customs* (Routledge, 2001).

# Select Bibliography


Boym, Svetlana, *Common Places: Mythologies of Everyday Life in Russia*, (Harvard University Press, Cambridge, MA, 1994).

Bromley, J. S. (ed.), *The New Cambridge Modern History, VI: The Rise of Great Britain and Russia, 1688-1725* (Cambridge University Press, 1970).

Buniyadov Z. M., *The History of Caucasian Albania in the Seventh-Eighth Centuries* (Baku, 1962).

Burnaby, Frederick, *A Ride to Khiva* (Oxford University Press, Oxford, 1876; reprinted 1997).

Buxton, H., *Transcaucasia* (Faith Press, 1926).

*By the Light of Day: Stories by Soviet Writers* (Progress Publishers, Moscow, 1968).

Cartier-Bresson, Henri, *The People of Moscow* (Simon & Schuster, New York, 1955).

Chahin, Mack, *The Kingdom of Armenia* (Caucasus World, Curzon, London, 2001).

Chaqueri, Cosroe, *The Russo-Caucasian Origins of the Iranian Left: Social Democracy in Modern Iran* (Caucasus World, Curzon, London 2001).

Chaumont, M. L., *Encyclopaedia Iranica*, vol. 3, pp 17-18.

Cidylo, Lori, *All the Clean Ones Are Married, and Other Everyday Calamities in Moscow* (Academy Chicago Publishers, Chicago, 2001).

Cornel, Svante, *Small Nations and Great Powers: A Study of Ethnopolitical Conflict in the Caucasus* (Caucasus World, Curzon, London, 2000).

Cox, C., & J. Eibner, *Ethnic Cleansing in Progress (War in Nagorno-Karabakh)* (pamphlet; Institute for Religious Minorities in the Islamic World, 1993).

Croissant, Michael P., *The Armenia-Azerbaijan Conflict: Causes and Implications* (Praeger Publishers, Westport, 1998).

Davidson, H. R. Ellis, *The Viking Road to Byzantium* (George Allen & Unwin, London, 1976).

de Waal, Thomas, *Black Garden: Armenia and Azerbaijan through Peace and War* (New York University Press, New York, 2003).

Deutscher, Isaac, *Stalin* (Penguin, London, 1990).

Diakonoff, I. M., 'Media', in *The Cambridge History of Iran, Vol 2: The Median and Achaemenian Periods*, ed. Ilya Gershevitch (Cambridge University Press, 1985).

Donabedian, P., 'The History of Karabakh from Antiquity to the Twentieth Century' in *The Caucasian Knot: The History and Geo-Politics of Nagorno-Karabakh*, eds. L. Chorbajian, P. Donabedian, & C. Mutafian (Zed Books, 1994).

Dorraj, M., *From Zarathustra to Khomeini: Populism and Dissent in Iran* (Lynne Rienner Publishers, 1990).

Drakulic, Slavenka, *Café Europa* (Abacus, London, 1996).

Efendiyev, Rasim, *Arts Craftsmanship of Azerbaijan in World Museums* (Baku, 1980).
Elliott, Mark, *Azerbaijan with Georgia* (Trailblazer Publications, 1999).
Essad-Bey, *Twelve Secrets of the Caucasus* (Viking Press, New York, 1931).

Farson, Negley, *The Lost World of the Caucasus* (Doubleday, New York, 1958).
Frye, R. N., 'The Political History of Iran under the Sassanians', in *The Cambridge History of Iran, Vol 3(1): The Seleucid, Parthian and Sassanian Periods*, ed. Eshan Yarshater (Cambridge University Press, 1983).
Fuller, E., *Azerbaijan at the Crossroads* (pamphlet; Post-Soviet Business Forum, Royal Institution of International Affairs, London, 1994).

Gabibov, D., & M. N. Nadzhafov, *Iskusstvo Sovetskogo Azerbaydzhana: Zhivopis, Skulptura, Grafika: Ocherki* [The Art of Soviet Azerbaijan: Painting, Sculpture, Graphic Art] (Moscow, 1960).
Garsoïan, N. G., 'Iran and Caucasia', in *Transcaucasia, Nationalism, and Social Change*, ed. Ronald G. Suny (University of Michigan Press, 1996).
Gnoli, Gherardo, 'Manichaeism: An Overview', in *The Encyclopaedia of Religion, Vol. 9*, ed. M. Eliade (Macmillan, London, 1987).
Gnoli, Gherardo, 'Zoroastrianism', in *The Encyclopaedia of Religion, Vol 15*, ed. M. Eliade, pp 579-591 (Macmillan, London, 1987).
Golan, G., *Russia and Iran: A Strategic Partnership?* (Royal Institute of International Affairs, London, 1998).
Golden, P., 'The Turkic Peoples and Caucasia' in *Transcaucasia, Nationalism, and Social Change*, ed. Ronald G. Suny (University of Michigan Press, 1996).
Goldenberg, Suzanne, *The Pride of Small Nations: The Caucasus and Post-Soviet Disorder* (Zed Books, London, 1994).
Goltz, Thomas, *Azerbaijan Diary* (M. E. Sharpe, Amonk, 1998).
Gordon, T. E. (General Sir), *Persia Revisited, 1895* (Edward Arnold, London, 1896).
Guliyev, I. S., & A. A. Feizullayev, *All About Mud Volcanoes* (Geological Institute, Azerbaijan Academy of Sciences, Baku, 1997).
Gunther, John, *Inside Russia Today* (Harper & Brothers, New York, 1957).

Hambly, Gavin R. G., 'Agha Muhammad Khan and the Establishment of the Qajar Dynasty', in *The Cambridge History of Iran, Vol 7: From Nadir Shah to the Islamic Republic*, ed. Laurence Lockhart (Cambrdge University Press, 1991).
Henry, J. D., *Baku: An Eventful History* (Archibald Constable, London, 1905).
Herzig, E., *Iran and the Former Soviet South* (Royal Institute of International Affairs, London, 1995).

Heyat, Farideh, *Azeri Women in Transition: Women in Soviet and post-Soviet Azerbaijan*, Routledge, New York, 2002).

Hitchins, Keith, 'Theme and Character in the Azerbaijani Novel, 1930- 1957', in *Twayne Companion to Contemporary World Literature Vol I*, ed. Pamela A. Genova (Twayne, 2003).

Hope, Christopher, *Moscow! Moscow!* (Minerva, London, 1990).

Hopkirk, Kathleen, *A Traveller's Companion to Central Asia* (John Murray, London, 1993).

Hopkirk, Peter, *On Secret Service East of Constantinople* (John Murray, London, 1994).

International Monetary Fund, *Azerbaijan Republic: Recent Economic Developments and Selected Issues* (IMF Staff Country Report, no. 00/121, 2000).

Issawi, 'Charles European Economic Penetration, 1872-1921 in *The Cambridge History of Iran, Vol 7: From Nadir Shah to the Islamic Republic*', ed. Laurence Lockhart (Cambridge University Press, 1991).

Juvaini, Ata-Malik, *Genghis Khan: The History of the World Conqueror*, trans./ed. J. A. Boyce (Manchester University Press, 1997).

Kaplan, Robert D., *The Ends of the Earth* (Vintage Books, New York, 1997).

Kaplan, Robert D., *Eastward to Tartary: Travels in the Balkans, the Middle East, and the Caucasus* (Random House, New York, 2000)

Kapuscinski, Ryszard, *Imperium* (Alfred A. Knopf, Toronto, 1993).

Karny, Yo'av, *Highlanders: A Journey to the Caucasus in Quest of Memory* (Farrar, Straus & Giroux, New York, 2000).

Katouzian, Homa, 'Khalil Maleki: The Odd Intellectual Out', in *Intellectual Trends in Twentieth-century Iran: A Critical Survey*, edited by Negin Nabavi (University Press of Florida, 2003).

Kazemzadeh, F., *The Struggle for Transcaucasia* (The Philosophical Library, New York; George Ronald, Oxford, 1951).

Kazemzadeh, F., 'Iranian Relations with Russia and the Soviet Union, to 1921', in *The Cambridge History of Iran, Vol 7: From Nadir Shah to the Islamic Republic*, ed. L. Lockhart (Cambridge University Press, 1991).

Keddie, Nikki and Amanat, Mehrdad 'Iran under the later Qajars, 1848-1922' in *The Cambridge History of Iran, Vol 7: From Nadir Shah to the Islamic Republic*, ed. Laurence Lockhart (Cambrdge University Press, 1991).

Kendrick T. D., *A History of the Vikings* (Metheun, London, 1930).

King, John, John Noble & Andrew Humpreys, *Central Asia* (Lonely Planet Publications, Victoria, 1996).

Langer, W. L. (ed.), *Encyclopedia of World History* (George Harrap, London, 1968).
Lapidus, Ira, 'Iran: The Mongol, Timurid, and Safavid Empires', in *A History of Islamic Societies* (2nd edn; Cambridge, 2002).
Lockhart, Laurence, *The Fall of the Safavi Dynasty and the Afghan Occupation of Persia* (Cambridge University Press, 1958).

Maclean, Fitzroy, *To Caucasus, the End of all the Earth* (Little, Brown, Boston, 1976).
Maclean, Fitzroy, *Portrait of the Soviet Union* (Henry Holt, New York, 1988).
MacMillan, Margaret, *Paris 1919: Six Months that Changed the World* (Random House, New York, 2002).
Madelung, W., 'The Minor Dynasties of Northern Iran', in *The Cambridge History of Iran, Vol 4: From the Arab Invasion to the Saljuqs*, ed. R. N. Frye (Cambridge University Press,1975).
Mamedov, R., *Archeological Finds* (Azeri History Museum, Baku, n.d.).
Manicom, David, *Progeny of Ghosts* (Oolichan Books, Lantzville, 1998).
Miller, Donald E., & Lorna Touryan Miller, *Armenia: Portraits of Survival and Hope* (University of California Press, Berkeley, 2003).
Mutafian, Claude, Alain Ducellier, & Eric van Lauwe, *Atlas Historique de l'Arménie* (Edition Autrement, Paris, 2001).
Muttitt, Greg, & James Marriott, *Some Common Concerns: Imagining BP's Azerbaijan-Georgia-Turkey Pipelines System*, (PLATFORM, The Corner House, Friends of the Earth International, Campagna per la Riforma della Banca Mondiale, CEE Bankwatch Network, & The Kurdish Human Rights Project, Abbey Print, Spalding, 2002).

Nahaylo, Bohdan, & Victor Swoboda, *Soviet Disunion: A History of the Nationalities Problem in the USSR* (Hamish Hamilton, London, 1990).
Nasmyth, Peter, *Georgia: In the Mountains of Poetry* (Caucasus World, Curzon Press, 1998).
Najafova, Nassiba, *Art Ceramics* (Baku, 1983).
Novruzova, G., *Sculptura sovetskogo Azerbayzhana* [Soviet Sculpture of Azerbaijan] (Baku, 1979).

Orbeli, I. A., *Hasan-Jalal: The Prince of Khachen* (Yerevan, 1963).

Paulston, C.B., & D. Peckham (eds.), *Linguistic Minorities in Central and Eastern Europe* (Multilingual Matters, Philadelphia, 1998).
Pipes, Richard, *The Formation of the Soviet Union* (Atheneum Publishers, New York, 1954; reprint 1968).
Pipes, Richard, *Russia under the Bolshevik Regime* (Alfred A. Knopf, New York, 1994).

Remnick, David, *Lenin's Tomb* (Random House, New York, 1993).
Riddell, John (ed.), *To See the Dawn, Baku, 1920: First Congress of the Peoples of the East* (Pathfinder, New York, 1993).
Robinson, Francis (ed.), *The Cambridge Illustrated History of the Islamic World* (Cambridge University Press, 1996).
Roemer, H. R, 'The Safavid Period', in *The Cambridge History of Iran, Vol. 6: The Timurid and Safavid Periods*, ed. P. Jackson & L. Lockhart (Cambridge University Press, 1986).
Rost, Yuri, *Armenian Tragedy* (St Martin's Press, New York, 1990).
Rypka, J., 'Poets and Prose Writers of the Late Saljuq and Mongol Periods', in *The Cambridge History of Iran Vol 5: The Saljuk and Mongol Periods*, ed. J. A. Boyle (Cambridge University Press, 1986).

Scarce, Jennifer 'The Arts of the Eighteenth to Twentieth Centuries: Textiles' in *The Cambridge History of Iran, Vol. 7: From Nadir Shah to the Islamic Republic*, ed. Laurence Lockhart (Cambrdge University Press, 1991).
Schwartz, M., 'The Religion of Achaemenian Iran', in *The Cambridge History of Iran, Vol 2: The Median and Achaemenian Periods*, ed. Ilya Gershevitch (Cambridge University Press, 1985).
Said, Kurban, *Ali and Nino* (Robin Clark, London, 1937; reprinted 1990).
Shaffer, Brenda, *Borders and Brethren: Iran and the Challenge of Azerbaijani Identity* (MIT Press, 2002).
Shaw, W., & D. Pryce, *Encyclopaedia of the USSR* (Cassel, London, 1990).
Shissler, Holly A., *Between Two Empires* (I. B. Tauris, London, 2003).
Smith, Hedrick, *The New Russians* (Random House, New York, 1990).
*Somewhere Over the Rainbow… Reconstruction and Rehabilitation of War-Damaged Areas in Azerbaijan* (UNDP, Baku, 1998).
Sulimirski, T., 'The Scyths', in *The Cambridge History of Iran, Vol 2: The Median and Achaemenian Periods*, ed. Ilya Gershevitch (Cambridge University Press, 1985).
Suny, Ronald (ed.), *Transcaucasia: Nationalism and Social Change* (University of Michigan Press, 1996).
Swietochowski, Tadeusz, *Russian Azerbaijan 1905-1920: The Shaping of a National Identity in a Muslim Community* (Cambridge University Press, 1985).
Swietochowski, Tadeusz, *Russia and Azerbaijan: A Borderland in Transition* (Columbia University Press, New York, 1995).
Swietochowski, Tedeusz, 'The Caspian as a Region in History' in *Oil an Environmental Security in the Black and Caspian Seas* (held on October 30, 1998; Columbia Caspian Project: www.sipa.columbia.edu/RESOURCES/CASPIAN/env_p11.html).

Tapper, R., *Frontier Nomads of Iran* (Cambridge University Press, 1997).
Thomson, Jason, *In the Shadow of Aliyev* (Bennett & Bloom, London, 2005).
Thubron, Colin, *Where Nights Are Longest* (Random House, New York, 1983).
Thubron, Colin, *The Lost Heart of Asia* (Heinemann, London, 1994).
Thubron, Colin, *In Siberia* (Penguin, London, 1999).
Tutaeff, David, *The Soviet Caucasus* (George G. Harrap, London, 1942).
Tyrell, Maliheh, *Aesopian Literary Dimensions in Azerbaijani Literature of the Soviet Period: 1920-1990*, PhD thesis (Columbia University, New York, 1999).

Ulam, Adam B., *Stalin: The Man and His Era* (Beacon Press, 1989).
Umnyakov, I., & Y. Aleskerov, *Samarkand: A Guide Book* (Progress Publishers, Moscow, 1972).

Vahabzade, Bahtiyar, *Selected Works* (Indiana University Turkish Studies, Bloomington, 1997).
Vaksberg, Arkad, *The Soviet Mafia* (Weidenfeld & Nicholson, London, 1991).
van der Leeuw, Charles, *A Quest for Identity* (Caucasus World, Curzon, 2000).
van der Leeuw, Charles, *Oil and Gas in the Caucasus and Caspian* (Caucasus World, Curzon, 2000).
Vatanabadi, Shouleh, 'Past, Present, Future and Post-Colonial Discourse in Modern Azerbaijani Literature', in *Twayne Companion to Contemporary World Literature, Vol I*, ed. Pamela A. Genova, (Twayne, 2003).

Wixman, R., *The Peoples of the USSR: An Ethnographic Handbook* (Macmillan Reference, New York 1984).

Yarshater, Eshan (ed.), *The Cambridge History of Iran Vol 3(1): The Seleucid, Parthian and Sassanian Periods* (Cambridge University Press, 1983).

Zarrinkub, 'Abd Al-Husain', in 'The Arab Conquest of Iran and its Aftermath', in *The Cambridge History of Iran, Vol 4*, ed. R. N. Frye (Cambridge University Press, 1975).

*

# Index